A Case of Witchcraft

The Execution of Urbain Grandier

EFFIGIE de la CONDEMNATION de MORT

& exécution d' Vrbain Grandier, Curé de l' Eglise S. Pierre du Marché de Loudun, atteint & conuaincu de Magie, sortiléges, & maléfices, lequel a esté bruslé vif en ladicte ville.

Portrayal of the sentence to death and execution of Urbain Grandier, parish priest of the Church of Saint Pierre du Marché of Loudun, accused and convicted of Magic, spells, and evil charms, who was burned alive in the aforesaid town.

Source: Frontispiece from Urbain Grandier, *Traicté du célibat des prestres.* Paris: Robert Luzarche, 1866

A Case of Witchcraft
The Trial of Urbain Grandier

Robert Rapley

McGill-Queen's University Press
Montreal & Kingston · London · Buffalo

Legal deposit second quarter 1998
Bibliothèque nationale du Québec

Printed in Canada on acid-free paper

Published simultaneously in the UK, Eire, and Europe
by Manchester University Press

McGill-Queen's University Press acknowledges
the support of the Canada Council for the Arts
for its publishing program.

Canadian Cataloguing in Publication Data

Rapley, Robert, 1926–
A case of witchcraft :
the trial of Urbain Grandier
Includes bibliographical references.
ISBN 0-7735-1716-2
1. Grandier, Urbain, 1590–1634 – Trials, litigation, etc.
2. Demoniac possession – France – Loudun – History
– 17th century. 3. Trials (Witchcraft) – France –
Loudun. I. Title.
KJV130.G73R36 1998   345.744'0288   C98-900060-5

Typeset in Sabon 11/13
by Caractéra inc., Quebec City

To my wife

Contents

Contents

Acknowledgments

I have been helped by many people. The mayor and municipality of Loudun made available to me through their archivist, Madame Sylviane Rohaut, a mass of important material. Further, Mme Rohaut has gone out of her way over many months to continue to provide me with useful details and information that have been valuable to me. Pierre Delaroche, doctor, author, and historian of Loudun, gave me an enlightening guided tour of the town and some of his own insights. Edwin Bezzina of the University of Toronto, who is currently preparing his doctoral thesis on Catholic/Protestant relations in Loudun, has freely made available to me his research findings as well as reading and commenting on his book. Alex M. Johnston of Ottawa kindly prepared for me the illustration of the torture of the *brodequins*. Carlotta Lemieux of London, Ontario, has done a great job of editing, going well beyond the call of duty.

To all of these, and to my family and friends who have read the book, assisted, and advised, I give my grateful thanks.

A Case of Witchcraft

Prologue

At five o'clock in the morning the judges met to deliver their verdict:

We declare the said Urbain Grandier duly guilty of the crime of sorcery, evil spells, and the possession visited upon some Ursuline nuns of this town of Loudun and of other laywomen mentioned at the trial, together with other crimes resulting from the above. For redress of these, he has been condemned ... to be taken to the Place of Sainte-Croix of this said town, to be tied to a post on a pile of faggots that is to be built in the said Place. There his body is to be burned alive ... and his ashes are to be scattered to the winds ... Prior to proceeding with the execution of the said sentence, we order that the said Grandier be subjected to torture ordinary and extraordinary on the truth about his accomplices.

Issued at Loudun, 18 August 1634.[1]

Twelve Good Years

Loudun was a magnificent sight, set on a hill in the middle of a wide, rich valley. On the peak of the hill sat the enormous fortress within its own walls, guarding the city and its ten thousand souls.[1] To approach the fortress, an enemy had first to get through the wall that encompassed the town, with its turrets, strong points, and defensive towers, and then fight his way over a succession of draw-bridges, each a major defence point in itself. Even then, he would only be outside the main defensive tower of the château. Loudun was a very strong town. Yet it was not the strength of its defences that first struck the visitor from afar but the remarkable white stone of the fortress and the walls surrounding the city. From a distance, it looked like a fairy-tale castle waiting for a prince.

This is what Urbain Grandier saw in early August 1617 – his first sight[2] of this town where he would spend the rest of his life, savour his triumphs, and, far in the future, endure his death. Even from a distance, the spire of his church, Saint-Pierre-du-Marché, Saint Peter of the Market, stood out from everything else in the city. It was such a prominent feature that the Jesuits in Bordeaux would have told him that as soon as he saw it he would recognize his church. It still stands today, the most noticeable landmark of the town now that the walls and the great fortress are gone – gone, indeed, even before Urbain Grandier was executed.

The enchanting view of the city must have added to Grandier's delight about his arrival at Loudun. No twenty-seven year old, brilliant, handsome, and catapulted suddenly into two rich appoint-ments, could have failed to be excited about his prospects: his own church, his own parishioners, so much work to be done in God's name.[3] And when success followed, as it surely must, the material rewards and honours of this world would be nothing compared with the rewards of eternal life that awaited a priest who carried out God's plans. At his age, Grandier probably did not even ask himself whether he was worthy of all that his benefactors in distant Bordeaux had so unexpectedly given him. But even if he had asked, he would have had good cause to feel that it was his own qualities that had won him his position. Of course, luck had played its part as well, for there were some others as well qualified as he, but luck always played a part in life – he knew that.

During his long journey from Bordeaux, the quiet of the church and seminary had been replaced by the hustle and bustle of the world outside, a world he had not known since late childhood; the grey institutional walls had been replaced by the brilliance of summer colours in the cities and fields, and the black robes of the Jesuits had been supplanted by the multicoloured clothing of the citizens in the towns he had passed through. Above all, the quiet tenor of a young priest's life in a community of men had been exchanged for the adventure of his journey and the opening up of a whole new world. In all of Urbain Grandier's life, few days could have been more full of wonder, satisfaction, hope, and anticipation.

Grandier was well built, tall, strong, and handsome, with dark eyes, a prominent but well-modelled nose, and a smiling mouth. Only his pale face suggested that he had been too much confined inside. He wore the moustache and small pointed beard that were common at the time and bore himself well. He was always clean and neatly dressed (in an age when cleanliness was a thinly spread virtue), and he had a ready wit; he liked to laugh and make others laugh. These were the first impressions. He also possessed energy, vitality, and virility. He was a man who would not be ignored even in a crowd. Other men would enjoy his company. Women would too, no doubt, if he allowed it. His inaccessibility as a priest might even be an additional attraction.[4]

The arrival of the new priest was an event of social as well as religious importance in Loudun. A parish priest fulfilled obvious and essential tasks – from baptism, through marriage, to death, and including confession, with its pardon and consolation, perhaps the most comforting service in an era when life was short and death could be fast and unexpected.[5] As well, the parish church was a meeting place for all Catholics. With its decorative windows and statues it was the centre for art; in its services it was the centre for

Urbain Grandier at age 37.
Source: A contemporary engraving, published in
Legué, *Urbain Grandier et les possédées de Loudun.*
Illustration provided by the Musée de Loudun

music; in its ceremonies it was the centre for theatre and drama;
and in its preaching it was the centre for education, entertainment,
and culture.

The parish priest of the large, rich church of Saint-Pierre-du-
Marché was assisted by four or five vicars and curates, but it was
he who set the tone, so the Loudunais were full of curiosity. When
the new priest arrived, the rumour mills did not have much to work
with; but a provincial town, with so much of its world encircled
within its walls, could survive on very little solid material, and some

word of Grandier's background had preceded him. It was no secret that he came of good bourgeois stock.[6] His father had been a lawyer, and his uncle was a priest of some considerable status in a town near Bordeaux; he was known to have close connections as well as some influence with the Jesuits of that rich city. It was this uncle who had seen to the boy's education and sent him to the great Jesuit college of La Madeleine in Bordeaux. Word went around in Loudun that young Grandier had been a brilliant pupil.

The Jesuits already had him targeted for greatness. He had been ordained at twenty-five, just two years ago, but had stayed on at the college to study further. Then his father had died, and his mother, in her early fifties, had been left in straitened circumstances with a large family to bring up.[7] The Bordeaux Jesuits had the right to appoint the parish priest to Saint-Pierre-du-Marché, a benefice that had recently become vacant, and by choosing Grandier they could look after one of their own pupils and at the same time ensure the future of the widow and her whole family. The Jesuits also had the right to appoint a priest as a canon of the collegial church of Sainte-Croix in Loudun. Few people knew exactly what duties this entailed, but everyone knew that it was a position with a substantial annual income and considerable prestige. This unknown young man had been given both appointments. Either of them would have been considered a plum by any of the numerous priests in the town and by their many relatives.

Consequently, some may have resented the arrival of the young priest, and indeed they had further cause for grievance. It was not just the priest who arrived; it was his whole family.[8] His recently widowed mother, Jeanne d'Estièvre, and his sister Françoise almost certainly travelled with him because, as the oldest son, he was now head of the family. His three younger brothers, François, Jean, and René, probably followed later; although they may have accompanied their mother, it is more likely that they stayed in Bordeaux to finish their education. Another sister was married and is never heard of. In due course, two of the brothers, François and Jean, also became priests, François as a vicar in Urbain's parish, and Jean as a priest in the town. The youngest brother, René, became a lawyer and a legal adviser to the city authorities of Loudun. Françoise, Urbain's sister, looked after his rectory as his housekeeper and was available to assist her mother in her old age. It seemed an ideal arrangement for the family.

A TROUBLED CITY

Magical as the white walls of Loudun looked from afar, it was in fact a troubled and perilous community, one that was tearing itself apart. Religious rivalries and hatreds were at the root of it all.[9] Loudun was an important town and inevitably had been caught up in the religious wars of the period. For nearly fifty years before Urbain Grandier arrived, Catholic and Protestant armies had swept back and forward over large sections of the south and west of France with fire and sword, murder and rapine, pillage and plunder. Both religions were certain in their cause. Loudun itself was besieged and taken on more than one occasion.

France was in general a Catholic country.[10] Like the rest of Europe it had felt the force of the Reformation, but the Protestant faith had not made such inroads as it had in England, Sweden, and parts of Germany. Less than 10 per cent of French men and women were Protestant. Their official status is perhaps best conveyed by the fact that government records always referred to them as members of the "so-called reformed religion" (rather than of the "reformed religion"). But although they were few in number, the aggressive vitality of their faith made up for any other shortage. Their religious founder, the great Protestant reformer John Calvin, had sprung from France in the 1530s.[11] His followers in France – uncompromising, rigorously Protestant, and zealously anti-Catholic – were known as Huguenots. Part of their strength came from their faith, of course, but part came from the fact that they were concentrated in certain areas. The close cohesion and cooperation of these Huguenot communities, their vigorous defence of the centres of their religion, and their determination to spread their faith gave them a military strength far beyond their numbers.[12] They were feared, yet they also feared for themselves, and with good cause. Within living memory, in 1572, on the eve of the feast of Saint Bartholomew and through the following months, Catholics throughout France had killed as many of the leading Huguenots as they could find.

Some twenty years before Grandier's arrival in Loudun, the Huguenots' fears had been somewhat allayed when Henry IV, the present King Louis XIII's father, had offered them protection through the Edict of Nantes, which arranged for their religious and personal security, even to the point where certain cities that contained significant numbers of Huguenots were given the status of

places of "safety." In these cities (and Loudun was one), the Huguenots were guaranteed their share of royal positions in the city
government, freedom to practise their religion, and control of the
city garrison. If the guarantees had been permanent rather than
renewable and changeable every few years, a stable peace might
perhaps have been achieved in the Huguenot-dominated areas. And
if the relative numbers of Huguenots and Catholics in these areas
had remained unchanged, the peace might have lasted. Above all, if
Henry IV had remained king for a normal span, the Huguenots
would have been reassured of sympathy and support from the
crown. But none of these things happened. Henry IV was assassi-
nated in 1610. Louis XIII came to the throne at the age of nine
under the regency of his mother, an ardent and aggressive Catholic
who was determined to eradicate the "heretics" and their power in
France. When Louis rebelled against his mother's rule and assumed
power for himself, his methods with the Huguenots were more
gentle, as long as they did not wage war against him, but his
underlying desire to see Catholicism spread was undeniable.

Catholicism did spread. In part this was due to a revived Catholic
Church in France with a greater emphasis on preaching and conversion, and a revived laity and clergy. Some of the leading Huguenots read the writing on the wall; in this country centred on the
crown, preferment would in future clearly go to those who accepted
Catholicism. The losses were not enormous in number, but the effect
on Huguenot morale was considerable. These same results could be
seen in Loudun. At the time of the Edict of Nantes in 1598,
Huguenots were probably a majority in the city, and they included
the governor and most of the holders of top positions; but by 1617
Catholics equalled Huguenots in number and exceeded them in
influence.[13] There had also been a shift in power. Although the
Huguenots still held some of the positions of importance, the majority of truly powerful positions were held by Catholics or their
sympathizers. The most powerful royal position in the city was that
of the governor. After the Edict of Nantes, the governor whom the
king had appointed was a firm, even aggressive, Huguenot. By 1617
his appointment was in jeopardy, and he was soon replaced by a
new governor who, though nominally a Huguenot, converted
shortly afterwards to Catholicism.[14]

The times were violent, and religion was a matter not only of life
and death but of eternal life or endless damnation. To kill a man
or woman in order to save their souls was considered an act of

mercy by the extremists on either side. In the climate of the times, the gradual loss of power by the Huguenots of Loudun represented a grave danger; they feared that the Catholics would rise in the city and put them to the sword. Among the Catholics, things were no easier, for they feared that the Huguenots would attack them in a pre-emptive strike and kill them in their beds. Fortunately, for most of the time the moderates on each side managed to find enough common commercial and social interests to maintain a peaceful coexistence. Despite some extreme religious enmities, a working relationship for daily living was a necessity, and a balance was achieved that included trade, friendship at times, and even intermarriage. But under stress, these relationships broke down.[15] The fears were always there, and they were not merely fears of overheated imaginations.

It is doubtful whether such thoughts disturbed Urbain Grandier when he first saw Loudun. He would have been thinking about the opportunity that lay ahead rather than the dangers. It was not just the promise of a good living and financial security for his family, though this would surely have pleased him; nor was it the virtual assurance of his acceptance into the best levels of society. It was the fact that he had been selected for this post by the Jesuits of Bordeaux because the parish needed new life. His ineffective predecessor, Father de Laval, had left a somnolent parish behind him. Loudun needed a charismatic priest who would convince many Huguenots to return to Catholicism.

Still, if the dangers within Loudun were perhaps dismissed by the young priest on his arrival, there can hardly be any doubt that he had been given plenty of advice by the Jesuits before he left Bordeaux. They knew his brilliance, his charisma, his great potential, but after having had him as a pupil, boy and man, they also knew of his inability to tolerate fools, his caustic wit, his tendency to insufferable pride, and his inability to forget an insult. They would have warned him to walk carefully. They would have told him to listen before he talked.

If all that Grandier had had to contend with in Loudun had been a division between Catholics and Protestants, his position would have been simple. As a priest, he would have been a leader of the Catholic party in the city. But the Catholics and Protestants were themselves divided. On each side there were extremists, and on each side there were moderates. A moderate Catholic could be as much an enemy to an extreme Catholic as any Huguenot was. The young

priest was soon to find that in choosing his friends, he was also
choosing his enemies. The Jesuits would have told him not to side
with one faction or another until he knew which was the stronger;
then he should find a powerful patron who would protect his
interests. The Jesuits knew how to spread their faith by becoming
friends and confidants of kings, princes, and powerful nobles. They
would hardly have failed to advise their protégé, far off now and
on his own, that the way to do his work best was to find new and
powerful friends.

Nor would they have failed to warn him that on his arrival he
would be resented by many of the townsfolk because he had been
preferred over local men – men who considered that at least one of
his two rich positions should have been theirs. They would not easily
forgive him. He should therefore learn who they were. He should
learn to listen, even to foolish men. They might have little to offer,
but they would resent him if he was too clever for his own good.

To complicate matters further, there were the usual family enmities that are to be found in any restricted society. Just as there were
Montagues and Capulets in Verona, there were Trincants and de
Brous in Loudun. On top of all this, there was the question of the
city walls and the château. After the religious wars and power
struggles of the last half century, the crown had come to the conclusion that only a strong central government could ensure internal
peace in France. This required that all the strongholds be demolished. Accordingly, a series of orders were issued for city and castle
walls to be razed. Some of Loudun's townsfolk supported the king's
intention to demolish the city's walls.[16] They agreed with his policy
of maintaining peace in France through a strong central government.
Those who were against were certain that the strength of their city
walls was their greatest protection. In their eyes, a Loudun without
its walls would be a rural town without significance. This was the
view held by most of the Huguenots, though it was also held by
some of the Catholics.

Despite all these hazards, Grandier at first made a good impression on nearly everybody. His erudition and wit soon made him a
favourite visitor to the great houses in the town. People flocked to
his church to hear his sermons. He was indeed an exceptional young
man. Many a mother with daughters of marriageable age must have
yearned for what had been lost when he entered the priesthood.
Meanwhile, as well as paying attention to the rich and powerful of
Loudun, Grandier gave much of his time to his ordinary parishio-

ners, including the poorest and weakest. He earned the reputation of having an open purse and of offering comfort to those in need. As well, since Grandier had been trained by the Jesuits, he was very likely imbued with the new idea that women could play a much more active part in the social and charitable work of their parish.[17] Right from the very beginning, he probably encouraged the women of his parish to become involved in the work of the church.

Grandier's first great ceremony in his new parish was his formal installation as parish priest, a celebration that was attended by all his parishioners as well as the priests of Loudun and the surrounding area.[18] Every town dignitary was there, or at least every Catholic dignitary. The scene was a mass of colour, a pastiche of ceremonial robes, both lay and religious, mixed with the multicoloured finery of all the lay men and women. Adding splendour and mystique were the solemn processions, the ringing of bells, the wafting of incense, the light and warmth of candles, and the sonorous voices raised in praise and thanksgiving.

It is possible that Grandier's bishop, Henri Chasteignier de La Rocheposay of the Diocese of Poitiers, presided at the installation of the new priest, for this magnificent event was designed, as much as anything, to send a message to the Huguenots, a message of the splendour, power, and majesty of the true church. Grandier had probably already met the bishop. He had likely made a courtesy call on him when passing through Poitiers on his journey from Bordeaux. And La Rocheposay's first impressions of Grandier were probably favourable, as most other people's were. Since the bishop was only thirty-nine years old, he would hardly have thought Grandier too young to run a parish. Indeed, that day must have confirmed what was already being said in the town, that the new priest at Saint-Pierre-du-Marché was a fine addition to Loudun, a man with a great future.

FRIENDS AND ENEMIES

One of the most important factors in establishing Grandier as a social star in Loudun was the friendship and patronage offered him by Scévole de Sainte-Marthe. Scévole was about eighty at the time, and nobody was held in higher esteem. He was a man of outstanding learning, respected throughout France, the friend and counsellor of kings, and a former treasurer general of France. Years before, when Loudun was under siege during the religious wars and was about to fall, Scévole had negotiated with the leader of the besieging army, and Loudun had been spared. The Loudunais regarded him as their saviour.

Retired now from active life, Scévole presided over a salon of music, arts, and sciences, which not only included every cultivated person in Loudun but attracted all the powerful and learned who passed through the country. Even England's Prince of Wales, the future King Charles I, went out of his way to visit Loudun and Scévole's salon. Although it could not perhaps compare with the great salons of Paris, it was a jewel in the crown of the provincial town. Scévole made a point of inviting all who represented something of cultural value: poets, historians, astronomers, philosophers, musicians. New ideas were aired at his salon, new challenges to thought, new discoveries; every opinion was not only accepted but welcomed, provided that it was grounded on rational argument. Grandier soon became a star at these gatherings, an attraction in himself. To be accepted and befriended by Scévole de Sainte-Marthe was to have arrived indeed.[19] When Scévole died in 1623, Grandier had the honour of giving the funeral eulogy. He declaimed an oration that was so learned and well composed in the style of the times that it made his reputation far beyond the walls of Loudun. It was so highly considered that it was published and circulated in Paris, where Scévole had been as well known as he was in Loudun.

One of the leading members of Scévole's salon was Louis Trincant, a parishioner of Grandier's, who soon became a trusted friend and admirer despite the fact that he was almost twenty years older than the priest. After Scévole's death, the two men together continued the salon, moving it to Trincant's home. Trincant was one of the most important men in Loudun, third in rank in the very formal structure of the time.[20] He held the position of *procureur du roi*, the king's attorney, or public prosecutor.[21] As well as being respected as a magistrate with an extensive knowledge of the law, he was widely known as a poet and historian; he was one of the finest examples of the high quality of men and women accepted into the salon of Scévole de Sainte-Marthe. Trincant was also a strict Catholic, and like most ardent Catholics of the Counter-Reformation he considered the Huguenots a threat to religion, the state, and the safety of his fellow citizens. He pursued them at every opportunity, and they detested him.

Trincant and Grandier became inseparable. They were drawn to each other by their common culture and erudition and by mutual respect. As well, both had the reputation of showing great courtesy to their friends, however much they might pursue their enemies. The difference in their ages does not seem to have affected their friendship, for although Trincant was almost old enough to be Grandier's father, Grandier was Trincant's priest and therefore his spiritual father.

In the early days after his arrival, Grandier made friends with other important men and their families, sometimes through the salon but often through his work as a priest. Many were at the very top of the city's social structure. The most important was the governor of the city, Jean d'Armagnac II, who in time became Grandier's most powerful friend and protector.[22] D'Armagnac especially valued Grandier for his shrewdness. We know from the correspondence between them that by 1629 Grandier was secretly acting as d'Armagnac's right-hand man in the city. During the governor's long absences with the king, the priest did all he could, on the governor's behalf, to prevent or at least delay the razing of Loudun's fortifications. This was to play its part in the ruin of them both.

The de Brous were another family that was to play a significant part in Grandier's future. René de Brou, the father, was one of Loudun's leading citizens. Like Trincant, he had a wide network of relatives. A full generation older than his new parish priest, he too soon gained great personal respect for the younger man. Grandier became the spiritual adviser to the whole family, including de Brou's wife and their daughter Madeleine. Of all Grandier's friends, Madeleine proved to be the bravest and most constant, remaining loyal to him until the last day of his life, even when her own life was at risk because of their friendship. Grandier was also respected by many of the Huguenot leaders of Loudun, including the Protestant ministers. Unlike most Catholic priests, who were violently anti-Huguenot, Grandier behaved with moderation in an obvious desire to see the two communities live peaceably within the walls of the city.[23] This inevitably drew some criticism from the most ardent Catholics, but because of Grandier's friendships among the powerful, the criticism was muted.

These were good days for the young priest. He was accepted, respected, admired. He knew everybody of note in the town, and the population was sufficiently small and so interrelated that everybody knew him. For years, Grandier's position in Loudun was unassailable. Yet even in these early days the seeds of his decline were already germinating. Much as the new priest was admired, the admiration was not universal. In the good years, until 1629, when most of Loudun was on his side, it made little difference if he created a few enemies. In the bad years that followed, some of these adversaries would prove to be mortal foes.

One particular event stood out. A year or so after Grandier's arrival in Loudun, a church procession took place in which the various priests of the town took their position in order of precedence.[24] Also taking part in the procession was a bishop who was only five years older than Grandier and was unimportant because he was in disgrace at the royal court and had been exiled from the king's side. Because his family home was close to Loudun, the young bishop spent part of his exile in the Loudun area, befriended by some of the local Catholics. Any bishop, even one from another diocese, would normally take precedence over a parish priest. But on this occasion the bishop was taking part in the procession not as a bishop from his own diocese but as the prior of an abbey in the Loudun diocese. In other words, he was there as the prior of Coussay, not as the bishop of Luçon. According to church seniority, Grandier, as a canon of Sainte-Croix, outranked a visiting prior. He not only outranked this bishop/prior, but when he discovered that the visitor was to take precedence in the procession, he made an issue of it and won his point.[25] Here was a new humiliation to be added to the bishop's disgrace and expulsion from the court. A proud and ambitious man, he was not one to forget. Although he was of little importance in 1618, this minor prelate was later recalled to the king's service and eventually became the king's first minister, the most powerful man in France – Cardinal Richelieu.[26] This did not bode well for Grandier.

The controversy over Richelieu's position in the procession probably did not pass unnoticed by Grandier's bishop. During Richelieu's exile, the two bishops became close friends, with La Rocheposay showing considerable kindness to the younger man. Bishop de La Rocheposay was not the type of man who would easily accept the humiliation of a friend – a bishop and a noble – by an upstart young bourgeois priest. His dislike for Grandier, which later grew to enmity, may well have begun in 1618.[27]

There were battles, too, against some local priests who resented his appointment. They crabbed against Grandier and criticized him on every occasion. Grandier gave as good as he got. He had a devastating wit and could make astutely cutting remarks. Thus, although he had many friends among the local clergy, there were

others who disliked him intensely. One of these was René Le Mousnier, who had been a junior priest at Saint-Pierre-du-Marché; but as
the result of an embarrassing situation connected with the church
administration, he had had to leave his post there and take up
another. Subsequently, he physically attacked a fellow priest, an old
man who was a friend of Grandier. The elderly priest was injured
quite badly and took Le Mousnier before the ecclesiastical court. In
February 1618 the assailant was severely reprimanded.

Throughout this affair, Grandier came to the defence of his friend,
harrying Le Mousnier with his caustic wit and raillery. One Sunday,
in front of an enormous crowd in his church, Grandier delivered a
cutting sermon against Le Mousnier. He then descended from the
pulpit, triumphant at having stripped the priest of all respect. What
he did not realize was that Le Mousnier had entered the church and
made his way to the foot of the pulpit. There, in full view of the
congregation, he assaulted Grandier. The blows flew freely on both
sides as Grandier retreated to his sacristy, where he nearly felled the
other priest. It may seem extraordinary for two priests to behave so
belligerently, but these were violent times. Only ten years later,
Cardinal Richelieu and the archbishop of Bordeaux led the French
forces against their English and Huguenot enemies, wearing full
armour under their robes. Physical fights were commonplace, and
a man, even a priest, was expected to defend himself.

This was not the last of the affair. Because Le Mousnier had
attacked Grandier in his own church and during a service, he was
clearly in the wrong, and Grandier followed up his victory by taking
the priest before the courts. In 1620 he obtained a judgment against
Le Mousnier,[28] and he made sure that it was strictly carried out.
His aim, in part at least, was to intimidate others from attacking
him in any way.[29] But in Le Mousnier he had made a mortal enemy,
as he would later discover.

Moreover, Le Mousnier had a nephew, a priest named René
Bernier who, angered by what had happened, had a violent alterca-
tion with Grandier in the sacristy of Saint-Pierre. This fight took
place without any witnesses, but apparently Bernier attacked Grandier and tried to beat him up, whereupon Grandier took to his fists
and threw Bernier out of the door.[30] A few days later, Bernier was
returning to his village late at night when he was set on by brigands
while making his way along a path through the forest. This type of
hold-up was not unusual in those troubled times, but Bernier had
taken no precautions, for he did not expect that anyone would

attack a poor parish priest who had nothing worth stealing. Even so, what little he had was taken, and he was grievously wounded. Despite his injuries, he managed to drag himself the rest of the way home, and next day he told his uncle what had happened. Both men came to the conclusion that the attack must have been planned and that robbery was not the real motive. They were sure that Grandier was behind it. They went to the authorities and accused Grandier, but the inquiry revealed that there was not the least shred of evidence to support their allegations against the popular young priest. As a result, they lost all respect in the town. Thus Bernier, like his uncle, was added to Grandier's adversaries.

There was one other man who detested Grandier from the first. This was René Hervé, Loudun's *lieutenant-criminel*, a position that combined the functions of a principal magistrate and the chief of police. Hervé was a Catholic of extreme opinions. Like Trincant, to whom he was related,[31] he distrusted the Huguenots and believed that, given the least opportunity, they would rise up and take over the city. There was perhaps some truth to this fear, for in 1626 there was some kind of rising or revolt in the city by a group of Huguenots. It was quickly put down by Trincant and Hervé with the help of the garrison, and Hervé was ennobled for his efforts. We know relatively little of the man himself other than the fact that he had a taste for history and belles-lettres. Yet the governor, d'Armagnac, later described him in a letter as a brutal man, and he probably was, even by the standards of the time.

We do not know for certain why Hervé and Grandier could not stand each other, but their enmity was deep, bitter, and very public. In 1618, for example, there was an incident similar to the Le Mousnier case. In this instance, Hervé publicly humiliated Grandier. The priest then went up into his pulpit, and employing all his wit and the most caustic epithets, he got his own back by making a fool of Hervé, to the delight of his guffawing congregation. Furious at such an attack from this bourgeois upstart, Hervé responded by threatening Grandier and encouraging two of his supporters to throw the priest out of the pulpit. Grandier was fortunate to escape.[32] The matter did not end there. Grandier took the affair before the court in Loudun, which found in his favour and gave a severe warning to Hervé, threatening the *lieutenant-criminel* with the most serious consequences if there was any repetition of his behaviour.

There have been various suggestions about why Hervé detested Grandier. One prominent author maintained that Hervé had in his household a young woman, a cousin whom he hoped to marry but who had eyes only for Grandier.[33] Another author says that Hervé had definite plans to marry her but she became Grandier's mistress, to Hervé's fury.[34] The young woman later entered an Ursuline convent in another town, and we know nothing more about her. That Hervé had a cousin in his household who was his ward and whom he wished to marry could well be true, but that she became Grandier's mistress is almost certainly untrue. It is difficult to conceive that men such as Trincant who were filled with the religious fervour of the times would accept as a close friend a priest who had seduced a young woman in the household of one of the leading citizens. It is far more likely that Grandier, as the young woman's parish priest, did no more than encourage her to become a nun – which would certainly have infuriated Hervé, especially if she had money. A short time later he married the daughter of Loudun's mayor, Mesmin de Silly.[35] Like Bishop de La Rocheposay, Mesmin de Silly befriended Richelieu in his exile. Consequently, when Richelieu became first minister, Hervé and his friends had a direct line to the seat of power in Paris.

It was not only individual priests who resented the brilliant and popular new arrival. There were also the Carmelites and Capuchins, two of the religious orders in the town. Grandier offended both of them. He laughed at the Carmelite priests, making witty remarks about their renowned statue of the Blessed Virgin.[36] It wept miraculous tears and attracted large numbers of pilgrims, together with their alms. Grandier was highly suspicious of a stone statue that wept tears more or less on demand, and he said that the Carmelites worked more predictable miracles than the Blessed Virgin herself. The whole town heard of his views. But although he made it amusing, he regarded it as a serious matter. He had no doubt that if the Blessed Virgin wanted to make a statue cry, she could do so, but he was certain that this was not how Christ usually worked – or how the Virgin did in his name. This was the way man worked.

Grandier may well have conjectured that the whole thing had started when a penitent, praying in distress before a statue, had imagined that it cried tears – and that, as word spread, others soon imagined they saw the same thing. Perhaps the priests believed too. But the statue did not always perform, so they helped it along, drilling tiny holes in the back of the eyes and letting drops of water through. They may have reasoned that they were doing nothing wrong. The faithful believed even more in God and his miracles,

and more and more people came to pray and praise God and the
Blessed Virgin. Who could argue that was bad? More Huguenots
heard of God's miracles in the Catholic Church, and there were
more conversions. Surely a little assistance to the statue was justified
for such results. It was all for the good of God and the Holy
Church.[37]

What troubled Grandier was that it was a lie. God's work should
not be done that way! There was bound to come a time when people
discovered it to be a lie, and then they would lose faith – and not
just in the men who had lied to them. They would lose their faith
in God. Grandier attacked the Carmelites because he was convinced
that they were dangerous to the true service of God. Similarly, he
disapproved of the Capuchins, because their appeal was to people's
emotions. They too placed great emphasis on miracles as proof that
the Catholic Church was God's vehicle for salvation. As well, they
stressed the importance of fearing God and his eternal punishment,
whereas Grandier held that one should love God, not fear him.
Grandier drew back into his fold the parishioners who had been
going to the Carmelites and Capuchins, and by doing so he reani-
mated the parish.[38] It was partly by ridiculing the simplistic
approach of the Capuchins that Grandier was so successful in
reclaiming many of his parishioners.

In some ways, Grandier was kinder to the Huguenots in Loudun
than he was to the Carmelites and Capuchins. Although he was
convinced that the Huguenots were wrong in their beliefs, he held
that they still loved God and were therefore owed brotherly love
and should never be hated. Such views were dangerous in this town,
and it was not long before both the Capuchins and the Carmelites
were suggesting to those few who would listen in these early days
that Grandier seemed to be a better friend to the Huguenots than
to his fellow Catholics. The Capuchins viewed the Huguenots as the
Devil's agents. Any friend of the Huguenots was suspect as a friend
of the Devil.

Unfortunately for Grandier, his greatest strength was also his
greatest weakness. He was intellectually far superior to most of the
people around him, and he let everyone know it. As publicly as
possible, he made his adversaries seem like oafs. These incidents
reveal other facets of Grandier's character. In most of them, someone
else started the dispute, but Grandier returned even the most minor
insult with interest. To defend himself, he used his office as priest,
his considerable intelligence and wit, and his fists, and when these

were not enough he turned to the courts, usually with success. In an age of litigation, he became a litigant extraordinary. The enemies he made could do little to harm him during the years 1617 to 1629. The friendship of the most powerful men and women in town and the general admiration for him were an ample shield against the criticism of the few whom he had insulted in some way. The fire of their humiliation could not touch him.

Disaster

Grandier had twelve good years. In his life as a parish priest, he was outstandingly successful, with a reputation as a preacher that extended far beyond the limits of the town. In the town itself he was accepted into the best society as an equal. Although of "good stock," he could not normally have aspired to be accepted on such terms by the cream of Loudun society. In the fixed social structure of his time, he had come up in the world. His advice was sought not only in matters of conscience and religion but in financial concerns and for general counsel. He was comfortably rich with the security of a well-established income from his benefices, and he lived in a prosperous city in a rich, warm, and bountiful region. Apart from this general good fortune, not much is known about Grandier's life in this period, but the lack of record is evidence that his life was untrammelled, for there was no such dearth of material once disaster struck.

In 1626 an event occurred that would have a momentous effect on Grandier's future. A convent of teaching nuns was established in the town. Nobody could have guessed that eight years later these nuns would bear the immediate responsibility for leading the priest to his death. They were Ursulines, an order recently established in France, and their advent was a major event for Loudun. The town had previously had no schooling for girls, but with their arrival they undertook to run a free school where any girl could go daily. There the children were not only taught religion and prayers, but they learned to read, write, and count and were trained in sewing, weaving, lace working, and other skills that would help them in employment. This was an immense step forward in both education

and social work. Richer girls also attended the convent, often boarding there. They too were educated to their social level and taught
the skills appropriate to their position.

Every community wanted one of these new teaching convents. In
time, any town that did not have one was regarded as a backwater.
The eight nuns who had been sent from Poitiers to start the convent
at Loudun were given a tumultuous welcome when they arrived. On
descending from their carriage at the gates of the town, they were
met by a great crowd of people and were then conducted through
the streets by all the priests and the principal laymen to the accom-
paniment of singing, candles, and music in a great welcoming
celebration.[1] But once the nuns entered their new home, they were
never supposed to be seen again in public. Theirs was an enclosed
order. The little girls could go to the convent for their lessons, but
the nuns would never come out.

Grandier was probably one of the many influential dignitaries of
Loudun who had encouraged the establishment of the convent; he
was always interested in progress. And it so happened that their
house was within his parish bounds. But as was usually the case,
the nuns had their own chaplain, so Grandier had no direct contact
with them either at the time or in the coming years. Throughout his
trial he always claimed that he had never met the nuns, and there
seems no doubt that this was true.[2]

Meanwhile, events far outside Loudun were affecting the beautiful
stronghold. The Thirty Years War, which had started in 1618, was
a constant though distant backdrop, wreaking devastation on much
of Europe. But of more immediate consequence to Loudun was the
rise of the once lowly Bishop Richelieu in the favour of the king.
Richelieu had been called back to Paris in 1619 to be one of the
king's advisers, and by the time of the Ursulines' arrival in Loudun
he was not only the king's first minister, but had been made a
cardinal, a prince of the church. The rise of Richelieu brought an
unexpected threat to Loudun. As noted above, his policy and that
of the king was to reduce the power of the nobles and the fortified
towns in France by razing the walls of all fortifications. The internal
strongholds of France were no small problem to the crown. In 1610
the seigneurs of 70,000 fiefs occupied châteaux furnished with
cannons as redoubtable as those of the royal artillery.[3] The initial
decision to demolish Loudun's walls and château had formally been
made known to the city in 1622, but its execution had been
deferred.[4] By late 1628, however, three successive Huguenot risings

elsewhere in France had determined the king to forestall any possibility of the Huguenots of Loudun rebelling and taking over one of the strongest fortresses in the kingdom.[5]

During the intervening years, the city was divided between those who wanted the defences strengthened (because they hoped to take over the town and its fortress if civil war broke out again) and those who wanted total destruction of the walls. Yet this was never as simple as a straight division on lines of Catholic and Huguenot. Without its walls, Loudun would become just another country town, open to any roving band of troops. So it was possible to be an active anti-Huguenot and still want to see the walls maintained. Similarly, it was possible to be an ardent Huguenot and yet feel that in the long run safety lay in losing the walls but keeping the favour of the central power, which alone could police the peace throughout the country. The entire town was fractured by these divisions.

There was one individual who stood to lose more than anybody else by the destruction of the walls, and this was the governor, Jean d'Armagnac. At the time of his appointment, the city had been one of the strongest in France, and the position of governor had carried enormous prestige, a testimonial to the world of one's standing as a favourite of the king. If the walls were lost and the fortifications of his château torn down, d'Armagnac would be governor of nothing more than a provincial market town. The razing of the walls would be a public statement that he had lost his influence with the king, that he was a man of the past, and that Richelieu was the man of the future. D'Armagnac had been doing everything in his power to persuade the king to save the walls of Loudun. Meanwhile, since he had to be at the king's side nearly all the time to carry out his duties, he relied heavily on the information sent him by his protégé Grandier about what steps the cardinalist party was taking to influence Richelieu or do his bidding.

Over the years, the bitterness between the "cardinalists" and the "localists" became more and more severe. The crisis reached a new level on the 28 December 1628 when a royal message from Paris informed the inhabitants of Loudun that their walls and castle were to be demolished within a few weeks. Even worse, Richelieu planned to create a model town some twelve miles away, which was to be named Richelieu after his family[6] and was to take over many of Loudun's legal and administrative functions. This news split Loudun's leaders even further, for while some were very much against the transfer of powers, others expected to gain from the move. With all this friction among the people of Loudun, choosing the wrong side could be dangerous, and Grandier did choose the wrong side. He was firmly in the camp of those who wanted to keep the walls strong. From this time on, acting ever more openly on behalf of d'Armagnac, Grandier did everything he could to frustrate the destructive plans of Richelieu and his adherents in Loudun. He was making more enemies – and strong ones.

Early in 1629, Grandier was suddenly struck by a personal disaster. Everything he had worked for – his career, his position in society, his reputation, the good name of his family, his own peace and tranquillity – were threatened overnight. It could hardly have been worse, and he could blame nobody but himself. Philippe Trincant, the twenty-five-year-old elder daughter of his great friend Louis Trincant, was pregnant, and he was the father.[7] What do we know about this event? Since there was never any documentary proof that Grandier seduced Philippe Trincant and that she had a child by him, how do we know that it did in fact happen? Since Grandier's death flowed from the enmity that developed between himself and the whole Trincant family, it is important to establish whether the source of this enmity was indeed Philippe's seduction.

The first author to tell the full story was Nicolas Aubin, a Huguenot minister who had lived in Loudun in his youth and later moved to the Netherlands, an area much more receptive to Huguenots than France was in the late seventeenth century. In his book *Histoire des diables de Loudun*, which was written about fifty years after the event, he described the seduction of Philippe. He could only have been repeating the Loudun rumours, since the Trincant family had gone to considerable lengths to hide the shameful event, and nobody ever had anything more than gossip to work on. But the fact that it was undocumented rumour does not mean that the story can be dismissed. Although Aubin was an old man when he wrote his book, it was widely read, and there must have been many in Loudun who could have argued with his assertion if it had been substantially false. So we may take it that there is a considerable likelihood that he was repeating something that was already common knowledge. Because Aubin was a Huguenot he told the story from a very anti-Catholic viewpoint, but while many Catholic authors later argued every possible point of contention about his book, none of them ever argued that Philippe's seduction was untrue.[8]

What other evidence do we have? Certainly, a very telling point is that Trincant, together with all his relatives and closest friends,

suddenly became Grandier's mortal foes. Clearly, some grievous
event occurred in 1629 that caused Trincant, the former devoted
friend, to become a deadly enemy. Beyond these circumstantial
indications of Philippe's seduction, there is one piece of documentary
evidence that indicates that she had a child whose legitimacy was
doubtful. Her seduction, or at least the resulting conception, must
have taken place in late 1628 or early 1629, probably between
January and March 1629.[9] Trincant and his allies began their first
attack on Grandier in the summer of 1629.

On 7 June 1629[10] Philippe married a man named Louis Moussaut.
Ten months later a child was baptized. The baptismal record is most
unusual. The child was declared to be the son of Philippe and
Moussaut, but the record is extraordinary because Philippe's father,
Louis Trincant, specifically asked that the baby be named not
Moussaut but Trincant-Moussaut.[11] The baptismal record reads:

On Tuesday the tenth April 1630 was baptized Louis, son of Maistre Louis
Moussault, lawyer at the parlement, nominated heir to the position of the
King's procurator at the royal seats (courts) of Loudun, and of demoiselle
Philippe Trincant, which Louis Moussault was born on the preceding day
between six and seven o'clock in the evening. The godfather was Maistre
Louis Trincant, the King's procurator in the said courts, the grandfather,
who asks that his grandson take the name of Trincant along with that of
Moussaut, together with his coat of arms. The grandmother was Rachel
Mesmin ... The baptism was performed by Messire Gervais Meschin,
priest.

Why would Louis Trincant want his daughter's first child to be
named after himself in this way? Such an event was unknown in
those days. And why would Louis Moussaut permit this extraordinary request? He could not be sure that he would ever have a second
son to bear his own name alone; it seems remarkable that he would
allow this first son to be called Trincant. When another child was
born to the couple in July 1632, there was no hesitation in giving
him the Moussaut name. The only reasonable explanation seems to
be that the first baby was not in fact Moussaut's.

It is true that Philippe's wedding and the baptism of the baby
were separated by ten months, which would seem to make the child
legitimate. But was the baptized infant in fact a newborn baby? It
seems more likely that the child was conceived before the wedding,
hidden away for some weeks after birth, and then presented as the

newborn offspring of Louis and Philippe. True, this would have needed the connivance of the priest, Gervais Meschin, for it would have been obvious to him that the baby was not newborn.[12] But as we will discover, Gervais Meschin later deliberately made false accusations in the courts against Grandier on Trincant's behalf. He was clearly Trincant's man. But why did Moussaut, having agreed to pretend that the baby was his, allow it to have the Trincant name? The baptismal notice may give a clue: he was nominated to become the king's procurator, the position currently held by Louis Trincant. Perhaps the promise of succeeding to his father-in-law's prestigious post was enough to tip the balance.

And what of Philippe's reactions? They are not hard to picture: her horror when her period was delayed; her growing certainty that it was not going to come; her first visit to Grandier with the dreadful news, most likely delivered to him in the confessional. And Grandier's reaction: shock and fear, followed by an examination of all the possible courses of action, and the realization that there were none. He could not marry. He could not admit publicly that he was the father – that would only make matters worse for both himself and Philippe. There was only one course open to him. He would admit nothing to anybody. Let Trincant find the way out for his daughter. In choosing to play his hand this way, Grandier held a trump card, for Trincant would never publicly state that his daughter was pregnant by the priest; the shame would be unbearable. And as long as nobody was able to accuse Grandier of being the father, he did not even have to deny it.

Philippe must soon have realized that Grandier would do nothing for her. She could only turn to her father. She must have dreaded telling the proud Trincant that she was pregnant by the priest, the untouchable man. Loudun was a town in which everyone of any importance knew all the others intimately, where families hung together because the reputations of all were tied to the reputation of any one of them. An embarrassment to any of the families was a cause of gossip.

In any other case, unless the child's father was already married, Trincant would have been able to force the scoundrel to marry Philippe. The baby could always be called premature. But that path was closed. So Trincant approached Louis Moussaut, who had long had eyes for Philippe. Already a senior lawyer in the Loudun administration, Moussaut was an ambitious man who had hopes of buying Trincant's office as *procureur du roi* when he retired – or perhaps of inheriting it. (It is possible that an understanding already existed that Philippe and Louis Moussaut would wed. The Moussauts were an important Catholic family in the town.)

Whatever the details, when Louis married Philippe he must have known about her condition and could hardly have been happy about it. But in return he was promised Trincant's position not years ahead but within a few months, and in fact he succeeded Trincant as *procureur du roi* about a year later.[13] Of course, the marriage did not stop the rumours, but it did stop public humiliation. Who was going to risk any insinuations against Philippe when the most powerful group of men in the town were personally involved? Trincant and Louis Moussaut were two of the crown's senior legal officers in Loudun, and Hervé, Trincant's nephew, was the harsh chief of police.

So Philippe was confined to her home and the baby was born. Both the doctor and the apothecary were relatives who were fully prepared to cooperate. The doctor was almost certainly the surgeon René Mannoury, who was Trincant's cousin and Mesmin de Silly's nephew. The apothecary was Pierre Adam, Trincant's nephew. Both were bitter enemies of Grandier for ever after.

Aubin adds some details about the birth of the baby.[14] According to him, Philippe had a friend, Marthe le Pelletier, who was not well off and lived with her as her companion. The story goes that when Philippe had Grandier's baby, Trincant forced Marthe to say that it was hers, and she took it as her own and gave it to a wet nurse to be raised.[15] There was indeed a Marthe le Pelletier. Her name appears from time to time in the baptismal records as the godmother of different children, including three for whom Louis Trincant signed as godfather, so she certainly knew the family.[16] Church records describe Marthe as "Dame" and "Honorable Dame," titles which show her to have been of good birth. There is no record of a baby being born to her in 1629 or 1630, though we know that she stayed in Loudun and was married later.[17]

So where does the story about Marthe really fit into the events surrounding Philippe's baby? The most probable explanation is that Aubin, writing fifty years later and working from rumour and gossip, did not get the facts about her correct. It is likely that Marthe was indeed Philippe's close friend, a girl of good birth but poor. Perhaps, as Philippe's companion, she connived at their secret meetings and bore some measure of blame in Trincant's eyes for his daughter's seduction. Perhaps Trincant forced Marthe, with money or threats, to remove the baby and bring it back as a "newborn" after Philippe had been married for more than the necessary nine months; we cannot be sure. What we do know is that this baby almost certainly did not have Louis Moussaut as his father.

With Philippe's marriage and the legitimization of the baby, Trincant had solved the immediate problem; his family was in the clear.[18] But his anger against Grandier was enormous. He had treated the priest as a favourite son, had opened his home and heart to him, only to be betrayed, humiliated, and made a laughing stock throughout the town – even if it was muted laughter behind closed doors. Despite the fact that Trincant was a noble who had great influence and authority in his own right as well as connections to the most powerful man in France,[19] he could not openly take any steps against Grandier for the crime the priest had committed. And it was indeed a crime, not just a moral offence. What Grandier had done was a crime in both church and secular law; a priest convicted of seducing a parishioner could be executed for it. But Trincant's hands were tied. Even if he discreetly made a formal complaint to the church authorities, there would have to be an inquiry, and word would get out.

To rub salt into the wound, Grandier was going about his daily life as if nothing had happened. Not only did he still carry on all his duties as a parish priest, but he continued to enjoy an untrammelled social life. He even went to the houses of mutual friends when Trincant was present, and acted quite normally.[20] As the weeks of Philippe's pregnancy went by, Grandier must have felt a growing relief. It looked as if he was going to get away with it. But Trincant was merely biding his time.

Here, a group of close family members enters the action. They include the apothecary Adam, a priest named Jean Mignon who was another Trincant nephew,[21] Mannoury the surgeon, and Hervé the *lieutenant-criminel*. Since these men all had professional as well as family involvement, they must have been told the truth quite early on and sworn to secrecy. We can be sure that Trincant kept this inner group as small as possible. Beyond this core there was a wider group of relatives who together supported Trincant no matter what the rumours about Philippe. From this time on, members of this family compact met secretly in the shop of the apothecary and plotted against Grandier to destroy him.

Trincant's immediate problem was that he had to cut Grandier off from his household at the very time when the rumours about

An etching of Urbain Grandier,
author and date unknown.
Source: Musée Charbonneau-Lassay, Ville de Loudun

Philippe's pregnancy were flying. Despite her marriage, there were
suggestions that Louis Moussaut was not the father. If Trincant
broke with Grandier at this time without obvious cause, it would
not take long for people to put two and two together and guess that
the priest was the father. Trincant therefore had to find a reason to
break openly with Grandier.

His solution was to announce that he had been offered evidence
that the priest had secretly been living a lecherous existence, and

that when he had faced Grandier with this, the priest had responded with such personal insults that Trincant felt bound to ask everyone to refuse him further friendship. In view of Grandier's well-known proclivity for insulting those who offended him, this explanation would be thoroughly convincing, especially when coming from Trincant. Not only did Trincant have a fine reputation, but he had lived in Loudun all his life, unlike Grandier, the "foreigner."

The first signs of trouble for Grandier, although ominous, were merely embarrassing. Trincant's family connections throughout the town began to avoid him and make it clear that he was unwelcome. Then the same began to happen with mutual friends. This was because word was being spread that Grandier had been consorting with all kinds of women. This supposedly model priest had been living a disgustingly immoral life, it was said, and he was becoming worse and worse. No man's wife or daughter was safe; the confessional, the site of forgiveness, had become the site of Grandier's approaches to the women of Loudun, a centre of lechery. As the Trincant family made it known that the priest was now *persona non grata*, every friend of Trincant's followed suit. To do otherwise would have been a personal insult to the family.

This exclusion of Grandier from certain sections of society in which he had formerly been welcomed was hurtful, but the hurt weighed lightly compared with what the result of his foolishness might have been. However, Trincant was not content merely to spread rumours. To give substance to his reasons for breaking with the priest, he needed to have specific accusations. These would serve a further purpose, for they would allow the Trincants to pursue the priest before his bishop for his supposedly libertine behaviour.

THE THIBAULT AFFAIR

To this point, Grandier believed that it was only his reputation that was being damaged, and he was sure he could repair that, given time. He thought the worst was over. He did not appreciate how deep was Trincant's hatred or how implacable his enmity. Trincant was determined that this jumped-up bourgeois who had wormed his way into the best society in Loudun must be chased from the town, must lose his rich benefices and be thoroughly disgraced. But this would take time. For the present, the Trincants continued to exert damage control to protect their reputation by fanning the rumours about Grandier's "newly discovered" immoral life. Before long, almost everyone in Loudun was gossiping about the priest's debauchery.

The chatter even reached into the Ursuline Convent through the grille – the mesh of iron bars through which all spoken contact between the nuns and the outside world took place. Although other nuns needed permission to talk with outsiders, the mother superior could use the grille at her own discretion. In the account she later wrote about the events in her convent,[22] Jeanne des Anges stated that once she had become mother superior and could do what she wanted, she spent far more time than was proper at the grille, talking to visitors about matters in the world outside. When the stories about the priest reached her, she most likely passed them on to others in the house.

Meanwhile, the Trincant family was pursuing its campaign of retribution. In the summer of 1629, soon after Philippe became pregnant, a formal complaint was made to the bishop that Grandier was taking decisions as a parish priest that were beyond his authority. The involvement of the bishop was an important step in Trincant's plan, for the only person who could remove the priest from his position in Loudun was Chastenier de La Rocheposay, the bishop of Poitiers. Grandier had granted a dispensation regarding the reading of marriage banns, which only a bishop had the right to do. Clearly, a haughty bishop such as La Rocheposay, who was jealous of his prerogatives and was never on close terms with his priests, would take objection to such effrontery.[23]

This initial attack was based on church law. From Trincant's point of view, it had the advantage of striking at Grandier without being connected in any way with Philippe's condition or the rumours that were floating around. Although the matter was not severe enough to get the priest banished, it was bound to annoy the bishop. La Rocheposay's animosity to Grandier in the years to come was undoubtedly influenced by this episode. Indeed, Trincant was carefully laying the ground for the more serious accusations he was planning. The bishop reacted as expected. He immediately instituted a formal inquiry by two senior priests, one of whom was Gilles Robert, a Trincant relative and an old antagonist of Grandier; the other was Father Moussaut, the spiritual director of the Ursuline Convent of Loudun.[24] He was an uncle of the Louis Moussaut who had agreed to marry Philippe Trincant.[25] The inquiry was thus to be directed by Grandier's enemies, and he viewed it seriously enough to complain that the archpriest Robert was known to be his enemy. But worse was to come, for Trincant made sure that the bishop heard the rumours about Grandier's immoral behaviour. As a result, La Rocheposay instructed the priests inquiring into the case to find out what else Grandier had been up to in Loudun.

A sudden and unplanned development now took place that thrust the whole Grandier affair in a totally unexpected direction. It was precipitated by a hot-headed soldier named Jacques de Thibault. Thibault was a member of the minor nobility and seems to have been a native of Loudun. He was one of the cardinalist party and an active supporter of the proposal to raze the city walls. As a longtime foe of Grandier's, he had suffered much from the priest's quick tongue. Perhaps even more relevant was the fact that he was related to Philippe Trincant.[26] Did he have some particular friendship with Philippe or some other member of the family? There must have been something to make this man act as he did. Hothead though he was, he must surely have been close to the centre of the affair to have involved himself so deeply.

We can see in this instance an example of how the Trincant cabal went about its task of destroying Grandier's reputation. Thibault went to one of Grandier's rich and important friends in Loudun[27] and told him lurid tales of the priest's lecherous behaviour. The friend, who was also very close to Trincant, would have nothing more to do with the curé. Grandier was deeply affected by this and could not hide his distress. When another acquaintance told him what Thibault was saying about him, Grandier was furious.[28] Shortly afterwards he happened to meet Thibault in the Place Sainte-Croix, the open space outside the Church of Sainte-Croix. As a canon of Sainte-Croix, Grandier was on his way there, fully robed, to attend a service. He was so angry with the soldier that he went up to him and demanded that he explain himself, and he used such strong and caustic language that Thibault lost control and beat the defenceless priest over the head with his cane. Grandier had enough sense not to take him on and make the situation even worse. Without a further word he retired, bloody, but with as much dignity as he could summon. This was in October 1629 when Philippe had been pregnant for some months.

Thibault was widely condemned for his outrageous behaviour, but this was not the end of the matter. To attack a priest when he was clothed in his vestments was to attack the church, one of the two great authorities in the land. It was a crime that could be heavily

punished if it was pursued by the priest, and pursued it was, for
Grandier was not a man to let an insult pass without response. The
very next day he left for Paris to plead personally to the king for
justice against Thibault. His departure and its purpose were widely
known in Loudun.

It now becomes evident that Trincant had for some time been
hatching more than rumours in his efforts to destroy Grandier. He
knew that the accusations of lechery had to be given substance; they
had to be supported by evidence that would be damaging enough
to cause the priest's banishment or even imprisonment. Trincant had
been creating this evidence. Thibault's precipitate action caused him
to make his move earlier than he had planned and before he was
really ready, but he had no choice. It would be much harder to enlist
the bishop's support if Grandier won a judgment against Thibault
for false accusations of lechery. Consequently, the cabal had to get
in its attack right away.

A letter to the bishop was immediately prepared which accused
Grandier of "having debauched married and unmarried women, of
being impious and profane, of never having said his breviary, and
even of having seduced a woman in his church." The plotters did
not sign these accusations themselves. They arranged for the complaint to be laid by two men of the neighbourhood, Cherbonneau
and Bougreau. This indicates that Trincant and his relatives had
been working at the scheme for some time. Only if the papers had
already been far advanced could he and his cabal have moved at
such speed. Furthermore, if Trincant had had time to build his case
more carefully, it would have been without loopholes. As a prose-
cuting lawyer, he must have known that it would not stand up to
serious examination. But Thibault's attack had forced his hand.

Trincant may already have known that the bishop was not going
to question the case too closely. As a leading Catholic and a leading
citizen of Loudun, he would know Bishop de La Rocheposay well
enough to confide in him, certain that anything he revealed would
be treated with the secrecy of the confessional. He had probably
told La Rocheposay, in the strictest confidence, that the priest had
seduced his daughter, and had asked him what redress was available.
Like Trincant, the bishop would know that nothing could be done
that did not involve revealing that Grandier had seduced Philippe,
but his anger with the priest would be immense. He would want to
punish Grandier almost as much as Trincant did, so the least he

could do was tell Trincant that if he was provided with any grounds, he would prosecute Grandier to the limit. The bishop's later actions, apparently so unjust, cruel, and arbitrary, become totally understandable if he knew about the seduction of Philippe.

Trincant and Hervé left immediately to see La Rocheposay, taking the letter themselves. They were warmly received. The inquiry set up in Loudun about Grandier and the marriage banns was now complete, and the report was placed in the bishop's hands at the same time as the new accusations against Grandier. The two documents reinforced each other and together were convincing enough for La Rocheposay to order Grandier's arrest. This he could do as a bishop exercising ecclesiastical authority over one of his priests. He issued the following order on 21 October 1629:

Henri-Loys Chastaigner de la Rocheposay, by divine mercy Bishop of Poitiers. In view of the charges and information provided to us by the archpriest of Loudun against Urbain Grandier, priest, curé of Saint-Pierre-du-Marché of Loudun ... and in view also of the conclusions of our Promoter on these submissions, we have ordered and do order that the said Grandier, the accused, be sent without scandal to the prisons in our episcopal seat in Poitiers ...[29]

This order of arrest placed Grandier at the mercy of his enemies, but they took care to keep its existence secret until they were ready to spring the trap.

In the meantime, Grandier had reached Paris. Thanks to the protection of his good friend Jean d'Armagnac, he obtained an audience with Louis XIII. The king, a pious man, was shocked to hear of the scandal that had been caused in Loudun by Thibault's beating and promised the priest that justice would be done. Within a few days, Grandier's case was referred to the law courts of the Parlement of Paris, the highest legal authority for that area of France.[30] Very quickly, Thibault, in Loudun, received an order to appear before the court in Paris. By chance, Thibault received this summons on the same day that Trincant and Hervé returned from Poitiers bearing the bishop's order for Grandier's arrest. The family cabal realized that the bishop's document could serve a dual purpose. As well as achieving Grandier's early arrest, it could save Thibault from a very serious penalty for his hot-headed action. He left immediately for Paris bearing the arrest order. It was agreed that he could use it against Grandier in any way that would do the priest the greatest harm and his own cause the greatest good.

At the appointed time, the two adversaries appeared before the court. Grandier's lawyer pleaded his client's case eloquently, and there seemed little doubt that Thibault would be severely punished for his attack. But just when Grandier was on the point of victory, Thibault asked to be allowed to speak. He described in the most vivid terms the behaviour with women that Grandier was being accused of in Loudun. He called the priest debauched and evil, and said that his immorality was scandalizing the whole of Loudun and that the best families in the town were in despair at having such a man as their parish priest.[31] These outrageous accusations, coming from a man who had already behaved with violence against the priest, shocked the judges. There was the priest standing in front of them, a man of fine bearing and good deportment, neatly and cleanly dressed, a man who had spoken well and eloquently before them. Everything that Thibault said seemed only to confirm the justice of Grandier's cause. But Thibault played it well. At the perfect moment, he pulled from his pocket the order for Grandier's arrest, issued and signed by the priest's own bishop. He then read it to the judges. Grandier was totally confounded. Moreover, the judges immediately ordered that Grandier be sent to his bishop to be tried in the ecclesiastical court.

THE LOUDUN ACCUSATIONS

While all this was going on in Paris, a new inquiry, ordered by the bishop, was proceeding in Loudun. Its purpose was to find the truth about the specific accusations of immorality that had been made against Grandier. The commissioners whom the bishop appointed for this inquiry would seem to have been an excellent choice. One was a very senior priest and qualified administrator in the diocese; the other was an outstanding lawyer and judge and a leading Catholic layman. Nobody could criticize the appointment of such eminent men. Still, they were hardly likely to be totally objective, for one was Gilles Robert, to whom Grandier had already objected as an enemy, and the other was Louis Trincant.

Had the bishop already made up his mind that Grandier was guilty when he appointed these men? And had he in his own mind already found Grandier worthy of severe punishment? It is hard to believe otherwise. If the bishop knew about Philippe's seduction, he had on his hands a priest who had committed a most heinous crime for which he could not openly be accused without destroying the Trincant family. Yet the priest had to be punished. So it would seem only sensible to appoint to this inquiry men who would not be swayed by the priest's charisma.

It is in this inquiry that we find some of the earliest evidence of the family enmities in Loudun that were to play their part in the Grandier affair. One of the priest's close friends and constant supporters was the most important man in the hierarchy of Loudun after the governor: Guillaume de Cerisay, the *bailli* of Loudun.[32] The *bailli* was the officer of the crown responsible for the administration of justice in the town and a wide area of surrounding countryside. The most startling allegation that had been sent to the bishop was the extraordinary contention that the *bailli*'s mother-in-law, Madeleine de Dreux (who had died recently), was one of the women with whom Grandier had had carnal relations in his church. To accuse her was to dishonour all her relatives. These included de Cerisay and his two closest associates, Louis and Charles Chauvet. Swept into the same net were the de Brou family, all related to de Cerisay and the Chauvets, and particularly Madeleine de Brou, who was a friend of both Françoise and Urbain Grandier. This accusation gives some indication of the hatreds that were seething in Loudun. Madeleine de Dreux had lived a blameless and virtuous life, but she was dead and could not defend herself so was a convenient target for such an accusation.

It seems that Trincant took the position that anyone who remained Grandier's friend was automatically his own enemy. From this time on, de Cerisay, the Chauvets, and Madeleine de Brou were continually attacked by the Trincant family compact, even to the point of death.[33] But there was another reason why the dishonouring of Madeleine de Dreux was attractive to the Trincants. An assault on the *bailli* and his relatives was, in effect, an assault on those who sided with d'Armagnac, who with Grandier's help was striving to keep the Loudun walls.[34] They were still fighting to prevent or at least delay Cardinal Richelieu's intended reduction of Loudun's power as an administrative centre.

Now that Trincant was heading the inquiry, a number of people came forward with charges against Urbain Grandier. One of the first was René Bernier, the curé of Trois-Moutiers, and his uncle René

Le Mousnier, who had been Grandier's enemies from his early days
in Loudun. They testified that he had committed the most heinous
crimes, and Trincant accepted it all without demanding proof. The
worst and most damaging of the depositions came from one of
Grandier's vicars, a priest named Gervais Meschin.[35] Why he was
so bitter against his curé is not known, but he went to Trincant's
house and in the presence of Trincant's nephew, the priest Jean
Mignon, and Hervé, the *lieutenant-criminel*, he signed a deposition

that he had found Grandier lying full out with married and unmarried
women in the Church of Saint-Pierre-du-Marché with the doors locked;
that at all hours of the day and night he had seen unmarried and married
women coming to find the said Grandier in his room and that some of the
said women stayed there from one o'clock in the afternoon to two or three
o'clock in the morning and had their supper brought by their servants,
who left straight away; that he had seen the said Grandier in the church
with the doors open and that some women having entered, he closed
them.[36]

Meschin added that Grandier never said his breviary. Even this was
a serious accusation. The breviary contained a set of prayers that a
priest was bound to say at certain times each day. Failure to do so
was a serious offence in the eyes of the church.

   Another priest also came forward, one Martin Boulliau. He provided the formal accusation against Madeleine de Dreux. He testified
that one evening at sunset he had entered Saint-Pierre-du-Marché to
make his devotions and had noticed Urbain Grandier walking alone
in his church. Preoccupied by something else, Grandier did not see
him. Boulliau suspected some intrigue, so he kept out of sight and
found a place in the sacristy where he could spy on Grandier without
being seen:

He saw that the said Grandier closed the main door of the church having
looked about, and a little time afterwards he opened the door of the
church, and shortly afterwards the now dead Demoiselle Magdallaine [*sic*]
Dreulx entered and she went in the Dreulx pew, where she knelt, as he
believed, and he saw the said Grandier enter the Dreulx pew having crossed
the church; that he saw them both standing and that the said Grandier
had his two arms on those of the said Demoiselle and that it was a lewd
action and unworthy of the said Grandier and of the place.[37]

When Boulliau had finished his deposition, Trincant had him sign it. Unfortunately for the priest, he did not to read it over and thus failed to notice that Trincant had substituted the words "that he saw the said Demoiselle in the sexual act with the said curé."

Despite the precautions taken by Trincant to keep Boulliau's testimony secret until it could be submitted to the bishop, word soon got out. Understandably, the *bailli* was furious about the accusation made against his wife's mother. He had Martin Boulliau hauled before a judge from the *bailliage*. Faced with this judge, Martin Boulliau was much more humble and was ready to admit that what had actually happened was quite different. The judge's record is clear:

Questioned by Philippe Martin [the judge] if he had seen Magdallaine Dreulx in a sexual act with the said curé:

Said no and that he had never spoken in these terms and that if it had been written down that way, it was wrong and against his intention ... Then he was asked if he had been threatened or intimidated to let the deposition stand as now written. He replied that nobody had intimidated him but that Gilles Robert, the archpriest, had told him that if he was to change the written testimony now and remove the accusation about the sexual act, there would be grounds for having him questioned under torture [presumably for perjury]. Now, in front of this judge, he reaffirmed that he had only seen the curé from a distance speaking to the said Demoiselle and having his hands resting on her arms without kissing her or performing an indecent action.[38]

This "clarification" was a clear denial of his earlier deposition. It was signed by both Boulliau and the judge and became part of the official record. The Dreux family and especially the good name of Madeleine de Dreux came out of this affair safe and sound, but it was a warning to Grandier as well as the *bailli* and all who might be affected by the Grandier case: there were no limits to how far Trincant and his friends would go to ensnare Urbain Grandier.

Even when the Boulliau story has been told, the question still remains, Why did he come forward in the first place if there was no truth to his testimony? The answer is straightforward enough; Boulliau was dependent on the Trincant family. He held his position on a rental from one of Trincant's sons. If it was withdrawn, he would lose his living. To Trincant he had seemed a particularly valuable witness because he lived in the rectory of Saint-Pierre-du-Marché in the room next to Grandier's. One could expect his testimony to have the ring of truth. For Grandier himself, the outcome was less than happy. Although the Boulliau deposition carried less weight than had been intended, the battle was far from over. Clearly, Trincant was doing all he could to collect fresh depositions, true or false.

Grandier and His Bishop

Grandier had been ordered by the Parlement of Paris to go to Poitiers immediately and hand himself over to his bishop, but he delayed for a day before leaving Paris in order to see his patron, Jean d'Armagnac. Grandier may have considered this essential, but it was typical of him to think that his powerful friends and his own exceptional qualities permitted him to interpret the parlement's decision the way he wanted to. It was foolish to disregard the court order. D'Armagnac made it clear to Grandier that he was as appalled as the priest at the accusations that had been concocted by Bougreau and Cherbonneau, and he assured him of his continuing support. The governor had many powerful friends, and his influence could be valuable in small ways as well as large. He counselled Grandier to go to Poitiers straightaway and deliver himself into the hands of La Rocheposay. He should not risk anybody saying that he was treating the bishop's arrest order lightly. In addition, d'Armagnac gave Grandier letters of introduction to a number of influential men in Poitiers, and he promised to write personally to La Rocheposay, with whom he was on good terms.

Grandier was greatly reassured by all this support and hastened back to Loudun, which was on the way to Poitiers. When he got there he found that Thibault had arrived the day before, having gone straight from Paris rather than delaying for a day as Grandier had done. Grandier's friends informed him how actively Trincant was working to collect new depositions against him. This was disturbing news, and it finally struck the priest that he should get to Poitiers and hand himself over to his bishop as quickly as possible. Unfortunately for him, this became known to his enemies, who laid plans to have the bishop's order of arrest executed before Grandier arrived at La Rocheposay's residence. If the priest could be made to look as if he had been taking his time, that would put him in a much worse light when the prelate dealt with his case.

Grandier left Loudun first thing the next morning. On arriving in Poitiers after his lengthy and dusty journey, he went to a hostelry to clean up and attend to his appearance before reporting to the bishop. But Thibault, who had preceded him, discovered where he was staying and went straight to La Rocheposay to tell him that the curé was in Poitiers and had not given himself up as he had been ordered. He sought authority to have him arrested, and this was granted. A short time later, the chief of police, accompanied by his men, burst into Grandier's room. The priest protested against this unnecessary act of arrest when he was already about to hand himself over to the bishop, but it was to no avail. The record of the arrest said that Grandier was "found in this said town of Poitiers, in the hostelry run by the widow Litault in her house."[1] The wording left no doubt that as far as the authorities were concerned, Grandier had had to be "found" because he had avoided giving himself up. The date was 15 November 1629.

At the bishop's prison, Grandier was placed in a damp, ill-lit stone cell – at this coldest time of the year – and was refused any kind of comfort. His family was not allowed to provide him with warm clothing, nor was his mother allowed to visit him or send him anything that might sustain him in his confinement. Even his strong constitution could not stand up against such treatment, and by the end of two weeks he was running a violent fever. Since there was no sign of activity on his case, his only recourse was to throw himself on the mercy of his bishop, to whom he now wrote:

Monseigneur, I have always believed and even taught that affliction was the true path to heaven, but I have only experienced it since your goodness, moved by the fear of my loss and the desire for my salvation, has thrown me into a place where a fortnight of misery has brought me closer to God than did forty years of prosperity. By which I recognize that God, who uses both good and ill for his own glory and our benefit, in his wish to guide the work of my conversion, has happily coupled the face of man with that of the lion. I hear of your moderation with the passion of my enemies, who wishing to see me lost like another Joseph have brought about my approach to the kingdom of God. The profit that I have drawn from their persecution has changed my hatred to love, and my appetite for vengeance into the desire to serve them, which I would do better than ever if it pleased you to permit me to do it, which I would wish to do if I were released from here, where I have stayed long enough now for the healing of my soul and too long for the health of my body.[2]

On this occasion and throughout the rest of his life, even under torture, Grandier pleaded innocent to the charges of lechery while at the same time hinting at serious but unstated sins:

Although I am innocent of what I am accused of I am nevertheless greatly at fault before God [for many other things]. He wishes, for my own good, to use this false accusation as a means of chastising my true iniquities. But if it is true that God, and you by his example, look to the chastisement of a sinner only for the changing of his life for the better, I beg you to recognize that I have made great progress in my own improvement and beg you to put an end to the chastisement.

To the modern reader there are too many words – just as, to the Emperor of Austria, Mozart's music had too many notes. But this is because, like the emperor, we are not accustomed to the style. In the form of its day, the letter was finely phrased. If the tone sounds sycophantic, it was a reflection of the period. Those in power expected a proper degree of respect and expected it to be shown fulsomely. Besides, imprisoned in the bishop's cells, Grandier had no court of appeal other than the bishop, who in his own diocese was a law unto himself.

Grandier's letter had no effect. The conditions of his imprisonment were not relaxed. Even a letter to the bishop from his own superior, the archbishop, brought no immediate results. Henri de Sourdis, the archbishop of Bordeaux, enters the Grandier affair for the first time at this point. He came from a noble family and enjoyed fine living, though this was not unusual for people of his class. During his tenure, the church made many advances in his archdiocese, which included Poitiers. Like most other aristocrats who went into the church, Sourdis had been raised with a military background, for nobles were expected to lead in battle. Like Richelieu, he donned a suit of armour under his church robes when the need to arose. Only the previous year, 1628, at the siege of the Huguenot stronghold of La Rochelle, Sourdis had been Richelieu's right-hand man. Richelieu had led the soldiers, and Sourdis had gathered together a fleet to complete the isolation of the city by cutting it off from the sea. But although Richelieu and Sourdis were good friends, La Rocheposay had no liking for his archbishop, and he resented any interference in his diocese.

This letter about Grandier to La Rocheposay came about because d'Armagnac had sought Sourdis out while he was in Paris and asked him to write. Sourdis also wrote to one of the leading law officers in Poitiers and to the archpriest of the city, seeking their support for the curé. Although he wrote at the governor's request, it is evident that he knew Grandier personally and had a high opinion of him. We have no idea how this came about, but since the priest was living far away in Loudun from 1617 on, it is likely that any relationship must have developed in Bordeaux when Grandier was studying with the Jesuits. However it began, Sourdis was interested enough in the priest to intervene on his behalf.

While all this was going on, La Rocheposay was away at his country chateau of Dissay. He certainly knew of Grandier's arrest, but he may have decided to let the priest cool his heels, literally. However, he could not totally ignore appeals from Governor d'Armagnac, who had the king's ear, or from his own archbishop. So although there was little immediate improvement in Grandier's condition, there was enough pressure on the bishop for him to allow a letter from d'Armagnac to be delivered to the priest in his cell. It had been written in Paris on 6 December 1629:

I have been told that Sieur Thibault set after you as soon as you left and that he had you taken prisoner on your arrival in Poitiers to deliver yourself up. It has been very much frowned upon here that Thibault, who committed an outrage against you, has been permitted to have you arrested. I have already written to M. de Poitiers [the bishop] and am doing so again through my cousin de Tricon. Further, in case you are denied justice and are not set at liberty to pursue the [Thibault] outrage that has been committed against you, I am sending two letters that the archbishop of Bordeaux has written to [the bishop and the archpriest of Poitiers].

D'Armagnac went on to give a commitment that must have been very precious to Urbain Grandier in his cold and damp December cell: "I will never abandon you, I will help you to the end." He continued: "Thibault has had propositions made to me as if he were on your side, but I have not wished to delay [taking the actions that I have] in view of your innocence, and Messieurs the ecclesiastics here who are interested in your case have advised me against delay."

D'Amagnac concluded by sending Grandier warm salutations. It must have been heart-warming for Grandier to know that his powerful friends were active on his behalf. Although his dungeon was as deep as ever, he now had cause to hope.

Encouraged by this support, Grandier wrote again to his bishop, who was now back in Poitiers:

Monseigneur, your return has given me joy, and my joy gives me a foretaste of my imminent deliverance, which I wait for expectantly, based partly on your justice and partly on your kindness, for the first by its rigour has preserved my soul for heaven, and the second has preserved my honour for the world, in which I wish to live only to have your wisdom admired by means of the change in me, which I will prove through my actions which will render you much pleasure and will render me much more worthy ...

This letter has a very different tone from the pitiful plea in Grandier's first letter. Is it reading too much into it to believe that he now felt himself to be making his request from a position of relative strength?

D'Armagnac now wrote to Grandier saying that Thibault was prepared to make an offer of peace and restitution, but Grandier replied from his cell with a firm refusal. He said that an accommodation would be a concession unworthy of a man who was strong in his innocence. In this affair, he said, his honour was in question, and as a result he wanted justice to be rendered to him fully and completely.[3] Only a few weeks earlier he had written, "Their persecution has changed my hatred into love, and my appetite for vengeance into the desire to serve them." Now he had reverted to his instinctive reaction to any enemy: never to run away, to demand total victory, and to make sure that all the world knew of the enemy's defeat. Earlier, he had seen himself as a man utterly dependent on the mercy of his bishop. Now he saw himself as an innocent man with powerful friends who would make sure that he was treated justly and released.

This change of attitude became even more evident a day or two later when Grandier felt sufficiently sure of himself to write another letter to La Rocheposay: "Monseigneur, the passion of my enemies ought to be sated by the pains they have made me suffer under your authority, which I would wish to use in my turn to get justice against those who have offended against me." He went on to mention "the

friends whom I have close to the king" and asked the bishop to give
him an opportunity to obtain justice. He continued: "Some prelates
of this kingdom with whom I have but a distant connection of great
respect are very much interested [in my case]." Not only was there
a new assertiveness in this letter, but there was an implied threat.
This was not the way to gain the support of a noble and haughty
superior.

Meanwhile, the witnesses against Grandier were arriving in Poitiers.
Only the more important of them gave their testimony with Grandier present – Trincant, Le Mousnier, Meschin, and the curé Boulliau. The others were heard in his absence, and only their
depositions were read to him. The principal accusation was that of
having debauched married women and girls. This Grandier denied,
and he had a valid defence, for not a single woman had come
forward and laid a complaint against him. It was all hearsay.
Grandier not only refuted all the accusations, but he attempted to
show that this whole affair was an intrigue to get him chased out
of the Loudun area, where his influence was an annoyance to his
adversaries. We do not know for sure what explanation he gave
about why he had enemies and why they wanted to see him gone,
but the documents suggest that he may have claimed that the
Loudun priests were still jealous for his preferment over them. This
was probably true, for a number of the persons whom Trincant
persuaded to sign accusations against Grandier were priests from
the town. Moreover, in Loudun, Grandier's enemies were so confident that the decision would go against him that already his benefices and other sources of income were being divided up among the
local clergy.

The bishop would not be making his decision alone; he was being
advised by a panel of judges, most of whom were priests. To their
number was now added a lawyer named Richard, who was a relative
of Trincant. With this development, a favourable decision seemed
even more remote, and Grandier objected strongly. He protested
that it was against all justice and the laws of the church – but to
no avail. On 3 January 1630 he wrote again to the bishop in a
notably more abject tone, begging for mercy "in the examination
that is being made today of my doctrine and morals." He stated,
"If I have spoken too freely at times, your correction will be like a
burning coal that will purify my lips," and he promised that in
future he would never speak like that again. He added, "As for my
morals, I have no excuse to offer, but only a thousand pardons to

beg, with the promise of real improvement, in hope of which I beg you to reduce the rigour of your justice."

For the first time, we discover that one of the things on which Grandier was being judged was a question of doctrine that he had been teaching or preaching. Since we can be sure that Grandier never admitted to being guilty of anything he had not done, we can be equally certain that there was some truth to the charges that he had expressed doctrinal opinions unacceptable to the church authorities. They may have referred to Huguenots or Huguenot beliefs. It is quite likely, given Grandier's moderation towards the Huguenots, that he was attracted to some of their views. As we shall see later, he was sympathetic to Huguenot views on the married clergy, and he may have been indiscreet in what he said. From early 1630 on, some of the authorities questioned his full adherence to Catholic doctrine.[4] Grandier lived in a religious world in which a man who was doctrinally suspect would also be suspected of heresy, of being an agent of the Devil. When accusations of witchcraft were later cast against him, this suspicion made them easier to accept.

Meanwhile, his letter had clearly stated, "As for my morals, I have no excuse to offer," so he was guilty of something. Since he claimed innocence of the charges brought against him, what was this something? Could it be that the bishop, told the truth by Trincant, had privately charged Grandier with Philippe's seduction? This would explain the broad nature of Grandier's admission of immorality. It would also explain the severity of the sentence he received.

The sentence was passed the same day, and it was disastrous. Grandier was forbidden to perform the public functions of a priest for five years anywhere in the Diocese of Poitiers and forever in Loudun. With this decision, his livelihood was removed. He would be able to get only the most menial work as a priest in any other diocese with such a sentence. He would have to move from Loudun, publicly disgraced, with his whole family dishonoured. His benefices would never be returned to him. There would be no income beyond what he had saved. Short of death or condemnation to the galleys, there could be no more severe a sentence.

DELIVERANCE

Grandier was released from prison the day his sentence was delivered, 3 January 1630. His enemies thought him finished, but Grandier was a fighter. He knew that the charges that had been brought against him publicly were false, and he was determined to prove them fraudulent. Once that was done, he would appeal to the higher authorities in the church to have his sentence overridden. This was his plan from the day of his release, and he made no secret of it.

It was not going to be easy. The curé of Saint-Pierre-du-Marché, once so highly respected, had been the talk of the town for months, and there had been much sniggering and gloating. The damage done to the Catholic cause in Loudun was enormous. The moderate Huguenots as well as the extremists revelled in the embarrassment of the Catholics, whose prize priest had been found guilty of disporting himself amongst his parishioners. In such a climate, many innocents suffered. Any woman who had had anything to do with Grandier or had shown him the least sign of friendship over the years was now at risk. Many an old score was settled by an insidious suggestion about an enemy's wife or daughter. But there were some citizens, both Huguenot and Catholic, who simply did not believe the charges; they were aware that Trincant's method of collecting the testimony had been highly questionable. Thus, Grandier's parish – or, more properly, his former parish – was split between those who were convinced of his guilt and those who were convinced that an innocent man was being unjustly punished.

Grandier could not return to his parish, for he had been forbidden to practise as a priest in Loudun, but nobody could make him leave the city. He made it clear to all that he was going to appeal to his archbishop. When the Trincant party saw that Grandier was going to stay and fight, they wrote to the bishop complaining that the spirit of his sentence was not being carried out. La Rocheposay must have then sent a reprimand to the priest, for Grandier wrote to him:

Monseigneur, if the counsel of my friends, the testimony of my conscience, and the care that I am obliged to have for my well-being and honour have forced me to make an effort to escape the ill fortune into which I have fallen, it is not with the design of resisting your power or reducing the respect that I have for your person or position. For after having told me when I had the honour of taking leave from you that you had washed your hands of this affair, I believed that I was free without offending you to pursue my vindication, bringing to light the malice of those who have used such deception under the clothing of the truth to animate your justice towards my total ruin.[5]

Grandier still had many friends, including Loudun's governor, Jean d'Armagnac, who was busy writing to his powerful acquaintances in Paris and Poitiers seeking their support for an objective review of the testimony that had been brought against Grandier. He even wrote to La Rocheposay, asking for some measure of pardon for Grandier. The bishop's reply was evasive, but he did offer a concession. He promised to reduce the severity of the sentence if Grandier would undertake not to appeal his case to the archbishop. To Grandier this was an impossible suggestion. To accept the bishop's offer would be to declare himself guilty. What he demanded was a complete absolution by an authority superior to his bishop.

Grandier's relatives were active too. They had been appalled at La Rocheposay's sentence – and not only because of its effects on Grandier; the stain of dishonour marked the whole family. Grandier's mother, Jeanne d'Estièvre, made it her task to visit everybody of influence in Loudun and to plead for their support for her son. Meanwhile, his brother René, the lawyer, enlisted the support of a number of his colleagues, and in particular that of the *bailli*, Guillaume de Cerisay. The *bailli* did not need much persuading in view of the earlier accusations about his late mother-in-law's relations with Grandier.

Grandier needed all the allies he could find, for his counterattack posed a serious threat to Trincant and his supporters; if the testimony against the priest was proved false, they might well be severely punished, so they could not afford to sit back and let Grandier make the running. Two attempts had failed to remove him, one based on canon law and the other on accusations of debauchery. Now they planned a new one. No longer would it be sufficient to see Grandier removed from the region. His death was the only certain way of defeating him.

Trincant was a knowledgeable lawyer. What he needed, he decided, was a precedent – a criminal case in which there had been similar accusations to those made against Grandier. And he wanted one where the death sentence had been applied. If he could find such a case, he would be able to pursue Grandier in the criminal courts using the same charges on which the priest had already been found guilty in the ecclesiastical court. This was powerful stuff. A secular court presented with the evidence on which a bishop had recently found a priest guilty would not be likely to come to a different conclusion, and the punishment it meted out would be much more severe.

Trincant soon found the case he was looking for. Within the recent past, in November 1623, the supreme court for that region of France, the Parlement of Paris, had passed the death sentence on the curé of Beaugé. The charge had been almost exactly the same as the one against Grandier: "For crimes of lewdness and sacrilege." Trincant, Hervé, and the *avocat du roi* Pierre Menuau – another Loudun magistrate who was a relative of Trincant – took steps to have Grandier's case brought before the same court.[6]

There was just one problem. Trincant had to strike before Grandier could collect the testimony he needed to seek an overturning of the bishop's decision. Despite all his efforts, the law took its time, and the case did not to come to trial before the Parlement of Paris until 30 August 1630, eight months later. Grandier had a good lawyer on this occasion, but his enemies were equally well armed. Moreover, the crown prosecutor, who opened the case, was notably severe. After stating that Grandier's crimes were most serious, he specifically recalled the trial of the curé of Beaugé, "who was condemned to death by a famous decision for spiritual incest and sacrilegious lewdness."[7] Grandier could be condemned to death by this court on the same charge, he said. This looked very dangerous for the priest, but the prosecutor (who was a friend of d'Armagnac) then stated that it was not necessary for this court to try the case. It could, he said, be handled much better and more easily in Poitiers; that was where it should be referred, since the bishop's judgment had been issued there and the witnesses were all in the immediate area.

A trial in Poitiers would be much better for Grandier because d'Armagnac had close friends in the legal system there; but the suggestion did not sit well with the Trincant group. Their lawyer argued that it would mean a whole new trial with the witnesses having to be heard again, and he said this was unnecessary because the priest had already been found guilty by a competent authority after a proper investigation; and that all the Parlement of Paris need do was pronounce a criminal sentence against Grandier. In rebuttal, Grandier's lawyer informed the court that the priest's enemies had gone to extreme lengths to mislead justice. He outlined the improper manner by which testimony had been taken and recounted at length the story of the curé Martin Boulliau and the way his testimony had been altered by Trincant without his knowledge. At the end of all the arguments, the court decided that the case should be referred to Poitiers.

All this time, Grandier's brother René had been working on his behalf and had gone to Paris to see d'Armagnac, who had approached various friends in the legal community of Poitiers. D'Armagnac wrote to Grandier on 14 December 1630 to tell him that he had obtained assurance that "in Poitiers nobody would dare take steps to have you unjustly treated because of the appeal to Parlement where your case will be closely examined."[8] This was very important news to the Grandiers. If he were to be found guilty by the court in Poitiers, there would be a right of appeal to the Parlement of Paris, which would quickly establish whether justice had been subverted. It placed great pressure on any witness who had given false testimony earlier. Until this time, all adverse testimony had been presented in a climate where its truth had not been questioned. Now it would not only be questioned, but if it was found to be false, severe punishment from the court would follow. By this time everyone in the legal establishment of Poitiers was aware that the priest had powerful connections. It was no coincidence that the principal police authority of Poitiers[9] immediately began an inquiry of his own into the case and had the witnesses summoned and questioned.

By the time the trial opened, many of the witnesses who had made depositions for the case before the bishop had begun to withdraw their testimony. It was one thing to give testimony in front of Trincant, who was happy to have any stick with which to beat the priest. It was quite another matter to appear in Poitiers before a royal court and give false testimony. In his efforts to help his brother, René Grandier made the witnesses very much aware of this. One of the original witnesses was a priest named Bougreau, whose benefice depended on the goodwill of one of Grandier's enemies. Bougreau now declared that he was withdrawing his testimony; he confessed that, along with other witnesses, he had been solicited and coached by Trincant and his friends. This deposition made it clear how far Trincant had gone. Another retraction, this one by Gervais Meschin, was fatal to Trincant's cause. Under pressure from René Grandier, this priest declared that he had made his deposition against Urbain Grandier only under extreme pressure from Trincant and Hervé. Now, he declared, he was ready to make a complete retraction. Threatened or guided by René Grandier, he wrote:

I, Gervais Meschin, priest vicar of the church of Saint-Pierre-du-Marché of Loudun, certify that this document is written and signed by my own hand in order to clear my conscience. Rumours have been circulating that in the preliminary inquiry performed by Messire Gilles Robert, archpriest, against Messire Urbain Grandier, priest curé of Saint-Pierre, the said Robert urged me to depose that I had found the said Grandier with married and unmarried women lying at full length in the Church of Saint-Pierre with the doors locked:

Item: that on many and diverse occasions at all hours of the day and night I saw married and unmarried women come to find the said Grandier in his chamber and that some of the women stayed from one in the afternoon till two or three in the morning and had supper brought by a servant who left straightaway.

Item: that I never saw him say his breviary and that he would go to sleep at the altar.

Item: that I saw the said Grandier at all hours in the church with the doors open and when some women entered, he locked them.

Desiring that such rumours no longer be allowed to continue I declare that I have never seen the said Grandier with married and unmarried women in the church with locked doors, nor alone with them, for when he spoke to them they were always accompanied and the doors were always open. As to posture, I want to clarify what I declared when I was confronted with the accused, the fact is that the said Grandier was seated and the women at some distance from him. Further, I have never seen married or unmarried women enter Grandier's chamber either by day or by night. Although it is true that I have heard people coming and going very late in the evening, I cannot say who it was and one of Grandier's brothers always slept close to his chamber. I have no knowledge of either married or unmarried women having supper brought.

To add to the truth, I no longer declare that I did not see him reading his breviary; that would be untrue. On the contrary, on a number of occasions he asked me for my breviary and said his hours.[10] And similarly I declare that I never saw him lock the doors of the church and that on all occasions when I have seen him with women I have never seen anything untoward by way of touching or in any other fashion, and that if there is anything in my deposition contrary to the above, it is contrary to my knowledge. This has been read and signed by me to give witness to the truth. Done this last day of October 1630.[11]

From this and other retractions it was clear that witnesses had been suborned. Many withdrew their testimony, though Adam the apothecary (Trincant's relative and close accomplice) continued to maintain all his earlier accusations. But Grandier had a card to play here. Adam had publicly accused Madeleine de Brou of being Grandier's mistress, whereupon she had taken him to court in the Parlement of Paris and obtained a judgment against him for defamation of character. Grandier had this brought out in court. From then on, Adam's testimony carried no weight.[12] Hervé and Trincant had no better success with their depositions. Most of the witnesses affirmed under oath that the two magistrates had created the whole house of cards in order to damage the curé. Faced with this evidence, the court had little difficulty in rendering a verdict. The case against Grandier was set aside. It was not a complete and absolute discharge. The actual words used were that it was set aside or discharged "for the time being." The implication was that Grandier had been found innocent but that if new evidence came forth the case could be taken up again by the court without having to start a completely new trial. This was to be important some two years later.

The clear loser was Trincant. Although he was a senior magistrate, reputedly a man of probity, he had been proved to have suborned and threatened witnesses and deliberately assembled false testimony. He was forced to resign from his office and turn it over to his son-in-law Louis Moussaut. Because of his implacable pursuit of his enemy, he had sacrificed his name, his career, his reputation – everything he had worked for all his life. But for all the opprobrium heaped on Trincant in his own time and through the centuries, it was Grandier who had committed the original crime. And since that crime could never be revealed, Trincant had no doubt believed that his only recourse was to create false testimony so that Grandier could be rightfully punished. But Grandier had turned defeat into victory.

Grandier was fortunate in having a patron as powerful as the governor of Loudun. D'Armagnac's efforts had been considerable. It was no light matter for a courtier to leave the king's personal service to attend to somebody else's business as d'Armagnac had done for Grandier on a number of occasions. At the French court, one's influence was measured by one's closeness to the king, and a courtier who was absent even briefly left the field open to others. However, d'Armagnac's efforts on Grandier's behalf were not entirely disinterested. He needed Grandier to be free in Loudun to look after his interests there.

This mutual reliance between the governor and the priest had other implications, for the rumours of Grandier's overfriendly relations with Huguenots were not unfounded. Two weeks after the

priest's release from prison on 3 January 1630, d'Armagnac had
invited him to his country estate, saying he would send a horse for
him. He told Grandier that two of the town's leading Huguenots,
Gougeon and Le Blanc, were also invited but that Grandier should
journey separately because people would not understand such frat-
ernization.[13] This liaison – dangerous at any time for a Catholic
priest – had taken place while Grandier was still under full attack
by Trincant and his family; they would have been delighted to have
had word of it. It is a measure of Grandier's temerity, and perhaps
of his dependence on d'Armagnac, that he ran such a risk.

During the summer of 1630, d'Armagnac for once passed a
considerable time away from the king in pursuit of his own affairs.
His wife was pregnant, and he spent some months in Loudun with
her. Grandier was often a visitor at the governor's country house
during these months, and it is evident from d'Armagnac's letters to
him that Huguenot leaders were often present too. The January
meeting was but one of many. While d'Armagnac, as governor, had
reason to maintain good relations with the principal Huguenots,
Grandier was in a very different position.

In due course, the d'Armagnac baby was born, and the little boy
was baptized in June in a ceremony of some magnificence. The
christening brings into the Grandier story the man who was destined
to become the priest's inquisitor, judge, and, in effect, executioner
– Jean Martin, Baron de Laubardemont. D'Armagnac's intimacy
with the king can be measured by the fact that Louis XIII was
prepared to be godfather to his son. Since he could not himself be
present at the christening, he sent as his representative "the seigneur
and baron de Laubardemont, of Saint-Denis-de-Pile, Saint-Georges-
de-Guesboin and other places, king's counsellor in his councils of
state and first president in his court of aides of Guyenne." This
would have been a welcome choice, for at the time d'Armagnac
considered Laubardemont to be a good friend.

It is probable that Laubardemont met Grandier during his visit.
Grandier would have played no part in the christening, for he was
still under sentence from the bishop, but d'Armagnac may well have
introduced them, reckoning that Laubardemont could be a valuable
contact in Paris for the priest. More intriguing is the possibility that
Laubardemont and Grandier already knew each other. They had
been born in the same year and had studied with the Jesuits in
Bordeaux at the same time. While their interests were different –
the law for Laubardemont and the church for Grandier – and their

social circles were entirely separate, it seems probable that they were at least aware of each other. Whatever his earlier knowledge of the priest, Laubardemont was to rank, with Trincant and La Rocheposay, as the man who led Grandier to his death.

Laubardemont already had an association with Loudun. He had two sisters-in-law in the Ursuline Convent, and he was related to the mother superior, Jeanne des Anges. During his visit he met many of the elite, for a christening of such importance was a major event in the town and everybody of significance was invited. When Laubardemont was later sent back to Loudun by Richelieu to raze the walls, he already knew much about the people he would be dealing with – who would resist and on whom he could rely. But on this occasion he was received favourably by all.

ABSOLUTION

Grandier's next step was his appeal to the archbishop of Bordeaux – La Rocheposay's superior, d'Armagnac's friend, and Grandier's protector – to have his sentence from the bishop reversed. He went to see Archbishop de Sourdis shortly after the end of his trial in Poitiers and received a sympathetic hearing. This may have been warmed to some degree by the fact that Sourdis and La Rocheposay could not stand each other; it would not be an unpleasant duty for this archbishop to overrule the bishop. But it was not going to be an arbitrary decision. Sourdis was a man of considerable common sense and good judgment, and although he was on friendly terms with d'Armagnac and Grandier, the priest's absolution would have to be justified through a thorough inquiry.

Despite the archbishop's promises and expressions of interest, the investigation was delayed, for when Sourdis had to go to Louis XIII's court in Paris, Grandier's case was set aside for more urgent matters. D'Armagnac, who was also at the court, had to remind Sourdis in March 1631 of his promise to inquire into the priest's case. Only then did the archbishop at last give orders for a court of inquiry to be started immediately, and even at that it took months to complete its work. The whole case was gone over again, and both new and old witnesses were called. Again it became evident that the inquiry conducted by Trincant and the archpriest Robert had been carried out improperly. Finally, on 22 November 1631, months after Grandier's innocence had been declared by the civil court in Poitiers, the whole process came to its slow conclusion and the archbishop's decision was rendered. Grandier was present, having been told the evening before that the decision was to be issued. Great was his joy when it was read out to him:

Everything having been seen and considered, and the advice of the Council having been sought, and after invoking the Holy Spirit, We by our definitive judgment and sentence, have put, and do put, the sentence at nought ... [We] send away the said appellant absolved of the cases and crimes held against him, and raise definitively the interdiction *à divinis* [the order not to carry out any public priestly functions] noted in the said sentence. We enjoin him to carry out his duties well and modestly according to the holy canonical decrees and constitutions [the rules of the church], except that he may pursue reparations, damages, and interest in the restitution of his benefices to the extent that he sees it to be appropriate.

Done by us in our abbatial house of Saint-Jouin-les-Marnes, 22 November 1631.[14]

Grandier's archbishop had restored to him his honour, his benefices, his livelihood, his future, and the future of his family. Once more he had defeated Trincant and his relatives.

After the decision had been read by the clerk of the court, Grandier was given a copy. Then he had the honour and perhaps questionable pleasure of a long interview with his archbishop. We know some of what went on. This sensible and experienced archbishop was well aware that Grandier was guilty of moral laxity. The man was no fool. He undoubtedly demanded from Grandier an explanation of why Trincant and his party had been pursuing him so bitterly. Under the seal of the confessional he would require Grandier to accuse himself of the sin he had committed with Philippe Trincant. Only in this way could Grandier receive absolution in the sacrament of confession. So the priest confessed. Undoubtedly – and with utter sincerity – he pleaded that he was truly contrite for the sins he had committed. On the last day of his life, under torture and knowing he would meet his God within hours, Grandier admitted that he had had relations with women but swore that he had never again committed this sin after his arrest by the bishop in 1629.[15] On this occasion, when confessing to his archbishop, he would have pleaded those past two years of abstinence as proof of his contrition and his new life.

In the interview, Sourdis gave the priest good advice, warning him that his enemies in Loudun would pursue him even more vengefully, driven to greater extremes by the absolution he had just been granted. Further, the archbishop's overturning of the bishop's sentence was not going to sit well with La Rocheposay. While the bishop could do nothing but accept Sourdis's decision, Grandier now had an increasingly bitter enemy who would be all too ready to do him great harm if he committed the slightest fault. Beyond that, he would be returning to a parish that was split into bitter factions. If Grandier insisted on returning, the archbishop could not stop him, having just found him innocent, but he told the curé very plainly that he would be asking for trouble. Sourdis did everything possible to make it easy for Grandier to leave Loudun by offering to find him other appointments as fruitful as the ones he now had and under another bishop, but Grandier rejected these wise counsels. He was determined to return to Loudun despite every problem.

In view of all that had happened, it might be expected that Grandier would return quietly to Loudun, a wiser and chastened man, to take up his duties and lead an unobtrusive and exemplary life. But Grandier was Grandier. Victory had to be savoured. His enemies had to be publicly humiliated. On the afternoon of a late November day in 1631, as soon as he could get back to Loudun after the archbishop's interview, he made his entry into the town. His friends had already gathered a crowd of supporters, who lined the streets to cheer him. He arrived on horseback carrying a laurel branch, the mark of a conquering warrior from Roman times. It was a symbol well understood by all.[16]

Although Grandier was celebrating a victory, he was soon beset by troubles again. His parish was split between those who believed him innocent and those who were convinced that a guilty and lecherous priest had obtained an unjust reprieve. Many of his parishioners were scandalized that he was resuming his duties as their parish priest. How could they go to confession to such a man? How could they have their daughters married by him, their children and grandchildren baptized? Who knew whose wives and daughters he had seduced in Loudun? So many rumours had been spread about him during the past two years that it was hard to believe they did not have at least some foundation. Once again, the town seethed with suspicions. If one's daughter or wife went to church too regularly during the week – or, worse, to confession – how could one be sure that nothing was going on?

In mid-1631 a letter was sent to Bishop de La Rocheposay, signed by many of the leading parishioners, asking him to give them

dispensation from having to receive the sacraments in the Church
of Saint-Pierre-du-Marché. It was not only Grandier's sworn enemies
who signed, men such as Hervé and many of Trincant's friends and
relatives; the signatories included the two Chauvet brothers, Louis
the *lieutenant-civil* and Charles the *assesseur*. These two relatives of
Madeleine de Brou had always been friends of Grandier, but insinuations had been made to them that their wives had been Grandier's
mistresses.[17] Their defection was only temporary – they were later
counted among Grandier's strongest supporters – but it was a
measure of the divisions and rumours that were sweeping Loudun
at this time. The letter read:

To Monseigneur the Most Reverend Bishop of Poitiers.
   We the undersigned parishioners of Saint-Pierre-du-Marché of Loudun
humbly beg that because of the scandal that has been given and brought
about by the very libertine life of M. Urbain Grandier, curé of the said
parish, regarding which complaint and information was laid before you
on which you pronounced sentence against the said Grandier by which he
was forbidden *a divinis* and for which the said Grandier has obtained a
decision from Monseigneur de Bordeaux, a copy of which is attached, by
which the interdiction has been lifted permitting him to exercise all his
functions as curé, which he has already done and has made it known that
he has no intention of changing from his past life.
   As the result, Monseigneur, the supplicants request, if it please your
grace and authority, to dispense them from hearing mass in the said parish
as long as the said Grandier has the charge as curé and to permit them
and their family, both well and sick, to receive the sacraments in another
church and parish.[18]

The bishop of Poitiers did not hesitate to grant this request. It not
only satisfied the complainants but allowed La Rocheposay a public
means of protesting against the decision of the archbishop of
Bordeaux.
   So Grandier's pride, which had led him back to Loudun, brought
him mixed blessings. True, he had been publicly vindicated, had
regained his benefices and their income, and had seen Trincant
humiliated through his forced resignation. But his work as a parish
priest was seriously damaged and he was under the authority of a
bishop who was ready to give public proof that he still considered
him to be guilty as charged. Above all, Grandier had returned to
bitter enemies who were as unrelenting as he was himself. They

were prepared to wait for the moment to snare him, no matter what he did.

All these events were passed through the grille into ears in the convent that were only too eager to hear every detail. The nuns heard how attractive the priest was – so tall, well built, and handsome – and they certainly heard the rumours that no woman could resist his advances. When the possessions began, although the nuns had never seen the priest, they knew all about him.

In the summer of 1632 there were two other events of note. In the middle of July, Philippe Trincant had a second son, and it was arranged that the baby would be baptized on the sixteenth. Grandier, as the parish priest, decided that he would conduct this baptism, despite the fact that he had a number of vicars who, in the circumstances, would have been much more appropriate. What led him to this we do not know, but it was a deliberate decision on his part. Certainly, it was a way of saying to everyone that his parishioners could write to the bishop as much as they wished, but in his own parish he was master!

It was a foolish and provocative step to take, but the Trincant and Moussaut families were being equally foolish and provocative. They already had permission to have the baptism performed elsewhere, but this was their parish church, and they insisted on having the baptism performed in it by another priest. When Grandier presented himself, each side was determined to prevail. Moussaut referred to the dispensation that the bishop had issued permitting him and his family to receive the sacraments in a parish other than his own. But Grandier stood firm, insisting that he conduct the baptism. Finally, the whole family party walked out of the church and went to the other parish church in the town, Saint-Pierre-du-Martray, where the baptism was celebrated according to the wishes of the Trincant family.[19]

Around this time, Grandier went to the courts and sought and obtained damages for the losses he had suffered throughout the time he had been refused the right to perform as a priest in Loudun. The court's decision was costly to his enemies and fed their fires of resentment even further. Grandier's determination to humiliate his enemies applied to the Thibault case too. In all that happened to Grandier between 1629 and 1632, it is easy to forget that the immediate trigger was Thibault's physical attack on him. By the spring of 1632, Grandier was free to pursue his case against the soldier. Thibault had made various overtures through d'Armagnac over the past months seeking to know Grandier's conditions for making amends, and d'Armagnac had repeatedly pressed Grandier to settle. "Consider whether by pursuing this matter you will achieve your aim," he told the priest. "I don't think so. It is not that I want to excuse myself to you, or that I don't wish to carry your affairs to their end, but look at what might result and whether you can get satisfaction by gentler means."[20]

Grandier would have none of it, of course. He wanted corporal punishment, a fine, and costs. But he ought to have read between the lines of d'Armagnac's letter. The governor was getting tired of spending time and favours on this matter. The Thibault dispute dragged on in Paris, and not until April 1633 was the case judged. The result was humiliating to Grandier, for although Thibault was found guilty, he received only a nominal fine. He was sentenced to give "twelve Paris livres to the poor and twenty-four Paris livres to Grandier to cover his expenses, damages, and interest." Clearly, Grandier had lost far more than he had won. When d'Armagnac sent him the news, his impatience showed through: "I don't know why you wanted to pursue the trial of this case, for I believe that we would have got far more by a settlement; but there is nothing we can do about it."[21]

Grandier's victory over Thibault was in fact his first permanent defeat. More important, his most powerful supporters were beginning to weary of his constant battles and his refusal to accept sound advice. D'Armagnac was not the only one who might not be there when needed. There was also the archbishop, whom the governor had recently seen at court. "He speaks highly of you," d'Armagnac told Grandier, "but you know what these men are, you cannot always rely on them because they sometimes have bigger irons in the fire than your affairs."[22] This was to prove all too true.

Destruction and Plague

One reason why Grandier returned to Loudun was that d'Armagnac needed him there to protect his interests. The governor had been the priest's strong right arm during his long tribulations, but having such a patron implied giving service in return. The time for this had come. D'Armagnac had by now accepted that the château and the town walls would be razed, but within the château was the donjon, a great round tower eighty feet high with walls thirteen feet thick, surrounded by its own protective fortifications. It was his home in Loudun and the seat of his administration over the town and surrounding countryside. Although the order of destruction covered all the town's fortifications, d'Armagnac still had cause to hope that the donjon would be spared as a suitable signal of his importance as governor.[1]

He had grounds for hope. The king himself, as a favour to his old friend, had made him a secret promise that the donjon would not be destroyed when the rest of the Loudun fortifications fell. But Richelieu wanted all the strong points in France destroyed, and in these years the power was passing from the old friends around the king to the new breed of men around Richelieu, men such as Laubardemont. D'Armagnac needed Grandier in Loudun to keep him informed of the machinations of the cardinalists and their attempts to have the donjon destroyed along with the walls and château. Armed with this knowledge, he could take steps at court to block their plans. Grandier was in fact a spy or agent acting for the governor, and his involvement became increasingly obvious to the governor's enemies, who were in large part Trincant and his extreme Catholic friends – Richelieu's supporters.

Although the final decision to destroy the château and town walls had been made and published in 1628, it was not until September 1631 that a king's commissioner was appointed to oversee the work. The man appointed was Laubardemont. He was a good choice; he had already razed the walls of other towns on the king's instructions, and Loudun seemed to be a straightforward enough task since he knew the town. But the king had not told Laubardemont that the donjon was to be preserved for d'Armagnac as a sign of affection for him.

Every generation has its Laubardemonts – ambitious, smiling, clever, and extremely capable. They serve a master who has the power to raise them to great heights, and they carry out his policies without qualm or question. "I was only carrying out orders" is their slogan. Often they are charming and cultured – and not by chance; these are the qualities that lead to advancement. Laubardemont wore these qualities like a glove, and like a glove he readily removed them to deal with his master's enemies. Of all the people in the Grandier story, Laubardemont is by far the most sinister. Born into a noble family and trained as a lawyer, he was an excellent administrator, and although unprepossessing in appearance – tall, thin, bald, and short-sighted – he had proved so capable and versatile that he could be sent to cope with a crisis of almost any kind anywhere. Over the years, he had been a royal administrator in progressively important posts. When there had been an outbreak of witchcraft in the far southwest of France, it had been Laubardemont who was sent to put it down, to find the sources, identify the witches and their pupils, and burn them at the stake. He claimed later that he had discovered and pursued more than a hundred of them.[2] They were tortured to admit their guilt and involve their accomplices. Most of them perished in the flames. When a man was needed to oversee the dismantlement of the walls of Loudun – a diplomatic post as well as an administrative one, in view of the enmities and interests involved – Laubardemont was the obvious choice, and he was promoted once again.

The king knew that his promise to d'Armagnac would not sit well with some of his advisers, including Cardinal Richelieu, so he wanted to delay making it public until a suitable moment. Meanwhile, the news that the king in council had confirmed the order to destroy all the fortifications was joyfully received by the cardinal's supporters in Loudun. Grandier alone knew, through letters from d'Armagnac, that the governor had been promised that the donjon was to be preserved. He had told Grandier to keep this a secret, "as if it was told to him in the confessional."[3] Grandier had time to spare for d'Armagnac's affairs, for in the autumn of 1631 he was still waiting for the his case to be heard by his archbishop. Working on d'Armagnac's behalf must have taken his mind off his own troubles. Besides, to be working secretly as the governor's right-hand man would have done something to salve his bruised ego.

The governor wrote to Grandier that he was pleased with the appointment of Laubardemont because he considered him to be one of his friends.[4] He said that he had the king's word that in due course Laubardemont would be told that the donjon was to be exempted from destruction. In the meantime, since he could not be present in Loudun when Laubardemont arrived, he was sending his wife in his place, both to greet Laubardemont and to be on the spot to watch over her husband's interests; Grandier was to act as her adviser. The priest was also instructed to remind d'Armagnac's deputy (whom the governor rightly believed to be working against his interests) that nobody was to enter the area of the donjon and on no account was any demolition work on it to be allowed.

Despite these instructions, d'Armagnac feared that his enemies in Loudun would prevail, so a few days later he asked Grandier secretly to organize a rowdy public meeting, almost a revolt, to make the strength of the opposition to the demolitions very clear to Laubardemont.[5] This meant that the priest had to connive with the Huguenots who opposed the destruction. It is clear from the correspondence that Grandier had been having secret meetings with some of the leading Huguenots in pursuit of d'Armagnac's interests. As the governor's personal representative in the town, he had become almost a deputy-governor in the secret influence he was wielding. What d'Armagnac had done for Grandier certainly gave the governor every right to call on the priest in return, but what the priest was doing was both inappropriate and extremely risky, given the religious enmities of the period. Moreover, it was impossible to keep such sustained action totally secret. Grandier was providing sound evidence for the later accusations that he was a crypto-Huguenot.

In every way, the priest was swimming in treacherous waters. The decisions that were being taken about the walls of Loudun were both matters of state and matters of personal interest to very powerful people. Although the king's close friendship with d'Armagnac went back many years, he was torn between the governor and

his first minister. Then there was Laubardemont, Richelieu's creature, an ambitious man, a man rising to the fore. He knew that the
cardinal would measure him by the speed and efficiency with which
he completed the demolition. Laubardemont was close to the cross-
currents of power in Paris and had already come to the conclusion
that Richelieu's friends in Loudun would prevail. He had read signs
at court that were not evident in Loudun. His conclusion was that
Richelieu's interests were now more important to the king than
d'Armagnac's.

When Laubardemont arrived in Loudun in mid-November 1631,
he was still officially unaware of the king's intention to preserve the
donjon, though no doubt he knew of the machinations going on in
the background. He also knew that a powerful group of cardinalists
in Loudun had been pressing their friends at court to see that the
donjon remained on the order for destruction. Before leaving for
Loudun, Laubardemont had met with d'Armagnac and had assured
him that although the orders of the king would of course have to
be carried out, he would do all he could to protect the governor's
personal interests. Greatly relieved that such a good friend had been
chosen as the king's commissioner, d'Armagnac instructed Grandier
to see that Laubardemont was given a magnificent reception.[6]

On arrival, Laubardemont showed great courtesy and friendship
to both parties; certainly, he gave no open sign of favour to one side
or the other. He was back among the friends who had first warmed
to him when he visited Loudun as the king's representative for the
christening of d'Armagnac's son. He even treated Grandier courte-
ously, though he undoubtedly knew the priest's history. Madame
d'Armagnac, who had come in from her country estate with her
children to accord the honours of the château to the royal commissioner and his wife, was greatly encouraged by Laubardemont's
charm and by his protestations of friendship for her husband – so
much so that against her husband's expressed wishes, she told
Laubardemont of the king's promise that the donjon would be
spared. She said he would receive the royal message in a few days,
and she swore him to secrecy. Yet the very next day, Laubardemont
revealed the information to Mesmin de Silly, the enemy of d'Armagnac and Grandier. This gave Mesmin and his friends the opportunity to bring further pressure at court to have the donjon included
in the destruction.[7] When Laubardemont did receive the king's letter,
he did not make it public or have it entered in the town's official
records as he should have done. Instead, he continued to act and

talk as if everything was to be destroyed. This was significant because the king's orders received official status locally only when they were formally recorded in the city records and published for all to see; failure to do this implied that the order could or would be reversed. Clearly, Laubardemont was allowing time for the king's decision to be withdrawn.

By the end of December 1631, six weeks after Laubardemont's arrival, d'Armagnac at last realized that the commissioner was working against him, and he began to use all his influence at court to ensure that the king's instructions to preserve the donjon would be observed. The battle over the donjon was now openly joined at court, but this did not delay the destruction of the city walls. For the next few months, Loudun was almost totally taken up by the demolition. Even some of those who had wanted it must have been sad to see the beautiful walls gradually coming down. The view of the city from the distant hills and surrounding fields changed day by day. The dust and the noise of the work were never absent; there was no place in the town so far removed from the walls that it could be ignored. Many of Loudun's citizens must have wondered what was going to happen to the town of their childhood now that they no longer had any protection from the world.

By early January 1632 the work of destruction was progressing so well that Laubardemont was able to leave for a while to attend to other duties. He still had not published the king's order that the donjon was to be preserved. Grandier passed this information to d'Armagnac, adding that the demolition crews were nearing the donjon and showed no signs of stopping. The governor then arranged for two of the king's senior counsellors to write urgently to Laubardemont enjoining him to execute his instructions. On hearing this, Grandier took it on himself to stop the demolishers. He went so far as to bar the way to the donjon with soldiers of the garrison whom d'Armagnac had put at his disposal.[8]

There was one climactic event in June 1632. D'Armagnac arrived in Loudun unexpectedly, hoping to catch his enemies in open revolt against him. Grandier had learned through one of his agents that a packet of letters was about to be sent by courier to d'Armagnac's enemies at court, and he had taken the extraordinary step of having the courier attacked en route and the letters seized.[9] One of these letters, written by Hervé against d'Armagnac, his superior, was particularly compromising. The others were from Mesmin de Silly, Trincant, and Thibault, all asking Richelieu to finish with Loudun and put an end to what they referred to as the exactions of the Huguenots. Grandier's advice to the governor was to call a general town meeting and reveal the correspondence publicly. This d'Armagnac did, and when the letters were read out, it became clear to all just how far Mesmin, Trincant, and the rest of the cardinalist party were prepared to go to have every fortification in the town destroyed. Such "treachery" inspired fury in those who wanted some stronghold to be preserved where the people of Loudun could withdraw in the face of an attack. But although Mesmin de Silly and his friends suffered a temporary setback, their party was too strong to be permanently damaged by these revelations. From then on, they conspired openly for destruction of the donjon. And from then on, Grandier was openly acting against the leading Catholics of the town. This was especially dangerous in view of the fact that his protector, d'Armagnac, was losing influence at court; new men now had the ear of the king.[10]

MADELEINE DE BROU

Grandier had other troubles too. His insistence on returning to Loudun after the archbishop overturned his sentence is often held to have had a further cause – his love for Madeleine de Brou. According to Legué (and virtually all modern authors follow his story of the events occurring after Grandier's break with Trincant), René de Brou had three daughters, of whom Madeleine was the third. "She was a beautiful and timid young woman with a grave and austere air who was admired for her intelligence and graces and respected for her virtue and piety. She had no wish to marry and was hardly ever seen outside except on her way to the church, where she spent long hours."[11]

Grandier often visited the family and was well received by them. Indeed, her parents asked him to watch over and guide Madeleine after their death. It was not uncommon for parents to ask a man of probity to guide a daughter in legal and financial matters and in some cases to give spiritual advice as well. In this instance, it was a particularly suitable arrangement because Madeleine was much the same age as Grandier's sister Françoise, and they had become best friends; they passed a great deal of time together in Grandier's rectory, where Françoise lived. Like Françoise, Madeleine remained unmarried. Legué recorded: "Before long she was daily seen making her way towards the rectory of Saint-Pierre and stayed there longer than was suitable. At first it was understood that these visits were to her intimate friend Françoise Grandier, who lived with her brother. But public spite, which until now had not dared to pursue her, began to question the true ends of these long stays in the curé's house. Madeleine was spied upon, and soon it was no mystery to anyone that she was Grandier's mistress."

"The poor child little knew the curé of Saint-Pierre," stated Legué, who added that in order to persuade this "virginal creature" to take such a terrible step, Grandier wrote his "Treatise on the Celibacy of Priests,"[12] a work that later became infamous. In it, Grandier argued that it was an accepted maxim that nobody could be compelled to do the impossible and that if one was forced to attempt such a thing, "the powerlessness to do so dispenses one from the obligation of doing it." He stated, "A priest does not embrace celibacy for the love of celibacy but only to be admitted to holy orders ... The priest's vow of celibacy does not proceed from his own will but is imposed on him by the Church, which obliges him, willy-nilly, to observe this harsh condition without which he cannot exercise the priesthood." He concluded the treatise by quoting the apostle Saint Paul that "it is better to marry than to burn."[13] According to Legué, Madeleine was persuaded by this argument and gave herself in secret marriage to Urbain Grandier.

"How was this marriage carried out?" Legué then asks. "Who officiated at it? We can only reply that it was totally outside any ecclesiastical laws. One night, these two beings became united in the Church of Saint-Pierre, in front of Christ, a mute witness to this sacrilege in which Grandier dared to be at the same time the priest and the spouse ... From that time on, Madeleine ... sacrificed her peace of mind, her rest, her reputation, and gave herself completely to him, accepting any humiliation with the calm and dignity of a woman whose conscience was untroubled."

It was the apothecary Pierre Adam, Trincant's nephew, who first began to spread this story about Madeleine and Grandier, as well as other shocking tales about her. We know this because eventually she sought the protection of the law and Adam was punished. Another man who became her implacable enemy was the king's advocate, Pierre Menuau, who had hoped to marry the beautiful and rich young woman. Legué tells us that when he realized that Madeleine loved somebody else, "he resolved to discover who his rival was and get his revenge. His anger was enormous when he learned that Madeleine had become the curé's sweetheart (that is what they called her in Loudun). From that day forward, a violent hatred took the place of the feelings of affection that he had had for her, and he became one of the craven persecutors of this young girl."

Legué's story of Madeleine's marriage is a great anecdote but mainly fiction. For example, Madeleine was not a young girl; she was a mature woman of thirty-four, hardly the "poor child" described by Legué.[14] We know that her mother was still alive in 1625, when Madeleine was thirty-one years old, because among Grandier's papers at the time of his arrest in 1634 was a record that he had lent money to her that year (as he did to many people). This "relationship" is supposed to have developed after the death of Madeleine's mother. Further, it was supposed to have developed after the seduction of Philippe, which probably took place in 1629. Thus, we can deduce that Madeleine was about thirty-four or thirty-five at the time.

The story of the secret marriage in Grandier's church is an obvious invention. In the first place, nobody could have known about the marriage if there had been only the two of them present. Secondly, Grandier's enemies clearly set little store by the tale. If there had been any substance to it, the story would have come out at Grandier's trial; it would have been far too good a stick to beat him and Madeleine with if it had been true. Yet this episode is very revealing, for it shows the vicious nature of the rumours that Adam and his fellow plotters were spreading around Loudun about Madeleine and Grandier; it shows that discreditable stories about Grandier cannot be accepted without question; and it shows just how hard it was to combat the lies, for this same story is still accepted centuries later even though much of it is patently nonsense.

Adam was the source of many of the anti-Grandier rumours that were circulated on behalf of the Trincant family.[15] In 1631 he was taken before the Parlement of Paris, where he was tried for having accused Madeleine de Brou of immoral behaviour with Grandier. When found guilty, he appealed the sentence, but the appeal was rejected in 1634. Thus, the court in Paris twice found his rumours to be without the least credibility. Adam was required to make a public and humiliating confession of his guilt in the Council Chamber of the Palais de Loudun. "Head bared and on his knees to say in a loud and clear voice that recklessly and wickedly he had uttered against the said demoiselle (Madeleine de Brou) atrocious scandalous words, for which he asked pardon of God, the King, Justice, and the said demoiselle de Brou, recognizing her as a good and honourable woman."[16] In addition, he was subjected to such a heavy fine that it nearly ruined him.

Grandier did in fact write the celebrated "Treatise on the Celibacy of Priests." It was found among his papers after his final arrest in 1634. Under questioning and torture he admitted to being the author, but even under the most terrible torture he never said for whom he wrote it or why.[17] He clearly had deep sexual drives that were so great that he felt it impossible to deny them, but he may well have written the treatise to convince Philippe Trincant rather than Madeleine de Brou. We do not even know whether Madeleine was in love with Urbain Grandier, and we can find no case against her on the basis of the available evidence, just as the courts could find no case. What we do know is that the picture of her as a naive, timid, immature young girl did not do her justice. Her personal bravery in adversity was enormous. In all that she later had to endure, she never flinched before the attacks of her enemies, not even when she was in danger of being burned as Grandier's accomplice. Firmly declaring her innocence, she accepted "any humiliation with the calm and dignity of a woman whose conscience was untroubled."[18] But all this was still in the future in 1632. Meanwhile, like the rest of Loudun, she had to suffer through the plague.

PLAGUE

In May 1632, before the city walls were completely razed and while Adam was still spreading his rumours about Madeleine de Brou, the plague came to Loudun.[19] It was so bad in June that demolition of the walls came to a halt. There was some abatement of the disease in July, but in August it returned in full force. Only at the end of September did it at last leave the town. In that short period of five months about 3,700 people died, between one-fifth and one-quarter of the population of Loudun![20] The first "possessions" started as soon as the plague was over. Without it, they might never have occurred.

"No man who has not lived through a great and incurable plague can possibly imagine the horror and despair that attend it. Appeals to human aid and divine intervention are alike in vain."[21] These are the words of Petrarch, who lived through the Black Death in the fourteenth century. Nothing in our experience allows us even to approach the terrors of the plague. The people of Loudun must have been in constant dread that spring, for they could see it coming like a thunderstorm as it swept through towns and villages, moving closer and closer until it finally burst over them.[22]

Partly through lack of medical knowledge and partly because the "plague" was not always the same disease, nobody knew what caused or carried it. This added to the terror. Was it carried by the air or transmitted through contact with others? And if carried in the air, was it the air itself that was diseased? Because nobody knew what caused the plague, it had no tangible shape that could be attacked. There were no medicines to cure it and only a few preventive measures that could be taken – some of them less than useless. This terror that flew by day and night carried to the common grave pits virtually everyone who fell to it, rich and poor alike. Often the whole social fabric of a town broke down under the strain.

In Loudun as elsewhere, the sickness spread easily because of the insanitary conditions. Bathing was unusual during the reign of Louis XIII; it was in fact discouraged by the medical authorities. "Bathing, outside the practice of medicine," said Théophraste Renaudot, a celebrated Loudun doctor, in a public conference, "is not only superfluous but very damaging to health."[23] Most houses were small, without gardens, set very close to each other and often consisting of a single room that gave straight onto the street. The streets themselves were narrow, badly paved (if paved at all), and filthy in the extreme. A visitor to Loudun recorded: "The animals relieve themselves freely in the streets, the houses for the most part have no sanitation, and the inhabitants profit from the cover of the night and the absence of lighting to relieve themselves on the public squares, in the streets, and at the crossroads."[24]

What went on in a town at the height of the plague can only be imagined.[25] In the houses the sick lay side by side with the dead, while the walls echoed with the groans and cries of the dying or the screams of anguish as a husband, mother, or child was discovered to be infected and thus condemned to die. Meanwhile, there was the regular sound of vomiting and, at night, the rumble of the carts coming for the dead. The smells were appalling – the towns full of putrid odours and the stench of the decomposing bodies. Every attempt was made to overcome these smells because they were seen as a mortal danger in themselves. The rich carried posies of flowers and sweet-smelling herbs, their houses were filled with the fragrance of aromatic burning wood, and their clothes were garlanded with little pockets and packages of scented herbs and flowers to provide a protective aura that would keep away the diseased and stinking air. The poor carried cheaper herbs and leaves – whatever they could find or afford that had a strong odour – and for the same purpose they burned wood that gave off clouds of strong-smelling smoke. In time of plague, sweet strong smells were the essence of life and, in everybody's eyes, one of its greatest protections.

Since this pestilence had no known cause, people looked for one. It had to be presumed that such a terrible scourge could be allowed by God only because he had cause for anger. So the search began for those who might be responsible – Jews, witches,[26] heretics, all of whom were viewed as adherents of the Devil.[27] As the town fell fully into the grasp of the plague, the disease ceased to be an individual disaster and became a collective one. It was the plague itself, not those who were infected by it, that filled all minds. The active element was no longer man, but evil.[28]

Those who could do so fled Loudun for their country houses. The notables, including most of the doctors, abandoned the town, leaving the people to their fate. It was not unusual for doctors to leave; it was a measure of how little value they placed on their own remedies. Others, led by the *bailli*, Guillaume de Cerisay, stayed to lead the defence. Loudun was better prepared than most towns. A plan had been drawn up some years earlier to cope with an attack of the plague, and a hospital had been built outside the walls especially for the purpose. All the accepted measures for sanitation were ready. The municipal officers stayed in the town throughout the crisis and met every day at five in the morning to plan their strategy. The streets were cleaned, and rules were put in place to stop public circulation as far as possible in order to prevent contagion.[29] The men appointed to collect and bury the dead wore long pointed masks, filled with herbs, and heavy black robes with a white cross on back and front, and they carried white batons. To warn of their coming and clear their way, they carried a bell. They were known as *corbeaux*, or "crows." With the carts for the dead trundling along with them, their appearance struck fear into everybody. As soon as it was known that somebody was infected, the "crows" were sent for to take the sick person to the hospital (or to remove the dead), though the hospital was unlikely to be able to cure the sick. There were times when the dead could not be removed or buried fast enough to keep up with the progress of the disease.

Few showed at their best under such horror, but one of these few was Grandier. His bravery and compassion, all his most Christian

Clothing for doctors and others who were required
to visit plague victims. This is a modern
reconstruction from old descriptions.
Source: Musée de l'Hôtel-Dieu, Lyon.
Photo B. Allard.

virtues as a priest, flamed to brilliance. Throughout these months
he comforted the sick and confessed the dying to ease their passing.
He took no care for himself, going everywhere, including the most
infected places. To those who had none, he brought food. He spent
freely from his own pocket to sustain the living, giving an example
of priestly charity that even his enemies had to recognize.[30] Terrible
as this time must have been for him, it was probably one of the

most peaceful of his life. All his problems of the past three years were lost in his work. His past sins were surely expunged by his selflessness and his dedication to his people as he put himself at daily risk of death.

Gradually the summer toiled its way to an end and September came. Then, day by day, things grew better. Each week the number of newly infected people dropped and the tally of the dying was reduced. Finally, on one sweet day there were no more. The living came out from their long siege, slowly, hesitantly at first. Then as hope turned to certainty, the pace of life picked up. Although it was now late in the year, it was springtime in the hearts of those who were still alive. Death had been conquered or at least cheated. Thoughts turned to living once again. During the worst of a plague, the urgent desire to die in God's favour had kept most normally decent people in a state of virtue. But as death retreated, it was as if there had to be a celebration of the return of life. The period after a plague seemed to bring with it heightened sexual activity, as if death could be finally overcome only by the most basic affirmation of living. It was often said that God took all the best during a plague, leaving only the worst people alive. Typically, promiscuity reigned for a while afterwards. There is no reason to believe that Loudun was different from anywhere else in this respect.[31]

Nor is there any reason to believe that the Ursuline nuns who had lived through the plague in their enclosed and cloistered house were miraculously unaffected by all that had happened or untouched by human fears and emotions. In the world outside, the relief from the past months could be responded to with concupiscence. To the young women in the convent this was unthinkable. But the same human needs had to be expressed in some form, and in this case they came out as dreams and hallucinations (for which the nuns could not, of course, be held responsible).

The day school had been closed down by the town authorities at the first sure sign that the plague was advancing, for children were particularly susceptible to the disease. Most boarders had been taken home by their parents, and only a few remained with the nuns. The sisters were thus left very much alone. Although a priest came to say mass daily (except perhaps at the worst time, when it was impossible) and although confessions were heard, all but essential visiting stopped. Nevertheless, some news seeped into the convent through the visitors who had to come, so the nuns knew of the progress of the disease. They heard about their students who had

died, and they heard of friends, benefactors, and parents of the
students, first stricken then dying. Worst of all, they heard about
their own relatives. They also heard of deaths in houses close to the
convent; they could feel the enemy approaching. And although they
could see nothing, for their rules of enclosure required high walls
so that nobody could see in or out, they could hear the wagons and
bells of the "crows" collecting the dead and dying.

The close confinement of the nuns was in fact a benefit, because
their scanty contact with the outside world reduced the opportunity
for infection. Throughout the whole period, not a single nun caught
the dreaded disease. But they did not know that they would be
spared, nor did they expect to be. And they were aware that if the
infection breached the walls of the convent, they would be trapped
inside with it. Each day they prayed for the dead outside and for
the grace of God to keep the scourge from them. The fear of the
plague was with them every minute, day and night. These young
women were as terrified as anyone else, and with both their day
and boarding school closed, they had time to worry and to agonize
over the fear of death.

The young, inexperienced mother superior, Jeanne des Anges, had
more than enough to worry about and was unsuited to cope with
stress. For the past three years, she had been under the care of the
doctors for nervous disorders. Now her mind became overburdened
with her fears and responsibilities; she fell into a condition of severe
anaemia and became prey to a series of nightmares and stomach
problems.[32] If this was the condition of the mother superior, many
of the other young women must have been under similar stress.
Jeanne des Anges was the type of person who would have shared
her fears. On top of everything else, Father Moussaut, their old
confessor, died.[33] His death almost certainly took place during the
plague. He was the one man whom the nuns saw regularly, their
spiritual guide and mentor. He knew their deepest and most secret
thoughts from the confessional.

Suddenly, for Jeanne des Anges, a whole series of threads from
the past and present came disastrously together – the years of gossip
at the grille, the laxity of her rule in the convent and her own poor
example for her nuns, the death of her confessor, her extensive
reading of the mystics, the end of the plague, and nature's impulse
towards sexuality with the final release from the fear of death. In
addition, there was her fascination with all she had heard about the
libidinous priest in the town.[34]

Possession

There is a common view that convents were places where young girls were forced to go against their will. It is widely assumed that they were locked up for life by parents or other authorities because they were unable to find a husband or were suffering from unrequited love; or because they were too poor to marry or were so wild or difficult that it was best to put them in a convent before they caused any more trouble. According to this portrayal, these misfits lived a life of boredom, saying their prayers regularly but being open to all sorts of temptations and diversions to fill their useless time. This picture is very distorted.[1]

At the time of the Loudun possessions, the newly founded Ursuline houses all over France were being filled to overflowing by eager young women, many of them from families of the nobility, both major and minor.[2] The Loudun convent opened in 1626 with eight nuns; six years later there were seventeen, an enormous increase but typical of the period.[3] Far from being idle, an Ursuline's life was filled to the brim – teaching the day-school pupils and also looking after the boarders, training the new nuns, keeping the house, praying in common, and doing all the work that went with running and administering a growing community. The normal day started at five in the morning and continued until nine at night with every minute accounted for in a closely controlled schedule.

If the convent of Loudun was unusual (and it most certainly was), it was partly because the nuns were so young and partly because of its unsuitable mother superior. In 1632 Jeanne des Anges, thirty years old, was superior, or prioress, of a convent of seventeen nuns whose average age was only twenty-five.[4] Jeanne came from a noble family; she was the daughter of a baron. She had not been an easy child and at an early age had been given over to the care of an aunt, the prioress of a convent. But Jeanne could not adjust to the discipline and routine of a convent education – or was not prepared to – and at fifteen she was sent home, where her quirks and aggravating behaviour did nothing for her parents' peace of mind.[5]

Despite her childhood experience of convent life, she eventually decided to enter the new Ursuline house that was established in Poitiers. She later said of her early days there that she had been an inadequate nun, missing her prayers, inattentive to her duties, with an exaggerated opinion of herself. She considered most of the others to be below her, in both capabilities and knowledge, for she was well read. She resisted all counsel, advice, and discipline from her superiors. But when, a few years later, the convent decided to start a house in Loudun, Jeanne was determined to be one of the eight nuns to go and did everything possible to be sent. On arrival, she went out of her way to be the perfect nun, in appearance at least. She set out to be the mother superior's indispensable right hand, and when, within a year, that senior nun was recalled to go elsewhere, Jeanne des Anges seemed the obvious choice as her replacement.

She was a very short young woman, only four feet tall, and one of her shoulders was slightly deformed, which gave her a slightly hunchbacked appearance. But she had a very pretty face and a charming smile, which together made people unconscious of her physical defects. This, along with her ambitions for the convent, her intelligence and drive, her obvious ability to lead, and her natural facility to adjust her approach and character to suit the circumstances, seemed to make her an ideal choice. From the beginning, she made no secret of the fact that she was determined that her convent would become an outstanding success, drawing to it large numbers of aristocratic young women. But although the choice of this ostensibly much-reformed young nun to lead the convent seemed highly suitable at the time, in retrospect it proved to be a disaster. She was strong willed, manipulative, highly strung, and a brilliant actor in the parts she designed for herself. When she set out to assume a particular character, whether one of great charity, great learning, great mysticism, or great possession, others would follow. Even worse, not only had she the chameleonlike ability to assume a character, but she had the psychological weakness of believing that the assumed character was her own.[6]

Like Jeanne des Anges, most of the nuns came from "good" families. She herself was related to Laubardemont through her mother. Claire de Sazilly, a lay sister, was related to Richelieu. Anne d'Escoubleau de Sourdis was related to Archbishop de Sourdis, Grandier's patron. The two Mademoiselles Dampierre were Laubardemont's sisters-in-law. Others were related to notables in the town or in the surrounding region. These relationships were to be important. From the very beginning of the strange happenings at the Ursuline Convent, many of their relatives found it imperative to believe that some spell had been cast on the nuns from outside. They could not possibly accept that their sisters, daughters, cousins, or nieces could themselves be responsible for what was going on.

The drama began on the 22 September 1632. The priests' records started eleven days later, when it was decided that there was a true case of possession and that exorcism was required. Thus, their initial report was based on what the nuns told them of what occurred during those eleven days and what the convent confessor recalled. After that, their reports were based on the exorcists' own observations:

On the night of the twenty-first to the twenty-second September 1632 there appeared to Sister Marthe [one of the junior nuns, twenty-five years old] between the hours of one and four the form of a churchman, dressed in a greatcoat and cassock, holding in one hand a book covered in white parchment. And holding it open he showed her two pictures, and after having held many discourses on the said book, he wanted to force her to take it. She refused saying that she never accepted any book except from her superior. [This was normal procedure in a convent.] The spectre drew back, became silent, and stood for some time at the foot of her bed crying. In the end the young woman was terrified, and the spectre began to tell her that he was in great pain, that he could not pray to God, and that she should pray to God for him. The [young woman], presuming that this was perhaps the soul of someone in purgatory, said that she would inform her superior. However, no longer being able to support the presence of the spectre, she called to her a boarder who was in a bed close to her own. [She was probably supervising a boarders' dormitory.] They both got up at the same moment but saw nothing further, except that being on their knees [praying] for an hour they heard a voice lamenting. After four o'clock in the morning nothing more was heard.

But in the main part of the building where the professed nuns had their quarters, the same ghost appeared separately to the mother superior and the sub-prioress [the second most important person in the convent hierar-chy], saying to one, "Have prayers said to God for me," and to the other, "Continue to say prayers to God for me."[7]

Furthermore, we have been told [wrote the priests who were recording the events] that on the twenty-fourth of the said month between six and seven in the evening, in the refectory, another spectre appeared in the form of a black sphere which violently threw Sister Marthe to the ground and the said prioress onto a chair taking each by the shoulders, and at the same time two other nuns present felt themselves struck in the leg, which left on their legs red contusions the size of a teston [a coin] for the next eight days.

Further, they told us that for the whole of the rest of the said month, they have not passed a night in which they have not been subjected to great perturbations, disturbances, and terrors. And even though seeing nothing, they often heard voices calling one or another. Others received fist blows, others slaps, others felt themselves involuntarily aroused to laughing uncontrollably.

Finally we have been told that on the first day of this month [1 October 1632] around ten o'clock in the evening, the prioress [Jeanne des Anges] being in bed, with a candle lit, and having seven or eight of her sisters about her to help her because of the attacks that she particularly had had, felt, without seeing anything, a hand which closed her own leaving three hawthorn needles [in it], which were handed over the next day to one of us to give advice on what should be done. And two days later it was found fit that the prioress herself should have them burned, which was done in the presence of the Father Guardian [the superior] of the Capuchins of this town.[8]

But it came about that the said prioress and other nuns, since the reception of the said thorns, had experienced strange changes in body and mind of such a kind that they lost all judgment and were agitated by great convulsions, which seemed to proceed from extraordinary causes. It was thought that the said thorns carried an evil spell, which caused them to be possessed, and in fact on the third day of this month, having seen occur the strange vexations and agitations to the bodies of the prioress, of Sister Louise de Jesus, and of Sister Claire de Saint-Jean [the lay sister who was a relative of Richelieu], we judged this to be a case of true possession and that it would be expedient to practise upon them the exorcisms of the Holy Church. Despite that decision, having waited until the fifth of this month, we have seen the continuation of the vexations and agitations to such an extent that seven to eight persons were incapable of preventing them and these vexations became more frequent after they received Holy Communion.

At the first exorcism of the said day, the fifth of the month, the evil spirits being commanded in Latin to say their name, said nothing other than two or three times "Enemies of God." And in response to litanies [a form of prayer that called upon the saints to help, one by one], on the words "Saint John the Baptist, pray for them," the prioress's demon cried out many times, panting, "Ha, John the Baptist." And during the exorcism of the prioress, [the demon] said three times while buffeting her, "The Priest." And repeated it during the pronouncement of the words of the exorcism.[9]

There is an interesting aspect of this event that was not recorded by the priests but does appear in another manuscript, one held in the municipal library in Tours.[10] This manuscript was written in the convent, probably some years later, and the part we are interested in was almost certainly dictated by Jeanne des Anges. It says:

Sieur Mignon [Trincant's nephew, who had become the nuns' priest confessor after Father Moussaut's death] having, during the month of September, directed the Spiritual Exercises [an established program of prayers and contemplations] of one of the nuns named Sister Marthe, it came about that on the night of the fourth day after the feast of the Nativity of Our Lady, being in bed and asleep, her spirit was greatly troubled by dreams of the dead Sieur Moussaut. The next day she was totally preoccupied with improper thoughts and had a violent desire that Sieur Mignon, her director, should fall into a great sin; further, she felt an extreme chagrin at having declared to him her secret thoughts.

She completed her exercises on the Sunday. The night between the following Wednesday and Thursday, it came about that, being in her bed wide awake, she envisioned a phantom.

This chronicle shows that the initial appearances recorded by the priests came to an already troubled mind and occurred some days before the official record noted the appearance of Father Moussaut's ghost. Probably, this was not recorded by the priests because it would have been embarrassing to them, for Sister Marthe was clearly suffering from a sexual obsession for the new confessor, Father Mignon. It is hardly surprising that the priests failed to record Father Mignon's involuntary involvement. He was the principal priest doing the recording, and even if he had had no responsibility for Sister Marthe's obsession, it would have been disconcerting to both him and the nuns to write it down in the official account.

At first reading of the priests' record, it seems that the ghost appeared to three separate nuns on the same night, but this is almost certainly incorrect. The events started with Sister Marthe. It was she who first saw (or imagined) a ghost, and it was she who, though she never saw the face, first assumed it to be the shade of a dead priest. The connection was soon made that it was the nuns' dead confessor, Father Moussaut, who had so recently died. The nightmare, if that is what it was, would have been a perfectly natural thing to have occurred so soon after the horrors of the plague. But to the nun, it was a terrifying experience.

The priests' report went on to say that "the same ghost appeared separately to the mother superior and the sub-prioress." When read quickly, it seems that these appearances took place on the same night as the appearance to Sister Marthe, and concurrently. The highly regarded Michel de Certeau, author of the best modern book on the possessions, says, for example, "During the night of 21 to 22 the prioress [Jeanne des Anges], the subprioress [Sister de Colombiers], and Sister Marthe de Saint-Monique ... saw appear in the night the shade of Father Moussaut, the nuns' confessor, who had died some weeks earlier."[11]

If the three appearances had happened at the same time, religious protocol would have insisted that the experience of the superior be mentioned first, followed by that of the subprioress and then Sister Marthe (and in fact that is the order in which de Certeau talks of them). To any churchman of the seventeenth century, precedence was as absolute as seniority is today in a military organization. But the order of sightings in the original record makes it very clear that it was the junior nun, Marthe, who received the first and most detailed visitation, for Sister Marthe's experience would never have been described before that of her superiors if it had not occurred first. Moreover, if it had not been the primary experience, the record would not have described in detail the appearance of a ghost to a junior sister while making only very general statements about its appearance to the two individuals of the highest status.

What fits the facts much better and matches the priests' account equally well is that on the night in question it was Sister Marthe alone who had the experience. She was in a building separate from the others, and not until the next morning was she able to go to

Jeanne in the main building and report her tale. The subprioress would have been brought in on such an occasion as a matter of course. The mother superior either then declared that she too had had an experience or, more likely, she and the subprioress, affected by the lay sister's story, had their own nightmares the next night. If the mother superior claimed to have had an experience that first night, she probably invented it. Given the character of Jeanne des Anges, one can be sure that no subordinate sister in her convent would ever have an experience that was not at least matched by one of her own.

The manuscript in the Tours library,[12] which appears to have been written some years after the event, gives us some more detail about what happened when Sister Marthe reported her experiences:

The same day this same phantom came to the mother superior in the same form; she believed that it was the spirit of the late Father Mousseau; he said to her, "Pray, and have prayers said for me to God," and then he disappeared. He then went in the same form to the subprioress and said to her, "Continue to pray to God for me," and then once more he disappeared.

At six in the morning Sister Marthe went to the mother superior's room and without telling her about the vision she had had she begged her to order the whole community to set about praying for the late Father Mousseau; the mother superior asked her what led her to make this request; Sister Marthe, reluctant to tell what had happened, said nothing for some time, until the superior ordered her to explain what was going on; the superior made her narrate all that had taken place, and at the same time the subprioress also went to the mother superior to report on her experiences. The mother superior, recalling her own experience, became convinced that what these two other sisters had just reported to her was no dream or illusion. A little later, Father Mignon having come to the Ursuline Convent, the mother superior recounted to him all that had happened during the preceding night and asked him to say mass for the repose of the soul of Father Mousseau and to have all the nuns receive communion. He agreed and it was all carried out.

On the surface, this record seems to bear out the contention that the apparition appeared to three people on the same night. But it does not ring true. The appearance of the ghost alone was extraordinary enough. But to appear to three separate people at the same time (and one of them in a different building) would be such proof of supernatural intervention that it could not fail to have been highlighted in the record. It could not have happened without special mention. It is almost certain that the appearance to Sister Marthe took place before (and probably the night before) the appearances to the other two.

There is yet another account of the events – at least, an account of the appearance of the spirit to Jeanne des Anges.[13] This is found in an official journal written in 1634 immediately after Grandier's execution:

During the night, resting on her little but very chaste pallet, the mother superior saw a ghost, encircled by some reddish light, clear enough for her to recognize what she saw, but in some way frightening. This ghost approached her, and she saw at once that it was the spirit of their dead confessor, who said to her: "My daughter, have no fear. I am your dead confessor come to visit you." "Alas, Father," this poor young woman said to him, "why have you come here? Where are you now? Do you want prayers or something else from us?" The ghost replied, "do not trouble yourself over me; I am where I have no need in the future of any assistance from your prayers. I have come here to console you and to teach you many things that I did not have time to do during my stay in this world. I have secrets to reveal to you which will serve to guide your actions."

The next day the phantom reappeared.

And as she resolutely followed his plan without the knowledge or consent of her confessor [Father Mignon], she suddenly saw a strange change in the person who was speaking to her. It was no longer the person of her dead confessor but the face and appearance of Urbain Grandier, who, changing his intent as much as his appearance, spoke words of love to her, urging her with caresses as insolent as they were lewd, and pressed her to grant him what was no longer hers to give and which by her vows she had consecrated to her holy spouse. She struggled, nobody helped her; she was tormented, she had nothing to console her; she cried out for help, nobody came; she trembled, she sweated, she invoked the holy name of Jesus.

The original story of Sister Marthe was recorded by the priests in October 1632. The story of Father Mousseau's appearance to Jeanne des Anges was published in 1634 and is clearly centred on the mother superior. The tone of the account has changed as well. The story of Sister Marthe's apparition has a nightmare quality to it; it has the tone of veracity. This later report of Father Mousseau's appearance reads as if it were an extract from the life of a saint – the brave, chaste mother superior.

The whole subsequent series of events indicates that a nightmare or hallucination placed a very minor nun at centre stage, with Jeanne des Anges playing only a bit part. Within days, Jeanne had taken the steps necessary to put the young nun back in her proper place in the hierarchy and to reassert her own position as the principal player at the convent. A minor event exemplifies this metamorphosis. The records show that during an exorcism on 31 October, "while Mme de Belsiel [Jeanne des Anges] was reciting this story [about the hawthorn needles], the lay sister had some convulsions to which hardly any attention was paid, for all the attention was naturally directed towards the superior. Indeed, the sister could hardly command any interest at all from those present."[14]

A more experienced mother superior, or even a more balanced one, would have heard Marthe's story carefully but with a good measure of doubt. A customary first step would have been to prescribe a good laxative. The common-sense approach of most ecclesiastical superiors of the time would have been to assume that anybody claiming to have had an extraordinary experience was mistaken or sick, or was a charlatan. The "sickness" often disappeared with a good purgative. Only after various reasonable medical tests had been performed would possession properly be contemplated as the cause of the disturbance. In this case, the fact that the mother superior was one of the first people "stricken" led to the by-passing of these sane steps and to the very early assumption of demonic possession.

Jeanne should certainly have handled Marthe's experience with considerable caution, but she and all the nuns had gone through the same stresses as Sister Marthe, and death was very much on their minds. Jeanne des Anges gave credence to Sister Marthe's story from the beginning, and since she accepted it as genuine, it had to become real to everybody. She was, after all, the mother superior. From then on, what had probably been simply a frightening nightmare of Sister Marthe's, followed by hallucinations, became a valid religious experience. It was recognized as such not only by the nuns who had immediate contact with it inside the convent but by those who first came into contact with it from outside. The mother superior's concurrence gave it respectability.

Now Jeanne des Anges' character came into play. We already know enough of her to see that she was not one to take a back seat.

If one of her nuns had a religious experience, she would have to have a bigger and better one. This is not to suggest that she deliberately set out to duplicate and then lead; it was probably an unconscious reaction, part of her nature. Nevertheless, both she and the subprioress now professed to have had the same kind of dream, and obviously they did not hesitate to spread word of it. This in itself was a mistake, for it created alarm throughout the convent. There was a sense of crisis, which was increased by the prayers which the nuns recited together for the soul of the dead priest. Nobody thought or talked of anything else; night was dreaded. Can it be wondered that, within days, half of the nuns were having nightmares and imaginings?

The first outsider to be notified of the strange events was the confessor, Father Jean Mignon. He undoubtedly believed that what was happening was supernatural and to be feared. He tried to give spiritual assistance to this group of young women, who by now had entered a highly emotional state in which their words and actions, even their prayers, encouraged one another to greater excesses. It was their outlet for the terrors that had been induced by the plague. All this was beyond Mignon's level of competence, especially when things began to get totally out of hand, with unseen blows and other violent actions. There was also a loss of self-possession on the part of some of the nuns. One started breaking into uncontrollable laughter over nothing. Mignon called for help from other priests in the town.

Up to this point, we can see how things developed. They are understandable. But the incident of the thorns appearing in Jeanne's hand was a dividing line. This could have occurred only by some supernatural intervention or by a deliberately misleading act either on her part alone or in concert with others. One can picture it. There she was lying in her chamber with her principal nuns gathered about her bedside, the centre of attention because her afflictions were by now worse than anyone else's. But she was still only first amongst equals, sharing the limelight with others. However, a simple little deception, quite harmless really, would put things in their right light. Perhaps she even thought that as the superior she should take the lead in this manner. What she almost certainly did not anticipate was that the incident would excite the nuns even further, herself included.

The subsequent onset of uncontrollable convulsions in a number of the nuns and their increasingly strange behaviour led inevitably to the conclusion that the Devil was involved and that a terrible

case of possession was under way. Mignon and the first of the
Loudun priests now in attendance on the convent reflected the
culture of their times when they believed the attack must be caused
by an agent of the Devil. Once convinced, they naturally began to
look for the human agent through whom the Devil was acting, a
witch or sorcerer.

More priests were brought in – eight, ten, twelve – all to no avail.
It was time to resort to exorcism, to bring in the full power of the
church to expel the evil spirits. Mignon called upon Father Barré,
a priest in the nearby town of Chinon who was a noted exorcist
and chaser of devils. (In this he had the approval of the bishop, who
by now had received word of the possessions.) Barré arrived at
Loudun leading a procession of his parishioners, who were determined that the witch or sorcerer would be unmasked. Clearly, the
good young women themselves were not responsible for introducing
the Devil into the convent, so someone else must have done so,
someone who had cast a spell on the nuns.

The first exorcism was carried out on 5 October 1632 and gave
an initial clue. There was a priest involved. But by now the nuns
were reporting a different kind of priest in their imaginings. Rather
than begging for help, the priestly figure had taken on the character
of evil. Nobody any longer thought of Father Moussaut. The second
exorcism[15] of Jeanne des Anges was held in the afternoon of the
same day:

The devil, required in Latin to tell his name, replied in French howling
and bellowing, "Ha, I've already told you."

And when pressed repeated, "Enemy of God."

And later in the exorcism he cried out saying, "You are hurrying me
too much, give me at least another three weeks. It has only been a
fortnight."

And a little later, "Ha, the wretch, he has been appointed to bring down
the whole community for me."

At the third exorcism, the prioress[16] was largely deprived of her senses
and reason. The devil commanded to tell his name, replied twice, "Enemy
of God."

Then pressed to conceal it no longer, said, "I have told you already."

Inquired as to how he had been admitted [into the convent], said, "A
pact."

And pressed said, "I am burning," crying out all the time. Then commanded to name the author of the pact, said, "The priest."

"Which priest?"

Then said, "Peter."

"Of what rank?"

"Curé."

He [the demon] was commanded to come out. After much violence, vexatious measures, howlings and shouting, and grinding of teeth, which was so violent that two back ones were broken, finally [the demon] left the prioress in complete peace and [she] declared that she was cured of a great spiritual trouble and severe heart palpitations, and believed herself to be completely recovered. She stayed in this state of peace all night, sleeping peaceably more than she had done since the first apparition.

The next morning, the prioress and the others, while being exorcized, at the time of Holy Communion, showed a great repugnance. Ordered to desist, the devils began their vexations, agitations, and contortions, but in the end, after persistent pressure, they let them [the nuns] confess.

When communion was brought to the prioress, the tortures and loss of judgment began, and the devil, pressed to let her bless God and adore him, said, "He is cursed." And then three times, "I reject God."

Finally pressed, [he] let her bless God. And when she was told to say "My God, take possession of my soul and of my body," the devil three times took her by the throat when she tried to say "of my body," making her howl out, grind her teeth, and stick out her tongue. At last constrained to obey, she received the Holy Sacrament although many times the spirit tried to make her spit it out of her mouth, inducing her to vomit.

When Holy Communion was taken to Sister Louise de Jesus, she was more than half an hour in receiving it, so agitated that even six or seven people could not hold her down. She did not wish to adore God; but in the end she opened her mouth and communicated peaceably.

The prioress was exorcized immediately afterwards in Latin, the vexations were renewed, the devils were interrogated:

"How were you brought in [to the convent]?"

"By means of a symbol."

"Under what symbol?"

"It is thorny [prickly, spiny]."

Interrogated, "Where was it placed?"

"I do not know. You know well enough." Then said, "O the power of the priesthood: it is all powerful. A priest put me there, a priest will not be able to remove me."[17]

The speedy progress from the first apparition to this state of violence, uncontrollable laughter, and denials of the God to whom the women had consecrated themselves all took place in about two weeks. The peaceful though frightening ghost of Father Moussaut was now completely forgotten. It had been replaced by the devils who possessed the bodies of the nuns. By this time, although half the convent community was afflicted, the nuns were taking second place to the priests; they were simply the field of battle where the priests fought the devils.

By this time, too, Jeanne des Anges had established herself firmly at centre stage. Her exorcisms form the centrepiece of the records. All the new information came from her. It is doubtful that she was deliberately leading the flock of nuns and priests along a path of her own choosing (though the chicanery of the thorns was certainly frand), but her need to remain the centre of attention meant that she had to be more afflicted than anybody else. She had to have everybody hanging on her words, waiting for her next revelation. And underlying all this was her obsession with the licentious priest, which had already begun to bubble to the surface in little pieces of new information. Nevertheless, she was as much the victim of her own sickness as the director of events.

Most of her contemporaries did not, of course, see it as a sickness. Diabolic possession was the obvious explanation in a society that accepted the idea of the Devil and his agents stalking the world, deliberately acting against God, and capable of taking over the bodies and souls of human beings. This was particularly true in a provincial town like Loudun, where the experience of possession was limited. All the priests brought into the case were mentally prepared to see the events in this light. Indeed, it would have been virtually impossible for them to believe otherwise. That would have required them to say that a whole convent of young women from good families either had suddenly gone mad or were perpetrating an outrageous hoax.

As they pondered the events, some began to conclude that all this might be God's will, that God might have permitted the devils to have their day for His own purposes.[18] Perhaps He had provided an opportunity for the priests to prove to the Huguenots of Loudun the power of the Catholic Church. The Devil would be conquered by the exorcisms, and then the Protestants would surely see that God was truly with the Catholic Church, and there would be a flock of conversions to the true faith. It was this conviction that permitted the fraud, deception, and trickery yet to come.

Grandier the Accused

Up to this point, only priests had been present at the exorcisms. This was natural because it was a religious matter without any criminal implications. But the nature of the case was changing. If an individual was about to be named by the devils as being responsible for introducing them into the convent, the civil authorities would have to be brought in, since sorcery or witchcraft was a criminal offence.[1] This presented the priests with a problem. When the civil authorities were brought in, acting for the king, who would now be in charge? If they thought that the exorcisms were being pursued in such a way as to put justice to the accused at risk, a real battle for power could arise. This was particularly true in Loudun, where the civil authorities were half Huguenot.

The name of the priest who had cast the spell on the nuns was revealed in an exorcism conducted on 11 October between seven and eight in the evening.[2] The record appears to have been made by Father Mignon. At this exorcism, at least two laymen were present, Guillaume de Cerisay de la Guérinière, the *bailli* of Loudun, and his *lieutenant-civil*, Louis Chauvet. The *bailli* had been invited by Mignon on the grounds that a criminal offence might be involved. The record of the event reads:

Under exorcism the devil was ordered to tell his name, and when he was pressed and pressed again, he at last in great fury said three times that his name was Astaroth.

Ordered to tell: "By what means did he enter the house?" Said,
"By a pact with the pastor of the Church of Saint-Pierre."

When we had proceeded with the prayers, the devil with a terrifying cry said in French twice, "O the wretched priest."

"Which priest?"

Said twice, "Urbanist."

And commanded several times to say clearly and distinctly who that priest was, replied screaming loud and long, and then hissing out, "Urbain Grandier."

Pressed to say what was the position of this same Urbain, said, "The curé of Saint-Pierre."

"Which Saint-Pierre?"

Said twice, "Du-Marché."

Pressed and pressed again to say "By means of what new pact was he [the devil] sent in?" said, "Flowers."

"What flowers?"

"Roses."

And all these replies were made only after so many attempts that it could be clearly seen that the devil had to be really compelled to speak. And even when he pronounced his own name, when he was ordered to reply he was so angry that he cried out once more shouting, "Ha, why did I tell it to you?"

At last the last demand pressed upon him for the evening was to tell "Why he had entered the monastery."

Said, "Animosity."[3]

Two new facts had been presented here. There was the clear accusation that Urbain Grandier was the source of the devils' invasion, and there was a revelation about how the devils were introduced into the convent. It seems to have been understood from the beginning that demons did not have the power to enter a convent on their own. They had to be introduced into it through a human intermediary who was in league with the Devil. Furthermore, they had to have some physical means of entry. Initially they had been introduced through the three thorns, according to the demon speaking through Jeanne des Anges on 5 October. But those were the devils who had caused the early disturbances and convulsions. Now impurity and immodesty had entered under the names of Astaroth, Asmodée, Iscaaron, and Balaam. They seem to have been introduced in a second invasion by means of some roses. During this exorcism of Jeanne des Anges it was revealed that she had picked up three branches of musk roses on the stairs, thinking that one of the nuns had dropped them while going ahead of her to the choir. This was about six o'clock in the morning:

She smelled the roses and put one-half at the crucifix of her oratory and the other in the belt at her waist. She felt a great trembling in her right arm and was seized with love for Grandier throughout the period for prayers, being unable to apply her mind to anything other than the picture in her mind of the person of Grandier.[4]

We have another word picture of the events that day, this one from a priest:

The mother superior having gathered [the bouquet] together, smelled it, as did some others after her, who were all uncontrollably possessed. They began to cry and call on Grandier, with whom they were so enamoured that neither the other nuns nor anyone else was capable of holding them back. They wanted to go and find him, and to do this climbed up and ran about the roofs of the convent, up the trees, dressed in their shifts, and standing right on the extremities of the branches. There, after dreadful cries, they endured hail, freezing temperatures, and rain. They went four or five days without eating.[5]

As noted earlier, sickness and health were closely tied to their associated smells, and the emphasis on sweet strong-smelling things as a protection against disease had been ubiquitous during the recent plague. What better way could there be for a demon to enter the convent than in a bunch of fragrant roses that would certainly be picked up? Furthermore, roses, especially musk roses, were associated with sexual love. They were the perfect vehicle for a devil of impurity, and this was understood in that way by all present.

What can possibly have led Jeanne des Anges, through the "demon" in her, to accuse Urbain Grandier of causing her demonic possession? And did she really believe she was possessed? She may well have done so. Her contortions, teeth grinding, and other extraordinary behaviour were almost certainly involuntary. Furthermore, the records make it clear that no matter how violent the episodes and convulsions, when one was over, she (and the other nuns also) became quite normal and remembered nothing of what had happened. Moreover, if she had any doubts about her condition, they were removed by the priests, led by Barré, who assured her that she was under attack by the demons.

The progression of Jeanne des Anges from a woman under severe stress to a subject of demonic possession was thus a mixture of imagination, mental sickness, deceit, and manipulation. But although we can recognize the ingredients, we do not know the relative quantities. We have no real idea of when and to what degree she was in control of herself and when she was just a desperately sick woman. Clearly, she was obsessed by Urbain Grandier. She said so herself: "At that time, the priest of whom I have spoken used demons to excite love for him in me; they gave me desires to see and speak to him. Many of our sisters were of the same sentiments without telling us. On the contrary, we hid from one another as much as we could, and after the demons had thoroughly aroused in us the passion of love for this man, he did not fail to come by night into our house and into our chambers to solicit us to sin."[6] She gave few specific details about her nights or about the "caresses as insolent as they were immodest by which he pressed her to accord to him that which was not within her liberty to grant."[7] Her temptations can be easily imagined:

When I could not see him, I burned for love of him, and when he presented himself to me and wanted to seduce me, our good God gave me a great aversion. Then all my feelings changed, I hated him more than the devil, and he was so insupportable to me that I would expose myself to all the furies of hell rather than give in to the least of his demands. It is true that I had been unfaithful in fighting against the thoughts and impure emotions that I experienced. I attribute it to the providence of a totally loving God that I was preserved from sin in the attacks of this wretched man.[8]

Later she said more about her own particular devils: "Thus I had seven devils in my body of whom the chief was Asmodée;[9] he continually operated within me, as much in imagination as in the mind, which he filled with unseemly things. Modesty prevents me from describing the details, for they are inappropriate." It is clear from these records that there was a tremendous sexual impulse in the woman. It is also evident that although she said that the nuns kept their temptations to themselves, her own excitements were transmitted to the others, who then became enamoured of the same man. Yet none of them, including Jeanne herself, had ever even seen him!

Some have held that the source of Jeanne's obsession with Grandier was as much spite as love. According to this interpretation, she wrote to Grandier and asked him to be the confessor, intending to create a situation in which she could have him close to her as much as possible, and she was furious when she was rejected. Curiously, much the same story is used by the enemies of Grandier. In this version, it was he who approached the convent, seeking unsullied fields for his amorous adventures, and he too swore revenge when rejected.

We have an example of this side of the story. In 1665, after Jeanne des Anges died, her nuns wrote a death notice that contained the following account:

Thus, a few years after this establishment [of the convent], when she [Jeanne des Anges] was in a ten-day retreat, her director advised her that the *superieure* was in touch with M. Grandier, curé of St-Pierre, who promised to confess the community gratis and to provide many good services. He counselled her to turn away from this step, telling her that this man was capable of bringing about their ruin. As M. Grandier had already been in the prisons of the bishop of Poitiers, Sister Jeanne des Anges had difficulty at first believing that the superieure had even thought of this matter; she begged her to tell her the truth; the *superieure* acknowledged everything, saying that it was a great advantage for a house as poor as theirs to find a man who wished to provide them with free services. All that the sister [Jeanne] could place before her was of no value; she begged her to at least write to the bishop of Poitiers. The prelate, warned, wrote promptly to the mother prioress to forbid her to undertake this engagement, and the prioress gave Sister des Anges the task of breaking it. She wrote without ceremony, on behalf of her *superieure*, to M. Grandier, who, seeing the letter, said before opening it, although he had never seen Sister des Anges and she had never written to him before, "I know what hand has flung this at me; she will pay dearly and drink deep."[10]

This item was used at Grandier's trial as proof that he had tried to approach the convent with the intention of seducing the nuns.[11] But it does not ring true. The incident would have to have happened after Grandier was released from the bishop's prison on 3 January 1630 and after the archbishop overruled that sentence in late 1631, because Grandier was not free to carry out any priestly duty until then. So it could only have occurred between about November 1631 and the beginning of the possessions in September 1632. It is unlikely that it happened while Father Mousseau was alive. He died in June 1632. So the incident, if it ever took place, occurred between

June and September 1632, during the plague. What is just possible is that after Mousseau died in the plague, it was hard for the nuns to find somebody to confess them at short notice. From what we know of Grandier's general behaviour during the plague and assuming that the nuns would be desperate to be confessed when death threatened all the time, he might have offered to help them out until a new priest was appointed – Mignon. The rest of it sounds like a fabrication.

Another story that might have a grain of truth to it is that some months before the possessions began, Madeleine de Brou visited the convent to talk at the grille to a young niece who was one of the pensionnaires. The superior was said to have had a furious argument with Madeleine over her supposed relationship with Grandier and to have told her that she was an unsuitable visitor to the convent. This was at the time when Madeleine was pursuing her legal case against Adam for the scandalous rumours he was spreading about her and Grandier. According to this story, Jeanne was already so enamoured of Grandier that she was determined to revenge herself on him for loving Madeleine and "rejecting" herself. It cannot be proved one way or the other, but it seems much more likely that the possessions crept up on the convent rather than being some kind of planned revenge.

The priests certainly believed that a true case of possession by devils was in progress, for they were daily observers of the inexplicable, violent, and apparently uncontrollable scenes. Thus, it is not surprising that they believed it when the "devil" in Jeanne said that the man responsible for introducing the demons into the house was the curé of Saint-Pierre-du-Marché. But the two magistrates present could not accept this so easily. We have the *bailli*'s description of what he witnessed on 11 October on his first visit to the convent: "Mme de Belciel [Jeanne des Anges] began to make violent actions and movements accompanied by sounds like the grunting of a pig, then thrusting herself down in her bed ground her teeth, and made other faces like a person devoid of her senses. There was to her right a Carmelite monk and on her left hand the said Mignon who put his thumb and index finger [the fingers used to hold the sacred host] in the mouth of the said superior and uttered exorcisms and incantations in our presence."[12] Whatever the two magistrates had been told, they could not have expected such scenes in the Ursuline Convent, and they were appalled when their friend Grandier was accused of being responsible. They wondered why they had not been brought in earlier. Whose work was this? The superior's? Mignon's? And was this true possession? Was this woman sick or bewitched?

It was at this point that the future course of the case was so fatally set. Father Mignon asked the *bailli* for a private interview away from the crowd around the nuns, and he then announced that this case "was somewhat similar to the story of Gaufridy, who had been put to death by virtue of the sentence of the Parlement of Aix, having been convicted of magic."[13] The reference to Gaufridy came like a bombshell to de Cerisay and Chauvet. They knew exactly what Mignon was referring to. Some twenty years earlier, in the Ursuline Convent of Aix in the south of France, a young nun had begun to have extraordinary dreams and lustings in which her whole body seemed to be possessed by some kind of being beyond her control. During these "possessions," the nun, Madeleine Demandolx de la Palud, appeared to be taken over by appetites of desire – not just taken over but actually controlled by some other being. Doctors were immediately brought in as well as priests, but it was decided that her problems were not medical. This was a case of demonic possession requiring exorcism. Madeleine responded well, and within a few months she was claiming that the author of her possession was a priest named Louis Gaufridy, who was her former confessor and a friend and spiritual director to her family. Gaufridy, a priest of high reputation, vigorously denied all the accusations.[14]

As Madeleine's exorcism proceeded, other nuns in the convent began to show marked signs of possession, and soon public exorcisms were being held so that all could witness the extraordinary contortions and sounds of these nuns and the accusations they made during exorcism. In time, the exorcists felt that there was enough evidence to force Gaufridy to answer charges of sorcery before the church authorities – to no avail, as it turned out. Gaufridy appeared and was questioned, but he had many supporters, including his own bishop, and they made it evident that they had no belief in the accusations. As a result, Gaufridy was permitted to return to his parish and carry on his normal priestly functions.

But now the civil authorities came into the case in the person of the principal law officer in Aix, who attended one of the exorcisms and became convinced that the possessions were genuine and that Gaufridy was responsible. The very next day he ordered the priest arrested. Accordingly, Gaufridy was imprisoned. Faced with an immediate and hostile investigation, including torture, he quickly lost heart and was soon ready to confess to anything he was accused of, including having made a pact with Satan and having enchanted Madeleine and many other women.[15]

Gaufridy's written confession stated that an uncle had left him a book of magic, which he had found among his papers some years earlier. When he picked up the book and started to read it, the Devil appeared to him. Gaufridy wrote that he was filled with desire for women and with lusts of the flesh to an uncontrollable degree and that this had led him into a pact with the Devil, to whom he had given all he owned, including his life. In return, Satan had given him power over any woman he wanted. Gaufridy claimed to have had carnal knowledge of more than a thousand women, including Madeleine. He said he had pursued her as a child in her parents' house even while professing to be their friend and giving her mother spiritual direction. He admitted also that he and Madeleine had been so consumed by each other that he had persuaded her to make a pact with the Devil as he had done. She had taken part in a sabbath with him, he said, and had gone through the most degrading of ceremonies. Meanwhile, Madeleine was telling much the same story and describing the same shocking secrets of the sabbath she said she had attended. She also described the Devil's marks of insensitivity on Gaufridy's body. When Gaufridy was tested, he was found to be marked as she described. Gaufridy made his confessions in the hope that although he might be punished, he would at least avoid the horror of being burned alive. It was a vain hope. He was subjected to the most frightful torture for three days to determine who his accomplices were, but he swore he had none. Then, on 30 April 1611, he was burned at the stake in front of a great crowd.[16]

Even at the time, there were unexplained points about the case that troubled some people. Still, the sceptics tended to keep quiet, for to speak out against the published events was to be in open battle against both the church and the courts, not a healthy position to adopt at that time in France. The case had been a major sensation throughout France, and because it represented the triumph of God over the Devil, all the details were permissible subjects for infinite dissection. There was an abundance of books and eyewitness reports on the subject in both private and religious houses, and everybody for years to come knew every detail of the Gaufridy case. It was proof that the Catholic Church would always prevail over the Devil in the end.

DEMONS AND WITCHES

The men and women of Loudun did not find it strange to believe
in angels, devils, and witches.[17] Their invisible world was as complex
and coherent to them as our material world is to us. If we find their
credulity naive, we should remember that we believe in atoms that
we cannot see, and that a table is mostly space. For them, the
supernatural was perfectly natural. In the seventeenth century there
were plenty of inexplicable events – plague, famine, untimely death,
unexpected sickness, impotence, sterility. If there was no material
explanation, then some other had to be found. We ourselves are not
totally removed from that same mind-set. In our own century, many
quite sensible people explain a number of inexplicable happenings
by the idea that there are visitors from outer space: intergalactic
rather than supernatural intervention. Many people believe in ghosts
or at least acknowledge the possibilty that such supernatural beings
might exist. And how many of those who scoff at ghosts would buy
a house that was reputed to be haunted by a troubled spirit? Deep
down, there are probably few of us who are totally convinced there
is no supernatural, and there are many who are convinced that God,
the Devil – good and evil, whatever we may call them – exist as
beings.

From the events of the time and from the art and writings, we
know something about how seventeenth-century men and women
in France thought. For instance, they viewed such a simple thing as
cleanliness in a very different light from us. Their streets were filthy,
washing was infrequent, and bathing more so. Toilets, when they
existed, were simple privies, but more often any convenient place
was used. There was practically no water piped into houses; public
wells served instead. People stank. They were not just copies of us
wearing different clothes and following a simpler life. Their whole
world was different.

Out of every hundred children born, twenty-five died before they
were a year old, another twenty-five never reached the age of twenty,
and a further twenty-five died between the ages of twenty and forty-
five. Only about 10 per cent of babies born ever made it to their
sixties.[18] Maternal death when giving birth, or shortly afterwards
from infection or disease, was commonplace. Consequently, second
and third marriages were equally common; the "folkloric commonplace of the wicked stepmother was an exaggeration based on a
well-known phenomenon."[19] Almost every family had its little

victims. Epidemics swept through and decimated the population: bubonic plague, smallpox, dysentery, and typhus, especially after armies had passed through. Each year in late summer the death rate rose as the heat and filth combined to create disease, probably gastric troubles caused by poor hygiene and diet.[20] The doctors knew little scientific medicine, and the drugs available to them were at best hit-and-miss. Operations, however major, were performed without any anaesthetic, for none existed, and the patient often died in agony.

Famine was common, sometimes covering great areas, sometimes being quite local, as the weather failed to give good crops or as hailstones, untimely cold, disease, or insects destroyed them.[21] Even a local famine could be disastrous, because the lack of roads, bridges, and canals made it impossible to bring in food. And what food there was rose and rose in price. People who lived at the bare subsistence level, and many did, simply could not afford to buy it, so starvation and disease took them off. Time and time again in the records of the period there is a reference to *cherté*, high prices; it was a term of fear, not merely a description. Animals, too, lived on the margin. Many a poor peasant family had a single animal, often a cow to give milk. Its death from a disease such as brucellosis was a major disaster. And in addition to all these natural calamities there was war, with its roving armies living off the land, stealing, raping, bringing their own diseases, and burning, flattening, or consuming the crops.

The period between the late Middle Ages and the early seventeenth century was a time of universal fear throughout Europe.[22] The Black Death, the deep economic crises that followed, the shocks and upheavals of the Reformation, and the recurring wars and plagues all caused people to believe that the Devil was intervening in the world with ever-increasing fervour. It made no difference whether one was Calvinist, Lutheran, or Catholic, all trusted in God, the source of goodness and hope, and all believed that the Devil was the evil one, who roamed the world seeking the weaknesses in people in order to tempt them and carry them to eternal damnation.

The Bible told the story of how Lucifer and other angels had rebelled in heaven through the sin of pride and had been cast into outer darkness. Lucifer, the angel of light, was from then on known as Satan, the Devil, the enemy of God, and the father of lies. But he remained a powerful rival of God, and his servants – the other devils, or demons – exercised strong powers, which flowed from their master.²³ Many of them had names and personalities. Jeanne des Anges had named several of them. Her first was Asmodée, the devil associated with lust and lechery. The second was Leviathan, who had filled her with pride, and the third was Behemoth, who opposed all her actions towards God. Then came Iscaaron who, like Asmodée, brought impurity; then Balaam, who also seems to have carried some variation of impurity, though she described him only briefly. The last two were Grésil and Aman; she said she knew about them but did not know how they worked because they were soon replaced by the others.²⁴

In the catalogues prepared by the exorcists of the sixteenth and seventeenth centuries, dozens of other devils were identified.²⁵ They had ranks, like an army on Earth. Asmodée, Leviathan, Behemoth, and Iscaaron were of the first hierarchy, with others below them. Thus, the world of evil was divided up; a major sin²⁶ was assigned to each principal demon, who had subordinates responsible for some area of that sin, and so on down to the nameless minor functionaries who served their master Satan in capturing the souls of men. In the convent at Loudun, each devil was recognizable by its distinctive characteristics, its "personality." When Asmodée was speaking through the mouth of Jeanne des Anges, for example, her face changed totally, as did her voice, her gestures – everything. Asmodée was expressing his personality through her person. If another of her devils was addressed during the exorcism or if another took over, there was a complete and identifiable change of face, voice, and movement.

Like the belief in devils, witchcraft had a long history, though it had not had much importance in the common view or been paid much attention by the church until towards the end of the fifteenth century. During that period, it was increasingly thought that the Devil's evil was being practised not only by demons but by men and women who worshipped him and used his powers malevolently on those around them. There were two essential characteristics to a witch or sorcerer: a pact of allegiance to the Devil, in which homage of some kind was paid to him, and a power that was given in return to do harm to others. Thus, witchcraft and diabolism were closely linked ideas.

The concentration on witchcraft and witch-hunting is generally dated from the late 1400s. The relatively recent invention of the printing press and the enormous expansion in the number of books made a considerable contribution to spreading the idea of witchcraft, along with the fear of witches. The height of the witch-hunting craze was from the 1580s to 1640s. By the beginning of that period, the ideas surrounding witches and witchcraft had solidified. All the characteristics by which a witch could be recognized and therefore taken before judges for verdict and punishment were well established. By the end of the witch-hunt craze, some 40,000 to 50,000 people had been executed, mostly by burning at the stake. About 75 to 80 per cent of these were women.[27]

Today, the common image of a witch is of an old hag: long nose reaching to a pointed chin; hanks or wisps of grey hair hanging below a pointed hat; long black clothes; and a dog or cat as companion. This is probably a true picture of the majority of those who were burned. Most were elderly village women who for one reason or another – by threat or curse, or simply by appearance – had aroused fear and dislike among their neighbours. Even the pointed hat was the common apparel of village women at the time. What caused them first to be suspected of witchcraft was usually an unfortunate event or disaster within the village. An animal or a neighbour would sicken or die; crops would wither or seeds fail; damaging wind and hail would destroy the harvest; or a newlywed husband would be impotent or would fail to impregnate his wife. Very often there was a perceived association between the witch, the victim, and the event. In the trial records it is common to find that the witch had asked for something – milk, food, a favour – and when refused had become angry and had perhaps cursed or threatened. Within hours or days a child or animal of the household had fallen ill, a baby had been stillborn, or an arm or leg had been broken in an accident. The obvious conclusion had been drawn: a spell had been cast on the house; the old woman was a witch, in league with the Devil, and was using his evil powers.

Few in the village would doubt the obvious connection. The old woman, commonly a widow, often had nobody alive to protect her. Already disliked and generally avoided because of her appearance and eccentric behaviour, she would have little defence against the accusation. Everybody would remember some incident in the past, some encounter followed by a calamity. All the inexplicable afflictions of the village would suddenly be understood. The witch would be taken before the judges in the local town, and there she would be tortured to obtain a confession and to reveal the names of accomplices and other witches she had met.[28] The tortures were horrifying. It is not surprising that the required confession was usually obtained with all the details the judges could want. Commonly, the "accomplices" were in turn pursued, tried, and executed. At times, it became an unending cycle of confessions, followed by new trials of the supposed accomplices, new confessions, and so on, raising fears on the part of many that they too would be accused.

It was generally believed that witches actively sought to bring others into their circle in order to get them to make their own pact with the Devil. This was one of the reasons for demanding names under torture. The other reason was the sabbath.[29] It was an accepted fact that witches went to sabbaths to worship the Devil.[30] Often they flew there (which is why representations of the witch, then as now, commonly show her riding the skies on a broomstick – a phallic symbol). There were always strong bars on windows and chimneys where a witch was detained; they prevented flight.

The shocking things that went on at a sabbath were well known. An authority of the time wrote: "Women take part nude and dishevelled ... [They] dance indecently, feast ardently, copulate diabolically, sodomize execrably, blaspheme scandalously, take revenge insidiously, search after every horrible, dirty, brutal desire, hold dear to themselves toads, vipers, lizards, and all sorts of fish, approach a goat ardently caressing him amorously, coming to him and copulating with him horribly and lecherously."[31] Sabbaths were "known" to take place everywhere; sometimes they were huge meetings, which a thousand or more witches attended. The great distances involved for some of the participants explained why they had to transport themselves magically on their broomsticks. Other sabbaths were purely local events. Many a village witch, when pressed under torture, stated that she had attended sabbaths where she saw other local people, whom she then named.

The judges at witchcraft trials always searched for admission of involvement in a sabbath and looked for a description of what had taken place and who had taken part – the trial records are full of these descriptions. The sabbath was the ultimate proof of the existence of witches. As torture brought forth the detailed confessions and the pattern of the sabbath became general knowledge, the next new-found witch knew what she had to admit to. Sometimes the details were so well established that an accused witch would describe the whole affair without even being subjected to torture. This naturally reinforced everyone's belief that sabbaths did in fact take place.

Another important element in every witchcraft case was locating the Devil's mark on the body of the witch. This mark, which was always insensitive, was a visible sign of the pact that had been made between the witch and the Devil.[32] Commonly it was in a secret area of the body, around the private parts. It might be a mole or skin blemish. Sometimes it was in the form of a teat, some growth that was supposedly used to feed the witch's familiar if she had one. Whether the accused was a village witch, a priest, or a member of the king's court, this was how the person was clearly identified as a witch.

The recognition of witchcraft and witches and how they should be tried and punished was almost universal in Europe in the century and a half when the witch craze was at its height.[33] If there were differences, they were of no benefit to the witch. Protestant clerics might place more emphasis on links between idolatry and witchcraft than Catholic priests, for they viewed Catholicism as being full of the worship of idols.[34] The Catholics, on the other hand, were more inclined to emphasize links between witchcraft and heresy, since they regarded Protestants as heretics. There were even differences among Catholic priests themselves. For instance, could the Devil, the father of lies, in some circumstances be forced to tell the truth, whether he wanted to or not, so that what he said could be used in evidence against the accused? This theological argument could make the difference between life and death, as we shall see. So while everybody agreed on the main body of facts, there was room for theological uncertainty. Did the Devil use the witch, or did the witch use the Devil? Were there situations in which the Devil needed a witch to perform his work, or could he always do it directly? Usually these were technicalities, but in the Grandier case it is possible to see a hint of this kind of argument in practice. In the incident of Jeanne des Anges and the roses, it seems to have been assumed that the roses carried the spell and that a human had to throw the roses into the garden; the devil could only enter the convent with human assistance. And only when Jeanne picked the roses up could he enter into possession.

Possession was closely connected with ordinary witchcraft (in essence it was a branch of it), but there were important aspects to it that made it a special case. In witchcraft, the Devil and the witch made a pact and then the witch used the power of the Devil to bring about evil. It was thus the witch who acted. In the case of possession, the possessed person's body was taken over physically by the Devil or his subordinates. The witch played an intermediate part only, introducing the demons into the body of the possessed person through a spell.[35]

Just as everyone at the time believed in witchcraft, everyone believed in possession. What varied was the approach to curing the possessed person. With a few exceptions, Lutherans and Calvinists believed that the expulsion of demons from the possessed person was to be accomplished by prayer. The Catholic approach of using exorcism as a therapy was largely rejected by mainline Protestants.[36] Exorcism had long been practised in the Roman Catholic Church, and there were established formulas of prayer for expelling the demons from the possessed person. But at the height of the witch craze, diabolical possession was a special battleground for Catholic churchmen, not only against the demons but against the Protestants.

In many cases, the private exorcism of an individual was replaced by public exorcisms, carefully staged and orchestrated, with enormous crowds attending.[37] In France, this developed particularly in areas where there was a significant Protestant population. The principal purpose was to prove to the world that the Roman Catholic Church was the true church because God had given it the power to expel devils. The secondary purpose was associated with this: to get the population to conclude that Protestantism was an evil fostered by the Devil. This association was not too difficult to make because in these great cases of public exorcisms the Protestants were often the people accused by the demoniacs.[38] As a result, exorcism became a weapon in the battle between the churches.[39]

MIGNON

Although the *bailli*, Guillaume de Cerisay, no doubt believed in the power of the Devil as much as anyone else in Loudun, he became very suspicious when Mignon compared the events at the convent with the Gaufridy case. Surely Mignon was acting on Trincant's behalf. This looked like another plot against Grandier. So in front of another priest, and of the Chauvet brothers who also were present, de Cerisay told Mignon that the exorcisms and questioning should be done by those who were not Grandier's enemies. This seemed all the more important when, after he and Louis Chauvet had retired to prepare the minutes of what they had witnessed, they learned that the mother superior had already been asked the same questions many times, often in the presence of Trincant and another of Grandier's enemies.[40]

Was it reasonable for them to assume that Mignon was behind the accusation against Grandier? Was Mignon putting leading questions to the nuns, especially to the mother superior? And was he coaching them outside the exorcisms in what they should say and do? All of these suggestions have been made by various authors, who have seen Mignon as a bigoted priest, blinded by his hatred of Grandier and working solely as the agent of Trincant and his family. Certainly, Mignon was not an impartial participant. Still, we cannot be sure that he was an active plotter. By this time, he might objectively have come to the conclusion that Grandier was involved in some way. It was Jeanne des Anges, after all, who had introduced Grandier into the case, and Mignon had been listening to her and the other nuns for some three weeks, since the very beginning. He had not been injected into the situation from outside, nor had he come into it as a member of the Trincant family. He had become involved as the confessor of the convent, even though he had soon included Trincant as a participant.

Furthermore, the early events he had witnessed had convinced Mignon that this was more than he could deal with alone, and he had called in more priests and experts to give assistance. When they arrived, they confirmed that he was dealing with a case of possession, indeed with half a convent full of possessions that were becoming increasingly more serious every day. It is likely, too, that from the very early days Grandier's name arose during the exorcisms and convulsions – not perhaps with accusations against him but at least with signs that some of the nuns were obsessed with him. And although Mignon's suggestion to the *bailli* about the Gaufridy parallel seemed to come out of the blue, the idea may have been developing among the priests for some days before the accusation was made in the exorcism of 11 October. All of them had been convinced by what they had seen and heard. Led by Barré, the expert, who never had any doubt about the reality of the case, they reinforced one another's belief in the possessions. Once they reached that point, it was only natural that they would recall the much-publicized Gaufridy case, which had occurred about twenty years ago. Since they had been young men at the time, they would remember it clearly. Moreover, Jeanne des Anges' obvious obsession with Grandier would have led them to ask the kinds of question that ultimately resulted in a direct accusation against the curé of

Saint-Pierre. It was therefore reasonable for Mignon to conclude that Grandier was truly behind the possessions – though it does seem curious that it was on the day the civil authorities were brought in that the the first clear accusations against Grandier were made. This suggests that there may have been some staging to the event.

There had, of course, already been rumours in Loudun about the events in the convent, but now it was truly out in the open. Within a day the whole town was talking. The Huguenots chortled at the idea of the nuns getting up to such antics; the Catholics were appalled. The embarrassment of those who were related to the afflicted young women must have been enormous. Like the priests, they could account for such extraordinary happenings only by believing in the possessions. They either had to disown their relatives as dirty-minded women or accept the much more reasonable supposition that the nuns could not be held responsible for the demons' invasion. For many people, the possessions had to be genuine.

At this time, too, the first rumours of Grandier's alleged involvement escaped from the convent. Soon they were expanded. Could it be that the cause of the plague, still only one month past, had finally been discovered? Had it been brought on them by the priest? Had God punished Loudun with the plague for harbouring the Devil's agent? And was this alliance with the Devil the reason why the priest had been able to move about during the plague, attending everybody, without catching the disease? How like the Devil to mislead mortals by encouraging his agent to look as if he was a saint when all the time he was acting for the enemy! Whether or not Trincant and his friends had been actively involved before, they certainly became so now. Trincant saw his opportunity and seized it. From this time on, it was no longer Grandier's banishment from Loudun that he sought, nor was it his total humiliation and the loss of all sources of income. From now on, Trincant sought the death of the priest.

Grandier's initial reaction to the news that he was being considered as a new Gaufridy was surprisingly low key. Certainly, he did not immediately recognize the full measure of his danger. Perhaps he placed too much trust in the ability of the civil authorities to correct the excesses of the ecclesiastical ones. On the morning of 12 October 1632 he sent a formal petition to the *bailli* in which he humbly requested that he be allowed to go "with Messieurs the other officers of justice to the nuns and to have them sequestered and separated, questioned and examined, and if it did appear that there was a case of possession, to exercise their office and to choose ecclesiastic persons who were of requisite standing and probity and were not suspect to the supplicant like the said Mignon and his adherents."[41]

This was the beginning of the battle for control of the case between the civil and religious authorities. But the civil authorities were split between Grandier's friends and enemies, whereas the ecclesiastics were all of one mind, unified in the view that this was a case for the church alone. Grandier initially placed far too much reliance on attempts to force the ecclesiastical forces to respond to the civil authorities. Above all, he overlooked the fact that the ecclesiastics already had the nuns under their control. In this case, possession was truly nine-tenths of the law.

De Cerisay could hardly introduce Grandier into the convent as the priest had asked. Grandier was, after all, the man who was being accused of causing the troubles. Nevertheless, the *bailli* assured him that from now on he would insist on being personally present at the exorcisms to ensure that justice was done. As a matter of principle, the priests had no objection to this senior official and his lieutenants being present at the exorcisms. There was no reason why they should. They were already convinced that the possessions were real, and no doubt they believed that the *bailli* would soon be of the same mind. However, allowing him to be present was one thing; allowing him to control events was quite another. They had no intention of letting the civil authorities dictate which priests would conduct the church's exorcisms.

As the exorcisms became more and more crowded, first with priests, then with magistrates and doctors, and before long with local notables, the nuns found themselves outnumbered by the onlookers. They had moved from being principal actresses in the theatre of the possessions to being at best participants and at worst theatre props, to be manipulated by the exorcists.[42]

When de Cerisay arrived at the convent on 12 October, he again raised the issue of whether priests hostile to Grandier should be involved. Barré and Mignon showed him an authorization which the bishop, La Rocheposay, had issued giving them specific authority to exorcize the Ursulines. There is no reason to read a plot into this by assuming that they were forearmed by the bishop because he disliked Grandier. He certainly did dislike Grandier, but his issue of written authority to specified persons to lead the exorcisms was perfectly normal; Mignon the confessor and Barré the expert were

the obvious choices. Since de Cerisay had no grounds for entering
into open battle with the bishop, he and his officers could do
nothing except watch the exorcisms.

It was not a good day for the exorcists. The record, which was
kept and signed by de Cerisay and other officers,[43] noted: "While
the said Barré said prayers and performed exorcisms on the superior,
there was an unexpected noise in the room and a cat was seen by
the chimney, and many attest to having seen it. The room was
searched everywhere and it was found. Pursued, it threw itself at
the bottom of the wooden beds: then, being taken, it was put on
the bed of the said superior where the said Barré made over it a
number of signs of the cross and exorcisms."[44] As the hubbub died
down, it turned out that the cat, taken to be a devil by the exorcist,
was none other than the convent pet, as terrified as everyone else
present. The magistrates withdrew, announcing that they would
return the following day.

Even this event had its parallel in the Gaufridy case, though there
it was even more embarrassing. It was alleged, and believed, that
Gaufridy left his room to transport himself to the Devil's sabbaths
by flying up the chimney in his room.[45] One day, while testimony
was being read to the judges in the large room where they were
conducting their inquiry, they heard a strange noise coming from
the chimney. It climaxed with the appearance of a large man, black
from head to foot, whereupon the judges assumed that the Devil
himself had come in this terrifying way to release his pupil from
their captivity. Every one of them fled, tumbling out of the room,
all except the court reporter, who could not get out in time. This
unhappy soul stood there, frightened out of his wits and trembling
all over, making signs of the cross against the demon as fast as he
could. The demon was in no better state, being equally terrified and
having no idea of what was troubling the magistrate. At last it all
became clear. The demon was a chimney sweep who had been hired
to clean the chimney of the next room and had come down the
wrong one.[46]

The cat incident, apart from its obvious humour and the
undoubted embarrassment of the exorcists, was typical of what
developed more and more as time went on. Since the ecclesiastics
were already convinced of the validity of the possessions, anything
that was seen or heard was interpreted in that light. Every unexpected event was seen as a sign that the Devil was at work, and as
each sign was accepted in this way, each one reinforced the belief

in the possessions. Things soon reached the stage where any observer at the exorcisms who searched for a natural explanation of an event instead of accepting a supernatural one would be accused either of being fooled by the Devil or of acting on the Devil's behalf.

It was already obvious to Mignon and Barré, the principal though by no means only priests involved, that de Cerisay and his officers were a disruptive influence. Apart from anything else, the whole town was chuckling over the cat story. If the exorcisms were to proceed in an orderly fashion, the priests had to discourage the royal municipal officers from attending; their scepticism was distracting both to the priests and to the nuns. Consequently, there was a sudden change in tactics, as the *bailli* reported on Wednesday the thirteenth:

The nuns were preparing themselves for confession, and [Mignon] asked us and the other officers to withdraw to a house opposite the said convent, saying that in a half or three quarters of an hour he would send us word that we could enter the convent and be present at the celebration of mass … We left the said convent to wait for the assigned time. Once it arrived we returned, and entering the chapel of the said place, we found that Mignon and Barré were at the grille, inside the convent, and the said Barré told us and the other officers undersigned that he had exorcized the said women and that they had just been delivered of unclean and evil spirits.[47]

Clearly, Mignon had deliberately lied to the magistrates. Not only had he not confessed the nuns, but in concert with Barré, he had in effect thrown the *bailli* and his officers out in order to perform his exorcisms without unwanted witnesses.

De Cerisay was furious. He admonished the exorcists, telling them that their procedure was improper. He left with a strong suspicion of fraud and with doubts about everything that had been said and done during the previous days, including the fact that he had found variations in what they said. He stated that Mignon had publicly defamed Grandier and accused him of having made a pact with the devils. Nothing, he said, should be done clandestinely. Everything ought to be done in the presence of the officers of the law. The priests had made use of a deliberate trick in asking persons of such official standing to wait half an hour, then performing their exorcisms on the allegedly possessed nuns. He warned that it called into question the whole procedure that was being followed.

The *bailli*'s outburst warned the two priests that they had gone too far. It was one thing to prevent the interference of the royal law

officers in the actual exorcisms, but to have misled and insulted the
king's principal officer in the Loudun region was a serious matter
and would be subject to firm action if they continued. Barré judged
it prudent to beat a retreat. The next day, he had word spread that
calm had returned to the convent and that since his further presence
would be useless, he was returning to Chinon. Once this visionary
left, the nuns had a little rest until mid-November.

Bishop versus Archbishop

Grandier knew that the exorcists would not give up now that they were convinced that demonic possession had taken place. When things had quietened down, they would feel compelled to return to their investigations and exorcisms; their spiritual concern for the nuns would demand that they bring everything to a conclusion. And if the exorcists returned, all of Grandier's problems would return as well, together with the accusation against him. Like de Cerisay, he soon came to the conclusion that it was not the exorcisms that were a threat to him; it was the fact that the leading exorcists were his enemies or were friends of his enemies. Justice could be served only if the present exorcists were removed and objective ones chosen. Furthermore, the nuns had to be separated from one another so that there could be no question of collusion. Grandier had hoped that the *bailli* would be able to insist on these conditions, but the matter was principally ecclesiastical and only secondarily criminal, and de Cerisay knew that he could not win a battle with the bishop over the issue; he therefore advised Grandier to appeal personally to the prelate.

Accordingly, on Friday, 22 October 1632, the curé of Saint-Pierre, accompanied by another priest, a close friend, went to where Bishop de La Rocheposay was staying in the country. When he arrived at the door and asked to be allowed to see him, the major domo replied that the prelate was indisposed and could not receive him. Grandier explained that he had come a long way and did not want his journey to be useless, and he asked the major domo if he could see the almoner, one of the bishop's senior staff. The almoner came right away, and Grandier told him the purpose of his visit, "which was to present him with the minuted record of what had happened at the Ursuline Convent and to lay a complaint before him about the deceptions and calumnies which were contained in it."[1] While the almoner relayed this message to the bishop, Grandier and his companion were left at the door, chilled to the bone. The almoner returned some time later and gave the prelate's response – that "Grandier should go before the royal judges and he would without doubt get justice [from them] in this affair."[2]

This can hardly have been a comforting reply to Grandier. After all, he had started off with the "royal judges" in the person of de Cerisay, the most senior judge in the Loudun area, and he had been unable to do more than put a temporary stop to things. It was clear, too, that La Rocheposay had no intention of withdrawing his authority from the exorcists he had appointed. And why should he? The bishop had been receiving reports from the many priests who had already become involved, both formally and informally. All seemed to be saying that this was a true case of possession. Even at this stage, since the bishop believed Grandier to be guilty of the earlier accusations, and since he probably knew of his perfidy towards Trincant and his daughter, it was no great step to believe that such a man might well have given his soul to the Devil.

Nevertheless, on his return to Loudun, the curé hastened to present a new petition to the *bailli* "in order to seek the king's justice, to be authorized to lay a complaint against Jean Mignon, his adherents and accomplices."[3] De Cerisay willingly acted on this request. Supported by the bishop's suggestion that Grandier put his case before the royal judges, he was prepared to take vigorous action against the exorcists, and he issued an order expressly forbidding "all persons of whatever condition or quality they may be to make any attempt on the person of Grandier or to do or say anything against him."[4]

Mignon, however, was not so easily dealt out of the game. Knowing that he was supported by those municipal and legal officers who were cardinalists, all enemies of Grandier, he now treated the matter as being no affair of the *bailli*'s. He went so far as to go to de Cerisay and tell him that this was a religious matter and that he was the Ursuline's confessor and the exorcist appointed by the bishop. He was not responsible for what the devils were revealing under exorcism, he said, and the *bailli* had no power to interfere in the church's decision to apply exorcism. He insisted that he would not accept the *bailli*'s jurisdiction; he and Grandier, both being priests, could have only the bishop of Poitiers as their judge. Mignon had enough right on his side to confuse the issue beyond solution. But de Cerisay, as *bailli*, had a considerable amount of personal authority, and even though he did not have the formal power to act, he did have the reflected power of his position. Using this, he warned Canon Mignon that he was prepared to treat the matter with extreme rigour.[5]

Mignon continued with his visits to the convent (which, as chaplain, he had every right to do). He probably also recommenced his exorcisms, though without fanfare. Still, nobody heard speak of the nuns during the early part of the month of November. The absence of Barré had been sufficient to restore a relative calm, and it was possible for Grandier to hope that the possessions and the accusations were at last going to stop. But things changed quickly when the mother superior fell dangerously ill. The surgeon René Mannoury and the apothecary Pierre Adam stayed at her bedside. Each day she had violent convulsions, and according to the reports of the doctors who visited her, she fell into a state of such feebleness that she could hardly walk.[6] Her disturbances, which had never completely been put to rest, had returned in even greater force.

Her afflictions were soon again communicated to her nuns: towards the middle of November Sister Claire, Sister Louise, and Sister Marthe had a great number of visions or hallucinations, and others were little better. The thought of Grandier was constantly on their minds, and the passion they experienced for him only seemed to grow. On 20 November, Jeanne des Anges was so afflicted and her attacks became so violent that Mignon, frightened, sent for Father Barré to return from Chinon to hunt out the evil spirits, which, he said, had returned more numerous than ever. At this news, Barré left at once for Loudun, where he began his exorcisms right away. But there was no immediate improvement. On the contrary, two days later half of the nuns were having convulsions. Both Mannoury and Adam were asked to treat them with medicines, but these had no effect in calming the patients, so a consultation was set up with one of the best doctors in town, Gaspard Joubert, a Huguenot. Before going to the convent, Joubert thought it proper to warn the *bailli*. De Cerisay encouraged him to visit the nuns and asked him to draw up – along with the doctors and surgeons of Loudun, who were going to accompany him – a formal medical assessment and record of the phenomena. That afternoon, Joubert presented the *bailli* with the following report:

We Gaspard Joubert, doctor in medicine, and many other doctors under-signed as well as René Mannoury and Charles Auger, master surgeons, have seen and examined the convulsions and outbursts that have attacked these Sisters ... We have advised Me. Jean Mignon and Sieur Barré, exorcists, that we are suspicious about the approach which they have continually taken with regard to the allegedly possessed women. We have very thoroughly examined them and recognize that they do appear to be totally changed in their behaviour and emotions, but it is our opinion that this is not the work of demons and spirits; rather, that the [extraordinary] strength they have manifested is due to the effect of some of the drugs, such as antimony[7] and other similar *liqueurs fomentées*, and it is our opinion that this alleged possession appears more illusory than real. Made in the presence of Messieurs the officers by us the undersigned doctors, except the said Barré and Mignon, priests, director confessor exorcists, who did not wish to sign.[8]

On hearing of this from de Cerisay, Grandier quickly prepared a new petition, in which he again asked to be permitted to go to the convent with the other officers to "be present at the exorcisms and to have the doctors present there." He added that "if some appear-ance of possession was seen, would he please have the nuns seques-tered and have them questioned by exorcists who were not as suspect as Mignon and Barré."[9]

The *bailli* gave these instructions to the *procureur du roi* Louis Moussaut, Philippe Trincant's husband. But far from carrying out the orders of his superior, Moussaut did everything possible to hamper any steps that would be favourable to the curé. When de Cerisay saw that his orders were being deliberately circumvented, he decided to go around the *procureur* and sent his own clerk to the convent to learn from the exorcists if the superior was still possessed. If they said the possessions were still taking place, the clerk was to tell Barré and Mignon that, by order of the magistrates, "they were expressly forbidden to proceed secretly with exorcisms." This the clerk did, only to be told by the two priests that the bishop of Poitiers had given them authority to exorcize and that conse-quently they would disregard the *bailli*'s orders. They did say, however, that the *bailli* could be present at the exorcisms and could bring any doctors whom he felt necessary.

De Cerisay was in a perplexing situation. The city officers were divided on the issue, led by himself and the Chauvets on the one hand and by Moussaut, Menuau, and Hervé on the other. To add to the problem, the civil and religious authorities had ill-defined and overlapping areas of responsibility. The opportunities for delay and confusion were everywhere. With division in the ranks of the magistrates, the *bailli* was not in a position to force Mignon and Barré to conform to his orders to stop exorcizing. Every time he gave such an order, the opposing magistrates told Barré and Mignon how to reply and what backing they would get; and each time de Cerisay lost a skirmish, a little of the authority of his office was lost as well. To make matters worse, the exorcists had covered themselves from open criticism by telling him that he could attend and could bring any doctors that he wanted. Even though on past experience he had reason to believe that they might in fact throw roadblocks in the way of his attendance, there was little he could do about it until there was an open confrontation.

Meanwhile, Barré refused to accept the jurisdiction of the *bailli*. He now revealed that the bishop had been brought up to date and was due to arrive in Loudun at any moment. Until his arrival, Barré said, he would continue to exorcize according to the instructions he had received. But the prelate was delayed. They waited in vain for him all day.[10] At this point de Cerisay decided that the best thing he could do was bring together all the officers of the *bailliage* with a view to taking the measures necessary to have the royal authority recognized. The *procureur* and the *avocat du roi*, both of the Trincant party, refused to participate on the grounds "that they believed in all faith that the nuns were possessed." Not surprisingly, once these very senior magistrates and their adherents stayed away, the remaining officers came to the conclusion that no account should be taken of the recriminations of the missing members. It was publicly recognized that they had every interest to believe in the possession. The whole assembly, with the exception of one member, a certain Moussaut de Menuau, decreed that "Sister Jeanne des Anges and the lay Sister [Claire de Sazilly, these two obviously being the worst cases] should be sequestered in private houses, that each of them should have a nun to keep her company, and that they should be accompanied not only by their exorcists but by women of probity and esteem and by doctors, etc., and that all others should be forbidden to approach them without permission."[11]

What appears to the modern eye as a reasonable proposal was really throwing down the gauntlet. Once a nun entered a convent and was professed, she could leave its walls only under the most extreme conditions, and this decision could be made only by the bishop or a person appointed by him. For the civil authorities to issue such an order was to attempt to override the bishop's authority. No nun and no priest could possibly accept such an order from the magistrates.

The *bailli*'s clerk, an officer of considerable authority, was sent to the convent to announce this decision to the nuns. Sister Jeanne des Anges was suffering too much to appear in the parlour, so it was the subprioress[12] who received the *bailli*'s envoy. She protested against the ordinance, which she quite properly called an attack on the vow of perpetual cloister. She declared that she would only submit to it under force. As the *bailli* was not prepared to use violence and all that it would have involved, he had to content himself with making a complaint to the bishop of Poitiers. La Rocheposay, no doubt furious with this interference in his area of jurisdiction over the nuns, did not reply.

The next day, 24 November, Grandier wrote the *bailli* another long petition, in which he said of the nuns that he had "*never seen or had any sort of communication with them*" (Grandier underlined the words in his letter).[13] Again he stressed how important it was that the nuns be sequestered and taken out of the hands of the "*mortal enemies of the petitioner.*" That same day, the *bailli* presented himself at the Ursuline Convent, and this time the exorcists made no attempt to delay his entry.

The exorcisms did not go well. The devil who possessed the superior replied in the most bizarre Latin to the questions put to him. A senior lawyer present could not refrain from remarking "that the devil did not speak very congruently." This was not just a grammatical criticism; it was a matter of extreme importance. The church had certain means by which it tested the reality of an alleged possession, one of these being that the person possessed (or more truly the demon possessing him or her) must speak clear sentences in one or more languages which the possessed person could not speak. Normally, nuns could not speak Latin, as the priests could do (though in some Ursuline convents they were taught to read it). They did, however, have some smattering of the language, which they had picked up because the mass and their formal prayers were recited in Latin. The devils, on the other hand, were expected to be well educated in their responses, so incorrect or ungrammatical replies threw serious suspicion on the possession. Throughout this case a great deal depended on the observer. Someone who was inclined to believe in the possessions heard the words, often grunted out or spoken through grinding teeth, as perfect Latin, whereas a disbeliever heard errors.

The next day and the following days, the *bailli* again attended the exorcisms with his officers. Every so often the demon was clearly caught out in lies. In one seance, when he was asked where Grandier was at that moment, he replied that the priest was at the château. The *bailli* immediately sent magistrates to verify this, and they found that it was untrue; Grandier was somewhere far removed. The same day, de Cerisay asked Grandier to take himself to the home of a mutual friend, and he then had the devil asked where the curé was. The demon replied that Grandier was walking in the Church of Sainte-Croix. This was again proved to be untrue.

The minutes prepared by the magistrates now openly questioned the validity of the possessions. But the fact that the officers and magistrates were divided into two opposing parties led to complications. A second set of "official" minutes giving a completely different picture of the exorcisms was being written and signed by the other officers, led by Hervé the *lieutenant-criminel*. These were the officers who had exempted themselves from the earlier meeting of the royal officials. There were enough of them and they were important enough for their minutes to carry equal weight, at least in the eyes of those who believed the possessions to be real.[14] Grandier, in a complaint addressed to Hervé, objected bitterly to these proceedings. He stated that Hervé had long been prejudiced against him and had pursued him as an enemy in the past and, furthermore, that since Hervé's first cousin was one of those allegedly possessed, Hervé should abstain from doing or writing anything about the case.[15] Needless to say, the *lieutenant-criminel* took no notice of Grandier's protest. He continued to draw up the reports, which he sent regularly to the bishop of Poitiers.

Faced with a situation that could clearly not be corrected locally by the *bailli*, the most important magistrate of the area, Grandier's only solution was to approach Jean d'Armagnac, who happened to be in Loudun at this time. He begged him to intervene with the *procureur général* in Paris (the senior law officer) to have these abuses stopped. But this got him nowhere. The *procureur général* was not going to become involved in a local dispute; he replied that "the matter being a purely ecclesiastic one, the Parlement [of Paris] could not take cognizance of the case." In the meantime, Barré had received further instructions from the bishop, obviously saying that the exorcisms were a church matter and that any orders from the civil authorities were to be ignored. In addition to these instructions, the bishop sent two more exorcists to help Barré, both of them relatives of Grandier's adversaries. This was a clear statement to the world that Barré and the other original exorcists had his full confidence and that he supported the position they had taken.

The pattern was clear. The case was an ecclesiastical one, and every attempt by Grandier's friends in the civil authority to influence the procedures was being blocked. Grandier's enemies were now totally in control of the situation. It must be remembered, though, that it was the *bailli* and his adherents who were trying to invade the bishop's areas of authority, not the other way around. The *bailli* was unsuccessful partly because he knew that if he pushed his demands to higher authorities, they would be rejected by both civil and ecclesiastical courts as interference in concerns that were the prerogative and responsibility of the church. Furthermore, the opposition to Grandier and the *bailli* was not all the result of outright enmity. Many observers were convinced that the possessions were genuine and that the devils were speaking the truth in attacking Grandier.

Something else had subtly changed. Mignon had become part of the background, no longer a leading figure among the exorcists. Now it was Barré who was in charge. And gradually the bishop was coming into the light as he stood behind the exorcists and progressively became more directly involved. Eventually, even Barré would disappear, and it would be the bishop's chosen men and then himself who would take over. The Grandier case was evolving from a local case to a diocesan one. By the end, it would become a national one.

It was not only a concern for Grandier, therefore, that led the *bailli* for a second time to bring together all the officers of the *bailliage*. They had to find a way out of the impasse. Before entering again into open battle with the senior ecclesiastical representatives of the bishop, the assembly, with common accord, decided to write one last time to Bishop de La Rocheposay. They asked him, in quite a belligerent manner, to put an end to what they viewed as the questionable procedures taking place at the Ursuline Convent. Their lengthy letter, dated 12 December 1632, told the bishop that what was going on was contemptuous of royal authority, and they asked him to have it stopped before they had to step in and apply the rigours of justice to the situation in the convent. They went on to say that if Barré and the others were sent away for six months, they were pretty sure everything connected with the possessions would stop. They said that although many people of worth believed in the possessions, such people were either simple or had a blind desire to see a miracle. They knew, they said, that it was "all cheating" and that "these so-called miracles" were being performed "in order to convert the Protestants." To support this contention, they included the *bailli*'s minutes of the exorcisms he had attended. As well, they emphasized that Grandier had never seen the nuns or had anything to do with them. If he had had demons at his call, they said, he would have employed them against those who were injuring him. They also pointed out that the two new exorcists appointed by the bishop were related to Grandier's bitter enemies. This letter, signed by de Cerisay and the two Chauvets, concluded by again asking the bishop to have the exorcisms stopped, which he could do "by a word from his mouth or three lines in writing."[16]

This was not a courtesy letter. It took issue with the bishop head on. It was adopted unanimously by those present at the assembly and was sent the same day. Grandier's adversaries were not present, and the tone of the letter suggests that a number of those who endorsed the letter were Protestants. The *bailli* had his minutes attached to the letter in the hope that the prelate would at last understand where the real truth lay. But the bishop was already too convinced by all he had heard to revise his earlier decisions. Like others, he must have noticed how similar this case was to the old Gaufridy one. He did not even reply to the letter, and the two new exorcists who had been added by the bishop were retained.[17]

By now every exorcism at the convent was crowded. First, there were the many priests, each of whom played his part. By force of circumstances, they were generally in the chapel with the nuns during the exorcisms. A second group consisted of the officers of the town, some of whom would be in the chapel and some outside the grille that in normal times separated the chapel from the world. By now there was also an increasing crowd of notables, who were present as spectators to the remarkable occurrences. In that society, any person of note, and particularly a noble, had almost a right to demand entry to see what was happening. The exorcisms had in effect become a public spectacle that was open to all who carried enough weight to attend.

In all of this, the *bailli* and his supporters were being pushed into the background. Although they were present, they had little restraining effect. The exorcists felt that they had a difficult enough task to do in wrestling with the Devil without interference from Huguenot-influenced doubters; it was not an unreasonable attitude. But everything changed with the arrival of Monseigneur de Sourdis, the archbishop of Bordeaux, at the local abbey of Saint-Jouin-les-Marnes. When Grandier learned that the archbishop was at the abbey, he hastened there to tell him about the events of the last few months. In fact, it was not news to Sourdis, because d'Armagnac had made sure that he received the minutes which the *bailli* had prepared throughout this period. The archbishop received the hard-pressed priest favourably, though he could hardly be blamed for saying "I told you so" and reminding Grandier how foolish he had been to stay on in the town where he had so many enemies who had sworn to ruin him. However, he did promise to concern himself with the affair. The *bailli* and his group of supporting magistrates also asked Sourdis to intervene in this matter, which was the source of increasing ill-feeling between the Catholics and Huguenots. As already noted, Protestants were prominent among those who doubted the validity of the possessions, for they, as much as the devils, were the true prey of the exorcists.

By this time, everyone connected with the possessions was far too influenced by local politics, family feuds, and religious differences to be able to take anything but a biased position. The archbishop, coming from a distance and with little in the way of preconceptions, was able to be more objective. Above all, he was able to judge whether the well-developed rules of the Catholic Church had been applied in determining whether there was a true case of possession. Once again he effectively overruled the bishop, this time by sending his own doctor to Loudun with instructions to see the possessed nuns and make an accurate report on their convulsions. He charged the doctor to make sure that he went to the convent accompanied by the *bailli*. This way, the doctor would be able to judge the opinions of the exorcists and the magistrates together.

For whatever reason, the devils were quiescent while the doctor was there – so much so that the nuns told him that they were no longer possessed. The doctor wrote down everything he saw and concluded that the nuns were not possessed. Grandier was overjoyed. This seemed the time to press home his advantage, and on 27 December 1632 he wrote to tell the archbishop that there was a group of people in Loudun who had coalesced against him. They had profited from the sickness of the Ursulines to denounce him as the author of the spell that had been cast over the convent. He complained that the nuns were surrounded by his most bitter enemies and he begged Sourdis

to forbid Barré, Mignon, and their adherents, both secular and regular, in the case of a new possession, to exorcize in the future ... and to have the alleged possessed nuns placed in the care of other ecclesiastic and lay persons not suspected of being enemies of the curé, to watch over the feeding, medication, exhortation, and exorcizing if necessary of the alleged possessed [nuns], and this in the presence of the magistrate, and in order to remove all suspicion, to order the said possessed to be sequestered in order that the full truth might be established.[18]

On the same day, Sourdis issued his decision on how the possessions were to be treated in future. First, he forbade Mignon to exorcize, and although Barré was allowed to retain his functions, the archbishop appointed two other exorcists to work with him, disinterested men of considerable experience. All others were forbidden to become involved in the exorcisms under penalty of the law.[19] The archbishop also immediately promulgated an order[20] on how future exorcisms were to be conducted if the possessions recurred. Among other things, the nuns were to be sequestered, as had been demanded so many times by Grandier and the magistrates. This sensible document outlined the correct way to deal objectively with a case of suspected possession:

ISSUED BY THE ARCHBISHOP OF BORDEAUX
TO THE BAILLI OF LOUDUN,
PROCEDURES TO BE FOLLOWED IN
EXORCISMS OF THE URSULINE NUNS
IN CASE OF NEW POSSESSION

First, at the moment that Sieur Barré is notified of it, he will call to his side Father l'Escaye, Jesuit of Poitiers, and Father Gau of the Oratory of Tours, and all three will in turn, and in the presence of the other two, perform the office of exorcism as may be necessary; separating the possessed person from the body of the Community, lodging her in a borrowed house that they consider suitable for this purpose, with nobody having any access to her except another nun who up to this time has shown no signs of being affected.

Arrangements will then be made to have her seen by two or three of the most able Catholic doctors in the Province, who, having observed her for some days, or having purged her if they consider that appropriate, will make their report.

After the doctors' report, attempts will be made by threats and discipline, as far as judged appropriate, or by other natural means, to discover the truth and whether the Possession is the result of sin, or unwholesome humours [a form of sickness], or of her own volition. After these things, if in the opinion of the three exorcists there still exist some effects that have the mark of being supernatural, such as:

responding to the thoughts of the three exorcists secretly exchanged with their companions, or responding correctly on many occasions at the instant that she is spoken to from a place beyond her hearing in such a way that it is beyond suspicion that she could know what was thought or said;

or that in many different languages she delivers a speech of ten or twelve words very correctly and well put together;

or that with hands and feet tied on a mattress laid on the ground, where she is left without anyone approaching her, she raises herself completely off the ground for some considerable time.

Then in this case, exorcisms are to be performed, fasts and the prescribed prayers being observed. And in the case that such exorcisms are necessary, all efforts are to be made to force the Devil to show some visible signs, beyond suspicion, of leaving the possessed person.

And in executing this present order, no other priests, unless they are called in by common accord of the three commissioners and are non-suspect, will become involved under pain of excommunication, or will speak to or touch the possessed person in any way whatsoever. And should it happen that there are a number of cases of possession at the same time, this same Order will be followed.

And in case some freethinkers may speak ill of the care that the Church brings to bear in such matters to know the truth regarding the possessions, and the loving help that its Ministers bear, the Honourable Magistrates the Bailli and the Lieutenant-Criminel only, and no others, are requested to be present at the carrying out of this Order and to sign the record which will be prepared by those appointed, who will have as their recording clerk the Prior of the Abbey of Saint-Jouin.

And to the extent that it is necessary to make major expenditures such as for the transport of the young women, the attendance of the doctors, the expenses of the exorcists, and of the women who are required to serve the sick, we have ordered, given that the house is poor, that the expense will be borne by us, and to this effect have from this time forward authorized Sieur Barré to call upon the Abbey of Saint-Jouin to provide all the monies he needs. And in case Father l'Escaye or Father Gau are not at Poitiers or Tours, or for some reason they are not available, the Superiors of their houses will choose priests of equal merit, if they can, to replace them.

27 December 1632

This was a worthy document. First was the order, in effect, to start off by doubting that there was any possession and to subject the afflicted person to purges, discipline, medical questioning, all in a search for natural causes. If there was still some belief that possession existed, there were strict tests to be applied, the speaking of unknown languages, the ability to know another's secret thoughts or words, the the ability to levitate while tied down. These were not the archbishop's own ideas. These were the tests long since developed by the church, and if scrupulously followed they would provide evidence of a condition that could not be explained as natural. Interesting too was the demand that all the exorcists must agree; even more so was the recognition that the civil authorities had a part to play. Although they were not to be involved in the exorcisms, they were to see that these rites were performed in a creditable way. Sourdis recognized too that Hervé, the *lieutenant-criminel* of Loudun, was openly acting as an enemy of Grandier; he was both a proponent of the possessions and a magistrate who was frustrating the decisions of his superior, the *bailli*. Consequently, Sourdis wrote to Hervé, as his archbishop, instructing him to exercise greater moderation and reminding him of his duties as a magistrate.[21]

It looked as if Grandier had won again – he seemed to have the luck of the devil – for the archbishop's instructions did cause a hiatus in the possessions. For many months a relative calm returned to the convent. But now that the possessions had ceased, embarrassing questions were being raised about the whole affair. Had the nuns really been possessed or were they just crazy? Many of the parents of the school's boarders had already withdrawn their daughters, and they had been one of the convent's steady sources of income. In other cases, relatives of the nuns, wishing to dissociate themselves from all that had happened, ceased to pay the money they owed on the modest dowries to which they had committed themselves. With all this, the unfortunate women were in a state of great misery. Mignon must be given his due; he never abandoned them. It was only through his help that they always had at least the minimum necessities.

Meanwhile, Grandier was still not totally reassured. The apparent calm that reigned in the convent could be hiding some new trap. He feared that the nuns, though much improved, were not really cured; the superior above all was still very sick, and her hallucinations had not stopped.[22] Grandier was afraid that his enemies would take advantage of this once Sourdis left the area, and on 21 March 1633 he petitioned the *bailli* to have the archbishop's letter and rules for exorcism formally recorded and publicized. The *bailli* immediately agreed. In the minutes drawn up on this occasion, Grandier arranged for de Cerisay to add the following words: "That from the instant the said order was made and sent, all word of the alleged possession of the said Ursulines ceased."[23] These precautions proved to be useless. The return to Loudun of the commissioner Laubardemont, come finally to raze the donjon, gave an unexpected lease on life to the possessions.

Arrest

By the beginning of 1633 the city walls had gone. Throughout that spring and early summer, the cardinalists openly conspired for the fall of the donjon – and successfully so. Eventually the secretary of state, who was both protector and friend to d'Armagnac, warned him that the battle was lost; the cardinal was determined to have the donjon razed. Any further resistance, he said, would be useless and would bring down on him the wrath of the cardinal and, eventually, of the king. From that day d'Armagnac left the field to his enemies. Sad, sick, and discouraged, he wrote to Grandier on 7 September, "I am very angry that this coarse brute of a *lieutenant-criminel* and his father-in-law [Mesmin de Silly] have begged for and procured the undoubted ruin of the town of Loudun." D'Armagnac was finished with Loudun; he never returned.[1] This was the last letter he wrote to the priest, and as far as we know, he never saw Grandier again.

The loss of his patron, his greatest protector, was chilling news to Grandier, for he was again under attack from his enemies, who had sent the bishop of Poitiers a new set of denunciations against him.[2] In May 1633 men hired by Moussaut, Hervé, and Trincant had created a series of disturbances at an important religious procession led by Grandier. Among other things, they had apparently shouted that he was not fit to lead on such an occasion. Grandier responded to these insults to a representative of the church by passing religious punishments on those who had taken part, but this simply engendered more protests. Moussaut, the *procureur du roi*, in concert with his friends, laid a complaint against Grandier which completely misrepresented the facts.[3] Only the protection of

Monseigneur de Sourdis sheltered the curé from the rancour of the bishop of Poitiers.

Towards the middle of August 1633, after receiving his orders from the king, Laubardemont left for Loudun to oversee the donjon's destruction, arriving in the first half of September. Perhaps to avoid looking as if he was siding with one party or the other in the city, he declined the offer of hospitality made to him by Mesmin de Silly and found lodgings with the mother-in-law of one of the local magistrates, a man named Champion.[4]

Although Laubardemont's task was to see that the donjon was razed, he took time to learn about the events at the convent since his last visit. He discovered that although the archbishop of Bordeaux had imposed silence on the demons, and the screaming and convulsions had stopped, the nuns were still disturbed and were far from well. He learned all this from Mesmin de Silly, who naturally knew all about Laubardemont's work against witchcraft in Béarn and was aware that the matter would be of interest to him. Laubardemont was especially interested because of his family connection through Jeanne des Anges and his two sisters-in-law, who were also Ursulines at the convent.

The story of the events that had reached Paris was considerably garbled, as might be expected, and the nuns were being laughed at, particularly since the possessions had stopped on the orders of the archbishop. Mesmin, Trincant, and other enemies of Grandier suggested to Laubardemont that he visit the convent so that he could hear from the mouths of his own relatives the true story of all that had happened. Accordingly, Laubardemont went to the convent next day. He received a warm welcome from his kinswomen, who clearly viewed Grandier as the sole author of all the attacks on them. With one voice, they accused him of having thrown a spell on the convent and of being the cause of their ruin (for the ordinances of Monseigneur de Sourdis had in effect told the world that they were either charlatans or sick). Although they did not say it in so many words, they made it clear that their powerful relatives (including Laubardemont) must either come to their support or share in their shame. In their own hearts, too, they must have known that to withdraw the accusations they had made, or even to go back to normal, would be an admission of foolishness. They had to press on, and therefore so must their relatives and allies. This meant, of course, that Grandier had to be pursued. Only the unmasking and punishment of the author of their possessions could clear the nuns and their families.

Laubardemont took all these things away with him and pondered them. Meanwhile, he promised to help the women. His appearance on the scene provided a heaven-sent opportunity for Trincant and Grandier's other enemies to revive their accusations against the priest. It is possible that if the commissioner had not had relatives in the convent, nothing would have been done. But as it was, Trincant could play on his personal interests. Once a man of Laubardemont's status became involved, Trincant and his friends needed only to take supporting parts, sufficient to make sure that the pursuit of Grandier was never abandoned.

Some days after Laubardemont's visit to the convent, the Prince of Condé passed by Loudun. Next to royalty itself, he was one of the highest nobles in France – a prince of the blood – and though widely known for his debauchery, he was nevertheless a man of great influence. At a dinner with Mesmin, Laubardemont, Trincant, and others, the conversation inevitably turned to the possessions. As a result, the prince was invited to go to the convent the following morning, along with the commissioner and the magistrates who were friendly to the Trincant cause. At the appointed hour Father Mignon, the director of the Ursulines, said a solemn mass which the whole community attended. The beginning of the office passed in perfect calm. But when the celebrant came to the communion, Jeanne des Anges, Sister Claire de Sazilly, and Sister Agnes, "the beautiful little devil,"[5] entered into convulsions. The prince was both fascinated and shocked. What he saw and heard convinced him on the spot that the possessions were genuine, and he demanded that Laubardemont inform the king and cardinal about the details right away. Something had to be done for these poor women.

Laubardemont, however, was not yet ready to act; he knew that the possessions had been received at court with incredulity and laughter. Moreover, the Prince of Condé was not a man for whose opinions Richelieu would have much respect. As an up-and-coming servant of the state, Laubardemont had no wish to be laughed at. There was also the fact that if he showed too much belief without some further evidence, his enemies might accuse him of trying to protect his relatives in the convent. He therefore decided to wait until he could find something that he could take to his master that would permit him to pursue Grandier.

This was the crux of the matter. The possessions would stop only when their author was found and punished; all of Laubardemont's

witch-hunting experience told him so. Meantime, as a good inves-
tigator, he made it his business to meet all the actors and make his
personal assessment of them. So he gave assurances to the prince,
but when he returned to his lodgings he received at his table
Grandier's friends and even Grandier himself. He treated them with
such kindness and courtesy that Grandier had no suspicion that his
future was threatened from that quarter.

Trincant and his friends understood Laubardemont's hesitation.
They realized that something had to be done that was startling
enough to make Richelieu and even the king look with fresh eyes
on the matter. It was up to them to find the key with which
Laubardemont could reopen the door to the case – and if they could
not find the key, they had to fashion one. This key would become
known as the "shoemaker's letter." To understand this letter, it is
necessary to go back in time.

Years ago, before Grandier and Trincant became close friends,
there lived in Loudun a girl named Catherine Hammon, a lively,
pretty young woman. Catherine had the good fortune to come to
the attention of the queen mother, Marie de Medici, at a time when
Marie, as regent during the king's minority, was staying in Loudun.
Marie became attached to this sprightly young woman and took her
into her service. She was also very generous towards the family.[6]
Catherine fulfilled all the expectations of her patroness and eventually became her appointed shoemaker, a recognized junior member
of the queen's household.[7] She so thoroughly captured the confidence of Marie de Medici that she was given secret missions to the
Prince of Condé and other potential rebels against the crown at a
time when the queen mother and the king were battling each other
for control of the country. Thus, Catherine was well versed in the
intrigues of the leading figures in France in the period before the
king came out the clear winner.

After the queen mother was exiled in 1617, Catherine returned
to Loudun. It was at this time that she met Grandier, who was her
parish priest. "The favour that she had for some time enjoyed,"
wrote the historian Anquetil, "gave her a certain air of importance
and caused the true or false details that she retailed on her return
to the curious of Loudun to be avidly received. Grandier was not
the last to take part in this pleasure of the idle of the town, and, as
he was caustic, he added to Hammon's stories piquant commentaries
that amused the circle."[8] Grandier visited Catherine frequently
enough, it appears, for a continuing friendship to be established

between them. His enemies later suggested that she became his mistress. Catherine stayed only two years in Loudun. At the news that the queen mother had returned to grace, she hastened to her side, but before she left she promised to write to Grandier often. It is easy to picture that a man of Grandier's ambitions would find the intimate news of court society quite fascinating. It took him beyond the narrow confines of the provincial town and made him feel part of the wider world to which he aspired.

Once in Paris, Catherine threw herself into the intrigues being woven against Cardinal Richelieu, who had been the queen mother's confidant and was now her enemy. It was at this period that she met a man named François de Baradat, who became an enemy of Richelieu. Richelieu succeeded in having him sent away from the court in 1626. And now we come to the letter. In 1627 a pamphlet published in the form of a letter addressed to M. de Baradat received wide circulation. It was entitled "A Letter from the Queen Mother's Shoemaker to M. de Baradat," and it caused a great stir. By any standards it was highly libellous, and Richelieu obviously found it so. It attacked his family, the other principal ministers of the state, and even the person of the king, whom it accused of fickleness, frivolousness, inconstancy, and (most shocking of all in view of his well-known virtue) "detestable impurities."

Richelieu was determined to find the author, for it soon became evident that the letter had not been written by Catherine Hammon and she could not be held responsible. But finding the true culprit turned out to be impossible, despite all the resources at Richelieu's command. We can get some idea of what awaited the perpetrator if he or she ever did get caught, for the printer was found, and although he had had nothing to do with the contents of the document, he was tried and condemned to be hanged. True, his sentence was commuted to the living death of the galleys, but the extent of Richelieu's continuing anger can be measured by the fact that years later he was still inquiring after the printer to make sure that the sentence was being carried out to the full. Despite the furore, within a few weeks a second "Letter from the Queen Mother's Shoemaker to M. de Baradat" was making the rounds with the same wide circulation. This letter was at least as scandalous and personal as the first, and it contained references which intimated that the author was someone who either lived in Loudun or had Loudun connections.

Some five or six years later, Grandier's enemies decided that the way to bring him down was to accuse him of being the author.

Trincant and his friends therefore reminded Laubardemont of the infamous letter and told him that Grandier knew Catherine Hammon well and that over the years she had sent him news of all the scandals of the court, including stories about the cardinal. (Her correspondence was no secret in Loudun). It was clear, they stated, that Grandier had written the letter. The importance of this allegation cannot be overstated. Champion, whose mother-in-law was lodging Laubardemont and who therefore claimed to be knowledgeable about the affair, claimed that it was "the true cause of the curé's death." Champion was firmly of the opinion that this was the means employed by the curé's enemies to influence the commissioner to act: "Now at this same time, there was a little pamphlet titled the Shoemaker of Loudun, which the curé's enemies were so crafty as to attribute to the curé, arguing that it was written in his style. This writing was a libel against those who were governing the State."[9] Laubardemont hesitated no further. In fact, a careful reading of the document would have revealed trivial expressions and considerable abstruseness, both qualities uncharacteristic of Grandier, who was an elegant writer.[10] But whatever the validity of the accusation, it provided Laubardemont with enough ammunition to take to the cardinal. He promised the Trincant group his full support.[11]

Grandier seems to have got wind that his adversaries were hatching a new plot against him that involved Laubardemont. Since the commissioner had been so pleasant to him in the recent past, he had no hesitation in calling on him at his lodgings and asking what Trincant and the others were saying about him. The commissioner received Grandier with extreme courtesy, assured him that he had nothing to fear, and even went so far as to promise him his support before the king. Champion, who was in the next room during this interview, declared later that the commissioner made the most beautiful promises to the curé. But after Grandier left, Laubardemont went to Mesmin's house and planned the details of how to get the cardinal to involve himself in the affair. Laubardemont was still somewhat reluctant to raise the matter directly with Richelieu. If it misfired he would look foolish, and his career could not afford that.

But Trincant and his friends had allies in the Capuchins of Loudun, who had been Grandier's enemies from the very beginning. They were only too ready to do anything they could to see Loudun rid of the priest.[12] They were convinced that he was responsible for the possessions in the Ursuline Convent, no matter what the archbishop said. The cooperation of the Capuchins had a particular value because their house had been set up by Father Joseph, the "Grey Eminence," the great friend and confidant of the cardinal. Father Joseph was aware of all that went on in Loudun through his continuing correspondence with this monastery. Grandier and the possessions certainly were thoroughly known to him. Moreover, he had set up the monastery in Loudun specifically to counter the Huguenots, and it would not have been lost on him that Grandier had been accused of making common cause with those heretics. A denunciation against the priest thus had every chance of receiving a favourable welcome from him. So when the Capuchins learned through Trincant and his friends that the author of the "shoemaker's letter" was none other than the curé of Saint-Pierre, they immediately wrote to Father Joseph. Indeed, they asked Laubardemont to carry the letter to him personally.

The commissioner could now approach the cardinal representing the whole question of Grandier and the possessions as an issue given him by the Capuchins. If Richelieu was convinced, Laubardemont could take full credit and give the matter his full support. If Richelieu was sceptical or laughed it out of court, Laubardemont could laugh with him and say that he had merely been doing the Capuchins a favour by carrying their letter. For a "senior civil servant" it was the perfect solution.

All this took place towards the end of October 1633. By then, the donjon had been demolished and Laubardemont was preparing to return to Paris to report the completion of his task. Before leaving, he again hosted a dinner for Grandier and his friends.[13] This farewell dinner was clearly meant to deceive the priest. Laubardemont received the curé magnificently, showed him great kindness, and promised to help him gain revenge on his enemies. The next day he departed, leaving Grandier in the belief that he was absolutely safe. But Laubardemont's promises were false. Passing through Chinon, he stopped for a day at the presbytery of Saint-Jacques, Barré's rectory, so that he could get a first-hand account of the exorcisms. Chinon now had its own cases of possession, and Laubardemont was able to see Barré at work exorcizing two of his parishioners. Later, Barré gave Laubardemont a full description of what had happened in the convent of the Ursulines during the months of October and November 1632. Laubardemont then asked Barré to provide him with the minutes of the exorcisms, which he had made secretly (against the formal orders of the magistrates).[14] These were of great importance. So far, only the *bailli*'s minutes had been sent to Paris, and it was because of them that the possessions of Loudun had been considered nothing more than a comedy. Laubardemont, in designing his case, was collecting the evidence needed to reverse the view of those in power.

On arriving in Paris, Laubardemont went straight to Father Joseph with the Capuchins' letter from Loudun. Then, together with Father Joseph, he went to see Richelieu. There is no record of this meeting, though Laubardemont almost certainly spoke about it to his peers in Loudun, and Father Joseph may have told his Capuchins. What has been passed down, therefore, is hearsay, but is probably substantially true. Apparently, Laubardemont described to Richelieu all that he had seen at the convent and heard in Loudun. No doubt he carried messages from Mesmin de Silly and other friends of Richelieu which supported his contention that the possessions were both real and serious. He made it clear that the religious parties were more divided than ever in Loudun and that because of one particular person, the hatred between the Catholics and Protestants was getting worse.

Richelieu, who knew through d'Armagnac about the *bailli*'s minutes, seemed somewhat incredulous at the commissioner's story. On the other hand, he knew of Grandier's reputation as a troublemaker, and he probably needed little reminding of the quarrel over precedence that he had had long ago with the curé of Loudun. And now Laubardemont revealed the suspicions of the Capuchins that Grandier was the author of the infamous satire of the shoemaker. Father Joseph confirmed what Laubardemont said, showed Richelieu the letter from the Capuchins, and asked him to rid Loudun of a priest who had long been the subject of scandal. In this very private, confidential meeting, Laubardemont may well have revealed to Richelieu the facts of Philippe's seduction (which would have been told him by Trincant or perhaps Mesmin). Nobody would have put that in a letter; but here, face to face, it could be raised with the greatest discretion. What we know for certain is that before this meeting the possessions of Loudun were not taken seriously at court and that from this day forward Grandier was a dead man. As will be seen, the wording and tenor of the order that was ultimately issued makes it clear that nothing and nobody was to be allowed to stand in the way of finding Grandier guilty and sentencing him. The investigation that was ordered was not designed to find the facts; it was designed to support a decision for death that had already been taken.

What would justify death? Grandier had crossed many people, including Richelieu himself back in 1618, but that was hardly sufficient cause. He was suspect as a crypto-Huguenot, a serious matter but not a mortal one. He had done all he could to prevent the walls of Loudun from being razed, but they had been destroyed and his opposition could do no further harm. He was thought to be a disruptive influence in the delicate religious balance in Loudun, and there may have been fears that he would cause an armed rising of the Huguenots in his support; but the Catholic party was already in the ascendancy in Loudun and, with the walls down, the threat of a Huguenot rising was much reduced.

The fact is that none of these things, individually or collectively, had enough seriousness or substance to warrant what was, in effect, a sentence of death before trial. Besides, there were much simpler means of getting rid of the priest than condemning him to death. The most common method was a *lettre de cachet* – an order by the king that could imprison an individual indefinitely without trial on the grounds that he was a threat to the good order of the state. The "shoemaker's letter" was not enough in itself. The fact that it never again enters the Grandier story is proof of that. It had served its purpose by opening the door to Richelieu's interest and active involvement; that was all it had ever been intended to do.

The Philippe Trincant affair was different. That a priest should seduce a young woman was far from unknown. But to seduce her in her father's house! And he was not just any father, he was the best friend and patron of the priest, a prominent Catholic nobleman who was an old friend of Richelieu himself; the girl was far above Grandier's station in life. This half-Huguenot town was still gossiping about the affair, yet there would be no punishment for the priest. That was the most shocking of all to Richelieu. Every time Grandier had been threatened with retribution he had escaped, laughing at the very people he had harmed and making public fools of them. To Richelieu, a priest himself, a noble, a bishop, the king's first minister, and the man responsible for the principle of good order in the state, this was totally unacceptable. Richelieu firmly believed that the good of the state justified overriding the good of the individual. He also cared deeply about the church. In the words of a great biographer, "Though Richelieu was a churchman without vocation, it would be a serious error to imagine that he was luke-warm in his religious convictions … He never caused a scandal and never gave the appearance of being a bad priest. Indeed … he was a very good bishop, attentive to the needs of his flock and active in nurturing it on the Church's teachings."[15] Thus, whether or not Grandier was guilty of witchcraft, it was clearly necessary for the state to be rid of him.

The cardinal raised the matter at the next meeting of the king's council, which took place on 30 November 1633. The king had already been well briefed by his secretary, Michel Lucas, a good friend of all the principal cardinalists in Loudun, including Mesmin de Silly, and he doubtless became totally convinced of the possessions. After all, his first minister was there to give him theological and state advice; his councillor, Laubardemont, who was experienced in matters of witchcraft, attested that he personally had seen the possessions and was convinced of their validity; and Father Joseph, who also was present, would certainly have supported this view. The king could hardly have come to any other conclusion. His decision was clear and unequivocal:

M. de Laubardemont, King's councillor in his councils of State, will go to Loudun and to other places necessary and inform himself diligently against the said Grandier on all the facts of which he has been earlier accused and other new ones brought against him concerning the Ursuline nuns of Loudun and other persons also said to be possessed and tormented by demons by the evil spells of the said Grandier. He will inform himself of everything that has occurred since the beginning on both the exorcisms and all other facts relating to the said possession. [He shall] have minutes prepared on these and other activities of the commissioners delegated to this; be present at exorcisms that are performed and prepare records of them and in every way proceed as necessary for the proof and verification of all the facts, arrange for the preparation and conduct of the trial of the said Grandier and all others who are found to be accomplices in these cases; to reach a final sentence without regard to any opposition, appeals or objections whatsoever.[16]

After the king had signed this commission it was handed to Laubardemont, who suggested that it would be prudent to arrest Grandier before making the order public and starting the inquiry. The priest had many good friends in Loudun, and they might hide him. Indeed, they might even storm the place where he was held. The secretary of state was therefore instructed to prepare the following arrest order: "Sieur Laubardemont will have the said Grandier and his accomplices arrested and made prisoner in a secure place."

On 6 December 1633, a cold and sombre winter evening, Laubar-demont arrived back in the Loudun area. To avoid giving warning of his return, he stopped at the neighbouring town of Chinon and stayed in the home of Paul Aubin, Mesmin's son-in-law, who lived there. The secret of his arrival was so well kept that Grandier and his friends had no suspicion of it. Grandier's enemies, on the other hand, had been apprised of Laubardemont's return and went to Chinon to meet him. Laubardemont read them his commission and told them that he had already visited the *lieutenant-criminel* of Chinon and given him orders to send armed police to reinforce those of Loudun; he thought that the Loudun police would be too few in number if Grandier's friends helped him resist arrest. The arrest was to be made by a royal officer of Chinon named Guillaume Aubin, and it was to take place the following morning.

Guillaume was the brother of Paul Aubin with whom Laubarde-mont was staying, but did not share his views. He could hardly refuse to carry out the orders he had been given, but he did secretly warn the priest about them. Nevertheless, Grandier refused to flee from the danger that menaced him. The next day, early in the morning, he left his rectory as usual to go to a service with the other canons in the Church of Sainte-Croix. There, Guillaume Aubin, who was waiting for him with numerous armed police, duly arrested him. Grandier's enemies had gathered in this same Place Sainte-Croix, where Trincant had his house, to enjoy the downfall of their foe. Grandier passed by them, calm and dignified despite their jeers and catcalls. Laubardemont had originally planned to have Grandier imprisoned at Saumur, a neighbouring town. But like Loudun, it had a strong Huguenot population, and it was too close to be safe from attack if the curé's friends attempted a rescue. He therefore sent Grandier to the prisons in the castle of Angers, with express instructions that he was to be closely guarded.

Appeal of Innocence

Immediately after the arrest on 7 December 1633, Laubardemont went to Grandier's house, accompanied by Mesmin, Hervé, Moussaut, the *avocat du roi* Menuau, and other magistrates. Trincant, of course, could not be there; he now had no official position, having resigned in disgrace. But he was well represented. When they entered the house, Grandier's mother, Jeanne d'Estièvre, was there. A determined old lady, she stood firmly at the door of her son's bedroom, barring the way and refusing to move. Hervé and another of Mesmin's sons-in-law grasped her and pulled her aside, holding her out of the way so that Laubardemont could enter the room. Their rough treatment made no allowance for her seventy years. Jeanne d'Estièvre complained loudly and bitterly at this invasion of the house, but the officers of the law were well within their rights and her objections were ignored. Once inside Grandier's room, Laubardemont laid hands on everything he could find that might be used in evidence against the priest. He took away all the papers he found, including money, as well as records of money owing to Jeanne d'Estièvre. After he left, she wrote to him asking for her papers to be returned: "You have taken, without making any inventory, many important papers, tax papers, loan records, obligations, and financial contracts, and have had them carried away to a place of your choosing, whereas the procedures call for restoration so that the supplicant may have the means of helping her son and of feeding and maintaining her large family, who it would seem must perish from hunger if they are denied food."[1]

The papers found in the priest's room included all the letters from d'Armagnac to Grandier, which ought to have been destroyed long ago, as the governor had instructed. There was also a printed copy of the "shoemaker's letter" (though that did not prove that Grandier was the author and, in any case, it could have been planted). The most damning paper was Grandier's "Treatise on the Celibacy of Priests." Not only did it appear to have been written in order to aid in the seduction of a woman, but it was a disavowal of one of the most basic rules of Catholicism; it smacked of freethinking and Huguenot leanings in its views on marriage. In the eyes of any devout Catholic, the author of such a paper would be capable of any devilry.

Besides being a strong weapon for Laubardemont to use against Grandier, the treatise could also be used against Grandier's friend Madeleine de Brou, for it gave Laubardemont the means of suggesting that the paper had been written for her. Ever since Mignon had suggested that this case was similar to the Gaufridy one, parallels had been sought at every turn, for witchcraft was believed to follow an established pattern. Thus, since Gaufridy had had an acolyte in his sorcery in Madeleine Demandolx, Grandier must have one too. It was only a matter of finding who she was. The treatise pointed in the clear direction of a woman who was very close to the priest, and Madeleine de Brou was the obvious candidate. (Of course, it pointed equally at Philippe Trincant, but her relatives were not going to draw that conclusion.) Menuau, the *avocat du roi*, was particularly pleased with this find and with papers concerning loans that Grandier had made to Madeleine de Brou, among other people. There was also a copy of the decision of the Parlement of Paris against Menuau's cousin, Adam, in favour of Madeleine. Menuau, who had been spurned as a suitor by Madeleine, blamed Grandier for having made her fall in love with him instead.[2] The treatise on celibacy gave him the chance to get his own back on them both.

Laubardemont also seized two sheets of verse that he said were dirty and lewd. Since he never allowed them to be seen, this allegation is somewhat suspect. In addition, he took the documents of the decisions of absolution given by the *présidial* of Poitiers and the archbishop of Bordeaux. He may well have done this so that Trincant and his friends could again raise the charges about Grandier that had been made in 1630. Very few copies were ever made of documents because everything had to be prepared by hand, so if a document was lost, it was almost impossible to replace it. Without these papers, Grandier was going to have a difficult time proving that he had been found innocent by the archbishop and the courts;

it left him with a large piece of his character defence missing. At least as important was the fact that the court in Poitiers had found Grandier innocent "as of now."[3] If new evidence of guilt came to light, the case could be reopened. And here was solid evidence found in the priest's house – evidence of sacrilege, heresy, and seduction. Thus, it was probably no coincidence that almost immediately all the old charges were brought forward again by exactly the same people and in the same words.

It was alleged later, at Grandier's trial, that among his papers was a book on magic, which supposedly had belonged to his priest uncle and had been handed down to him. This again was a deliberate parallel to the Gaufridy case. It will be recalled that Gaufridy's priest uncle was alleged to have given him a book of magic, which had introduced him to the world of the Devil. Since the book was never produced publicly in the Grandier case, it is doubtful whether it ever existed. But the significance of the allegation is not that evidence was being falsely created or alleged. Rather, it was the mind-set of the time that was having its effect: Grandier was a sorcerer, therefore certain signs must be associated with him; he was a Gaufridy parallel, therefore parallels of circumstance must exist; Gaufridy had a book of magic, therefore Grandier must have one too; if it was not found, it was because the sorcerer was too clever – but since it must exist, it could be created, in accusation if not in fact.

Laubardemont's duties for the weeks and months ahead were divided into two phases. First, he had to take testimony and hear every witness, including both the accused priest and the nuns. Then he had to set up a trial at which all this evidence would be presented to a body of judges who would find for guilt and impose and carry out the sentence. The first part of this work took the commissioner until July the following year, some six or seven months. The second took only a month.

On 12 December 1633, at the request of Louis Moussaut (the *procureur du roi* and Trincant's son-in-law), Laubardemont began an inquiry into all the accusations that had been made against Grandier in 1630. It was as if there had been no trial in Poitiers and no absolution from the archbishop. The argument was used that the witnesses who had retracted their evidence on the earlier occasion had been intimidated into doing so. This intimidation was said to have been done by René Grandier, Urbain's lawyer brother. Now the witnesses came forward again and made all the same accusations. This was clearly something that had been planned by Trincant and his relatives. By now, they had all their witnesses well coached. It had taken time both to organize the accusations and to make sure that the accusers would not renege again. But they had had as much time as they needed, and they were ready. For their part, the witnesses could be confident that they would be granted complete immunity and that their testimony would be accepted, for the tribunal was composed of the curé's enemies. The general public may not have had much respect for their evidence, but the tribunal did, and that was what mattered.

Even at this early stage of the inquiry, it was realized that anybody who stood up for the accused man was likely to be accused of complicity in witchcraft. Nevertheless, some brave witnesses dared to provide testimony favourable to Grandier. It was no help to him. Laubardemont refused to record their depositions and even threatened them. In all this it has to be remembered that Laubardemont's commission was to take testimony and try a priest who had already been found guilty by the king and his council. Moreover, it is more than likely that Laubardemont was completely convinced that the possessions were real and that Grandier was guilty of all the crimes of which he was accused; so he would have regarded witnesses who testified in favour of the priest as at best misguided and at worst highly suspect.

This case also gave Bishop de La Rocheposay the chance to get his own back on both Archbishop de Sourdis and Grandier. There was a well-established procedure by which a bishop could have published and read out in every church in his diocese a document that contained the charges that had been made against someone. The importance of this *monitoire*, as it was called, was that the bishop could compel anyone who knew anything about a case to come forward and give evidence. Failure to do so would automatically result in excommunication – which meant that if that person died without making amends, he would be subject to eternal damnation. This was pretty strong medicine in a society where religion was part of everybody's life and at a time when death threatened by day and night. In this instance, Laubardemont, as the king's representative, went to the bishop and asked for the *monitoire* to be published as an aid to his inquiry. The bishop very properly agreed to the request. The accusations contained in it were largely the same as those that had led to the original sentencing by him, and the wording was such as to say that Grandier had committed the crimes, not just that he was alleged to have done so. What this did in effect was tell the world that the bishop still believed in the priest's guilt; it clearly implied that the priest had always been guilty as charged and that the archbishop's absolution should be ignored.

In the meantime, Grandier was in prison in the castle at Angers. It was a bitterly cold place to be imprisoned in the depth of winter. His mother's first concern was to find friends who could get some comforts to him. One of the local priests, a canon, was given permission to visit him daily in his cell (it was always recognized that such a prisoner should have access to a priest), and through this canon, on 19 December, Grandier's mother was able to get a letter to him telling him that he was constantly in the minds of his family and that he had not heard from them earlier only because they had had no means of communicating with him. This letter gave him new hope because it confirmed that his friends were working to prove his innocence. Along with the letter, his mother was able to send him clothes, which he badly needed, and some money to meet his other needs and buy himself some comforts.

When the testimony on the events before 1630 was complete, Laubardemont went to the Ursuline Convent to gather evidence about the possessions. All seventeen of the nuns, headed by the superior, came forward. Nine were classified by the exorcists as possessed or obsessed,[4] and eight were considered to be normal or at least only mildly affected.[5] Since all had lived through the experiences together and all believed the convent to have been under attack by the Devil, they made a joint declaration:

that Grandier had penetrated into their house at all hours of the day and night over a period of four months, without their being able to give any explanation as to how he could have entered there; that he came to them when they were standing, attending prayers [this was their common prayer in their chapel when they would all be together], that he had incited them to sin, that they had been struck when they saw nothing, and that all these happenings had begun with the apparition of Prior Moussaut and been followed by that of Grandier.[6]

Ten seculars also came forward to give similar evidence; seven of them were classified as possessed or obsessed, and three were considered unaffected. Two of the seculars in particular, Elisabeth Blanchard and Susanne Hammon (the sister of the "shoemaker" of Marie de Medici), came forward to confirm these declarations of the nuns.[7] These two, especially Elisabeth Blanchard, were to be among the worst afflicted of the possessed.

René Grandier, Grandier's brother, who was a senior lawyer under the *bailli*, realized that he had to take issue against Laubardemont's practice of taking unsupported testimony from the possessed nuns and seculars. It could kill his brother. Only if he could throw doubt on Laubardemont's procedure would there be some hope of getting justice. On his advice, his mother therefore wrote to Laubardemont, outlining her reasons for objecting to the witnesses. This document, dated 27 December 1633, throws light on how Laubardemont went about his work, at least as seen by the family of his prisoner. Jeanne d'Estièvre started by saying that for five or six years the enemies of her son had "tried to destroy his reputation with lies and calumny, but to their confusion he was exonerated."[8] She stated that Grandier's enemies had used the nuns to accuse him of possession; that Laubardemont had been asked to take up the case by her son's enemies; that he had taken counsel with Barré on his way through Chinon; and that he had deliberately sought to be sent back as commissioner to Loudun. She went on to accuse Laubardemont of having met with Mesmin and Grandier's other principal enemies both before and after the arrest. She said he had taken lodgings in the town in a place where he could easily confer with her son's foes and that he had spent much time with them, far into the night. He had appointed a prosecutor in the case who was recommended by Menuau, one of Grandier's enemies; and even before his inquiry started, he had made others aware that he considered Grandier to be guilty. Moreover, he had ignored the decision of the archbishop of Bordeaux of 24 December 1632 on the alleged possession of the nuns. Further, he was related, through his wife, both to the bishop of Poitiers and to some of the nuns. For all these reasons he should withdraw from the case, she argued.

But Laubardemont was in no mood to change his procedure. Nor did he need to. His commission from the king stated very clearly that he should ignore any objections or interference. His power was absolute, and in his opinion – which was all that mattered in this case – the cause was just. He replied that he would continue without regard to the supplicant. The only effect of Jeanne d'Estièvre's letter and her later objections was that Laubardemont ordered her not to intimidate witnesses. It is unlikely that she had actually expected Laubardemont to give an inch. Nor would she have expected him to resign from the case. What this and her later letters did was build the grounds for an appeal to another court, the Parlement of Paris. The hope of the Grandier family and his friends was that no matter what happened in Loudun, the result could be appealed later. An adverse decision could be overturned on the grounds that the proper legal procedures had not been followed.

Next, it was the turn of Grandier's brother, François. In two documents, dated 9 and 10 January 1634, he objected to the publication of the bishop's *monitoire*.[9] He complained that the contents ran counter to the earlier decisions of the court in Poitiers and of the archbishop of Bordeaux. He formally asked for a copy of the *monitoire*, and he also asked that the *monitoire* be officially entered in the records of the court so that his objection could not be ignored. His purpose was clear. He too was looking for evidence for a future appeal. Obviously, he was planning to say that the bishop had no right to disregard the orders of his ecclesiastical superior, that Laubardemont was using an improperly issued *monitoire* to accuse the priest and gather witnesses, and that in taking these steps he was going beyond his legal authority. François' letters had no result.

Jeanne d'Estièvre tried again on 17 January 1634, when she once more accused Laubardemont of recording only testimony that was unfavourable to her son, of deliberately leaving out of the records testimony that was favourable to him, of leading witnesses, and of allowing magistrates hostile to Grandier to intimidate witnesses. In general, she accused Laubardemont of acting in concert with Grandier's enemies and performing procedures that were against the law and quite improper. She also accused him of publicly naming her son in the *monitoire* yet refusing to provide a copy of it, thus favouring the prosecution. Finally, she repeated that Laubardemont had close relatives in the convent and that he had a clear conflict of interest and should withdraw from the case.[10]

This very toughly worded series of accusations against his own person threw Laubardemont into a violent rage. He refused to answer and would not even give a reason for his silence. But this was a resolute mother, fighting for her son's life, and she was not going to be intimidated. As the result of her efforts, she had by now assembled the documents needed to make a strong appeal to the highest law court, the Parlement of Paris, and she instructed her lawyer to start the proceedings on her behalf. But the papers had to be processed through Laubardemont as the king's commissioner for the inquiry. He tore them to pieces and forbade the clerks of the court to bring such things to him again under pain of punishment.

Despite his reaction, on 27 January 1634 Jeanne d'Estièvre fought back by making public her intention to appeal, presumably in the hope of forcing Laubardemont to make some response in self-defence. It was useless. The commissioner remained silent.

To understand what the Grandier family hoped for from an appeal to the Parlement a minor digression is necessary. At that date, the powers of the king of France and those of the Parlement of Paris were not clearly defined. As a result, there was a constant though often low-key struggle between the two to gain or assert power. The Grandier case and the possessions of Loudun are a good example. This was a criminal case that had been initiated by the king, with a king's commissioner who had been given authority to do anything and had expressly been instructed to ignore any attempt to interfere with anything he did. This might be the perfect case for the magistrates of the parlement to say that their rights as the highest court had been infringed upon. Jeanne d'Estièvre's task was to get them interested. If she could do that, they might be prepared to interfere on her son's behalf, not for his sake but for their own.

The appeal to the Parlement of Paris was becoming of prime importance to the Grandier family, for it seemed to be their only hope. Sourdis and d'Armagnac, who in the past had supported Grandier at the seats of power, were no longer prepared to act. Sourdis was deeply involved in a personal power struggle with another noble at court. He had no time to spare for what was going on in Loudun. Besides, he probably felt that the priest should have followed his advice and left Loudun after his previous interventions. As for d'Armagnac, now that he no longer had interests in Loudun, he did not need Grandier. In any case, he must have been furious to hear that his compromising letters to Grandier had not been destroyed as ordered but were in the hands of his enemies. D'Armagnac needed all the favours he could get in order to preserve his own interests at court. So although he continued to involve himself on Grandier's behalf, his efforts had lost their intensity.

So Laubardemont proceeded on his way despite the murmurings from Grandier's supporters in Loudun. The *bailli* and his group of magistrates found themselves more and more isolated and began to fall under suspicion themselves as being involved too closely with a man who was clearly the Devil's adherent. Still, they continued to complain about Laubardemont's abuses of justice – whereupon he threatened severe punishment to anyone who showed signs of becoming involved in the affair. Meanwhile, the Ursulines remained possessed by their devils, despite many more exorcisms by Mignon. Once again it was necessary to call upon the expertise of Barré, the curé of Chinon. Within two or three days of his arrival, Jeanne des Anges, who up to that time had been possessed by no more than four devils, had seven of them; Sister Claire de Sazilly had six, and other nuns were almost as sick.

By this time, Laubardemont had all the accusations against Grandier recorded, and he was ready to go to Angers to interrogate the accused man. To assist him he took with him Canon Demorans, dean of the canons of Thouars, a relative and friend of the priest's enemies. He also took a young lawyer from the town, Pierre Fournier, whose father-in-law had earlier been found guilty of bearing false witness against Grandier and had been severely punished by the courts. While Laubardemont has been criticized by many authors for employing Grandier's enemies and their friends in his entourage, in fact he had little choice. His only alternative would have been to import staff from other towns at great cost to the crown, and that would hardly have sat well with the cardinal. By this time, anybody in Loudun who was of any consequence had long since become aligned on one side or the other, and Laubardemont would have been foolish to choose men for his staff who did not believe in Grandier's guilt.

When it became known that the commission was moving to Angers to take evidence, Grandier's mother sent a note through a close friend warning her son to say nothing. She informed him that Laubardemont was openly against him, as were his staff. To give substance to her advice, she attached her two unsuccessful petitions so that Grandier would be aware of how his enemies were proceeding. In the same letter she gave him news intended to encourage him, advising him that his friends were indeed working to have Laubardemont removed from the case. But even that could hardly have offered much relief to her son in his cold prison. It was very disquieting therefore for the priest to hear that the commissioner and his staff had arrived in Angers. This was on 4 February 1634.

Later that day Laubardemont went to the château prison intending to interrogate Grandier, but the accused man refused to respond to most of his questions. Laubardemont did not publish a record of that day's interrogation. He limited himself to noting in the registers of the commission that all the responses from the curé were negative. The next day he returned to the prison, this time with more success. When Grandier was presented with the "Treatise on the Celibacy of Priests," he admitted that he was the author. This was important because it was clearly a heretical document. But when Laubardemont tried to make him admit that he had composed it for Madeleine de Brou, the curé was immovable. The questioning went on until the 11 February, by which time it was evident that Grandier was not going to reply any further. The commissioner had him sign the record and left for Paris, furious.

In the meantime, Jeanne d'Estièvre's petition for the parlement's intervention had become a serious preoccupation for Laubardemont, because it looked as if the parlement might indeed take up the case. At all costs, this had to be avoided. If the parlement's magistrates declared that his procedures were improper, he would have embarrassed both the king and the cardinal, and even though he had been carrying out their orders, his whole career would be at risk. These matters took Laubardemont's full attention in Paris for the next two months, with the result that he had no time for his friends in Loudun. They became so concerned by his silence that they sent a representative to him to get his reassurance that they were not again going to be made a laughing stock while the priest went free. They need not have worried. Laubardemont had been putting his time in Paris to good use. He soon had Richelieu working to circumvent the parlement; the king's first minister had no intention of allowing it to gain a victory in its ongoing battle on the division of power with the crown. Richelieu obtained an order from the Council of State instructing the magistrates in the name of the king that no interference would be permitted in this case. Any steps so far taken by the parlement were to be annulled. The order said in part: "Ignoring the appeal placed before Parlement and the procedures begun in consequence, which His Majesty has dismissed, Sieur de Laubardemont is ordered to continue the proceedings begun by him against Grandier notwithstanding all opposition, appeals or objections." It went on to forbid the Parlement of Paris or any other magistrates to become involved under pain of a fine of five hundred livres.[11]

Armed with this piece of paper, Laubardemont arrived in Loudun on the evening of Sunday, 9 April 1634. The following morning he issued an order to have the priest brought back to Loudun under heavily armed guard. While the commissioner had been away, a solid prison had been prepared, secure against any attempted rescue. Grandier was to be incarcerated in a house belonging to Mignon. It was rented and occupied by a sergeant of the court named

Bontemps. He was Trincant's former clerk and had been one of the principal witnesses against Grandier in the last trial. Grandier was feared as a prisoner because of his special relationship with the Devil and the powers he could undoubtedly call upon. There was also the fear that his friends would try to storm the prison and release him. So he was placed in a most uncomfortable and unhealthy cell situated directly under the roof. The windows were walled for greater safety, leaving only the minimum amount of light. The chimney was blocked with enormous bars of iron. Word spread that these precautions were necessary to prevent the devils from coming to deliver the prisoner. In this dark and unhappy retreat, he was left in the care of Bontemps and his wife, who had the reputation of being a shrew. A strong armed guard was installed in the room on the main floor, and nobody was allowed even to approach the house.

Grandier had no bed to lie on except a bundle of straw. When his mother learned of his pitiful state, she had some provisions and clothing delivered. Laubardemont permitted this. Grandier sent a letter thanking his mother for her supplies and asking her to send him his own bed, "for if the body has no repose, the spirit succumbs." In addition, he asked for a breviary and a Bible for consolation. Finally, he expressed his hope that God would reveal his innocence. He was labouring under an illusion if he really thought he would be able to save himself.

The Exorcisms

Now that Laubardemont had returned to Loudun and Grandier had been moved there, the commissioner was able to turn his attention to the nuns once more. The first thing he did, with the bishop's agreement, was to have them sequestered. This was the step Grandier had been asking for, over a period of months. It was quickly accomplished now that it was Laubardemont, the king's commissioner, who was making the demand. In twos, threes, and fours the nuns were placed in the private homes of respectable people, who were to be responsible for their care. Two were lodged with one of Grandier's close friends, Canon Maufrat, but all the others were placed with friends or relatives of his enemies. However, all the nuns' hosts were unquestionably the kind of people whom most would consider to be the best of choices. One was a widow, an aunt of Canon Mignon. Another was the legal adviser to the convent. Another, a certain Nicolas Moussaut, was the uncle of the *procureur du roi* and brother-in-law of Mesmin de Silly. Though Grandier complained bitterly that the nuns had been placed in the care of his enemies, the people chosen fitted the normal requirements for such a task.

A new batch of doctors was now brought in. On the surface, at least, it seemed that Laubardemont could not be faulted in the arrangements he was making. Each household of nuns was to have a doctor to observe and treat them and to give independent witness about whether or not they were truly possessed or were simply sick. Grandier saw it in a different light: "One is from Fontevrault," said Grandier in his Factum, "who has never had letters and as the result was forced to leave Saumur; the same with those from Thouars, one having passed the greater part of his youth selling in a haberdashery in Loudun, the other similarly ignorant and convicted of extreme incompetence by the archbishop of Bordeaux and furthermore a close relative of Trincant's wife; the one from Chinon knowing nothing and kept unemployed by those of the town, also ill disposed in spirit, the one from Mirabeau the same, a relative of Mignon's sister. In brief, village doctors." This argument, whether just or not, was one that could not be won. Then, as now, the medical profession stuck together; a doctor was a doctor, and his competence could not be judged by a layman.[1]

Grandier became increasingly concerned when Laubardemont appointed Mannoury as the principal surgeon and Adam as the apothecary responsible for preparing the medicines for the nuns. In fairness to the commissioner, it should be pointed out that although these men were Grandier's sworn enemies, they were recognized in Loudun as highly competent members of their professions. Even so, Grandier must by now have realized that he was up against a different breed of man from those with whom he had battled before. Laubardemont had surrounded the nuns with a group of people whom any objective observer would agree were well chosen and well qualified. Yet all were strategically placed to influence events against the accused man. And Laubardemont had achieved this with the appearance of having done everything possible for the welfare of the nuns. Here the qualities of the experienced administrator were apparent.

On 14 April 1634 Laubardemont decided that the time had come to gather the nuns together to confront the accused man. Grandier saw this as one of his best chances to prove his innocence. He had never had any dealings with the nuns and he knew that they had not even seen him. He therefore wrote to Laubardemont, proposing that the same test be used as that devised by an early saint, Athanasius: "This great bishop, accused at the Council of Tyre by a lewd woman whom he had never seen, thought up a strategy that proved his complete innocence. When this woman entered the assembly to make her accusation publicly, a priest named Timothy presented himself to her and spoke to her as if he were Athanasius. She believed him, and by this means she herself manifested the falsity of her allegation."[2]

As might be expected, Laubardemont ignored Grandier's proposal and made a point of telling the nuns that the priest was being brought to them. They therefore had no difficulty in recognizing him and did not hesitate to declare that he was the man who came each night to visit them in their convent and solicited them to sin with him. Grandier asked Sister Claire how she could recognize him if she had never seen him except in the dark of the night.

To which the Sister replied that she recognized the resemblance to the description that had been given to her of what he looked like. The said Grandier having asked her in what fashion he had been depicted to her, she replied to him that she had been told that he was a tall man, having black hair, a pointed beard, a fine face, a large nose. The said Grandier replied that these were not the qualities by which he was recognizable because they were common to many men. To which the Sister made this reply, that she knew him by the strong emotion that she felt towards him and that thus it would certainly have every appearance that it was not natural.[3]

Grandier, of course, denied the nuns' accusations and objected to Laubardemont's procedure. Nevertheless, Laubardemont recorded that the nuns had told the truth.

The commissioner's next bit of business was to find replacements for Barré and Mignon, who had resigned after months of exhausting but largely fruitless work. Whether the resignations had been requested by Laubardemont we do not know, but its effect was to "prove" his objectivity. The replacements were not, of course, the priests chosen earlier by the archbishop of Bordeaux. The bishop of Poitiers was now fully back in charge of this case in his diocese, and it was he who chose the two new exorcists. No doubt once the king had appointed a commissioner who was prepared to work closely with the bishop, the archbishop had little right to interfere, even if he had wanted to. The two new exorcists were lodged with the nuns in the home of Nicolas Moussaut. However, the possessions continued to make such rapid progress that these exorcists were soon obliged to ask for reinforcements. Four Capuchins and two Carmelites were added to the team, and this proved sufficient. Thanks to Father Joseph, the head of their order, the Capuchins spent so much time and effort on their work that they were granted a donation of four thousand livres from the king's privy purse.[4]

These exorcists worked for months (and, in some cases, years) with the nuns. The names of two of them occur many times in the records of Grandier's trial and death: Father Gabriel Lactance and Father Tranquille. The former, a Recollet, was one of the two men appointed by the bishop, and Tranquille was one of the four

Capuchins (obviously agreed to by the bishop) whom Father Joseph installed. Tranquille and Lactance soon came to be the principal exorcists, and very early on they made a pronouncement that would ultimately build the funeral pyre around Grandier.

For many years the question had been debated whether the power of the church was so great that the Devil, under exorcism, could be forced to tell the truth. Some held that he could. Others held that as the prince of liars, nothing the Devil said could ever be taken to be true. This seems to be a fine theological point, but it had enormous implications in witchcraft trials.[5] During the exorcisms, the demons seemed to be speaking for themselves through the medium of the possessed nuns. Could the priests, using all the powers of the Catholic Church, demand that they tell the truth? Was the power that God had given the church great enough to force the Devil to tell the truth when speaking through a possessed person? To Grandier and the many others accused in witchcraft trials, the answer to this question was a matter of life and death. Most authorities in the Catholic Church held that in no circumstances could the Devil ever be assumed to be telling the truth. The Capuchins, however, were among those who held the opposite view. They had done so in the Gaufridy case, and they did so now.

Fathers Lactance and Tranquille together propounded their position, stating "that the Devil, under due constraint of exorcism, is bound to tell the truth". This was not expressed as an opinion which the people of Loudun could consider but as a fact which they had to believe. This meant that anything the nuns said while being exorcized was true. Thus, if Grandier was accused by any of them during an exorcism, the accusation must be accepted as true. Grandier could have no defence under this interpretation.[6] This theological decision was naturally welcomed by Laubardemont. It made his task much easier. He wrote to inform Richelieu, and the cardinal wrote back giving his approval.[7] Richelieu's support was important, and no doubt it was sincere, for he had made a considerable study of theology and his entourage included theologians whom he consulted frequently.[8]

It was not enough for Laubardemont to be provided with the pronouncement and its confirmation. He made sure that it was published in such a way that even to question this interpretation would be a serious offence. Thus, in all the churches of Loudun the priests were required to preach sermons based on the interpretation and to demand that all the people in Loudun accept it as true. Father

Tranquille's attack on a priest who held a different position shows how firmly this policy was pursued. From his pulpit, Tranquille proclaimed:

I find it wrong when Father Birette[9] in general advances the proposition that one cannot believe what the Devil says because he is our enemy. I challenge his position, for if it were not permitted to me in legitimate exorcisms to believe his [the Devil's] words and to accept his testimony, it would not be lawful for me to question him, as the Church requires me to do; for the only reason I question him is to get his replies. If then the Church judges that my interrogations are lawful, it presupposes that the responses of the Devil are true, for it cannot wish that I should conduct interrogations with the purpose of getting false responses. This good Father [Birette] ought to consider that when we believe the words of the Devil when he is duly under exorcism, we are not receiving the words as if they were from the Father of Lies, but we receive them from the Church, which has the power to force the devils to tell the truth.[10]

Of course, not everyone was convinced. The Huguenots certainly did not see the power of the Catholic Church in this light, and even some Catholics found it hard to swallow. This lack of faith and the arguments it provoked did not go unnoticed by Laubardemont. He therefore took further measures to make the belief mandatory. With his approval, Fathers Lactance and Tranquille began to preach that belief in the possessions was mandatory because the Devil said they were true. Those who failed to believe would be committed to hell when they died.

Not content with hectoring the public from the pulpit and calling those who were not of their view "heretics, atheists, libertines,"[11] Fathers Lactance and Tranquille declared that "the best proof of the reality of the possessions is that the king and the cardinal believe in it; those who doubt it are guilty of a form of *lèse-majesté* and become punishable as accomplices of the curé."[12] These intimidating words were certainly enough to convince most people. Nevertheless, the *bailli* and his band of Loudun officials held their own opinion right to the end.

THE PUBLIC EXORCISMS

Until this time, the exorcisms had been held in private, even though a large number of spectators (of the right sort) had been present.

Now the exorcists decided to make a public display of the power of the church over the Devil. They wished to accomplish two things. They wanted to prove to everybody in this half-Huguenot town that the church could force the Devil to leave the nuns; and in front of all Loudun, they wanted to identify the sorcerer who was responsible for the possessions. Four churches were designated for the purpose, and in each they planned to hold regular exorcisms of different groups of nuns in ceremonies that would be completely open to the public.[13] This was bound to attract spectators from far and wide. Such public shows at no cost would be the best theatre most people had been offered in all their lives. Each church became a stage, and each performance was "legitimized by a solemn procession where the possessed and their exorcists figured; the spectators numbered in the many thousands; the average length of each seance was from six to seven hours."[14]

At first the exorcists had little success, but once they became experienced in these public performances they surpassed even the effects of Mignon and Barré. The public sessions were noisy and crowded, and the nuns writhed and grimaced as usual, shouting wildly or grunting words through clenched teeth. The onlookers craned their necks, hoping to hear the exorcist repeat loudly and clearly the words that the demon was uttering through the nun. Many believed in what the exorcists said was happening, but not all. One eyewitness, who was clearly unimpressed, gave the following report:

While the friar read the prescribed adjurations contained in the formulary of the Church, the master exorcist ordered the demon to ascend to the head [of the nun] and to show himself by some colour in the face [i.e., by turning her face a violent red].[15] He repeated the words of the order many times. And when these poor creatures did not put themselves quickly enough on fire he sometimes shook their heads very roughly and putting their heads on his lap bashed the Holy Ciborium[16] on their foreheads until the normal result was brought about. [The observer went on to describe other examples] ... It is in this way that it seems to the ignorant that the devil obeys them [the exorcists] absolutely in everything he commands them ... Then the exorcist makes the alleged devils speak and by the force of exorcism and the virtue of the Blessed Sacrament obliges them to tell the truth about everything asked of them, and it is based on these statements that M. the Commissioner prepares the minutes of the exorcism. But these poor devils never said a word in our presence even when they were ordered under all sorts of exorcisms to give us an infallible mark of possession; they failed in all the signs that were proposed to them by many persons of quality, and myself having interrogated them in several western and eastern languages, they have shown very clearly that they understood nothing of any language in which I spoke to them.[17]

The exorcisms, of course, had to continue until the demons were ejected.[18] This was likely to be a lengthy process. If Grandier had made a pact with the Devil and was therefore in league with him, the demons could be expected to use all their power to avoid admitting any guilt on Grandier's part, for he was one of them. So the full "truth" about Grandier had to be forced from them painfully, bit by bit. But each admission wrung out of the demons with such effort was one more proof of the power of the Catholic Church over the Devil.

The evidence gained through exorcism was not the only way to prove that Grandier was a sorcerer; there were also the Devil's marks. The position of these insensitive points varied from one magician to another, but they were always there. Laubardemont, with his experience of hunting witches, knew that.[19] On 26 April 1634 he took part in the exorcisms with the priests and asked one of the devils possessing the mother superior to tell him where Grandier was marked. The demon replied that "Grandier was marked in two places in the most secret parts of his body, in the two buttocks close to his anus, and in the two testicles."[20] The surgeon Mannoury was given the task of testing for these points, which he did with terrible relentlessness. He employed the normal procedure for this test. A long thin needle was used, rather like a knitting needle, with one end blunt and rounded. "He had Grandier stripped naked, eyes bound, and shaved everywhere and probed and pierced right to the bone in many parts of his body."[21] This testing was so agonizing that Grandier could not prevent himself from screaming with pain. His cries were so loud that they were heard by the many people gathered outside in the street. However, Mannoury failed to find the points indicated by the demon.

Grandier's friends maintained that in order to find the insensitive marks, Mannoury then surreptitiously reversed the needle, pressing the rounded end on the places that had been mentioned by the demon. The blindfolded man naturally gave no violent reaction because there was no pain. Mannoury tried two or three times in the same places and then declared, for the sake of the record, that

"he had lanced in this place and that in this place he was insensible."
An apothecary from Poitiers, Sieur Carré, who was present, was far
from convinced. He took the needle from Mannoury and "pierced
Grandier, who reacted in such a way that it was quite clear that he
had full sense of feeling there." More than one report was prepared
in order to record the different opinions of what was seen. Laubardemont accepted only the one prepared by Mannoury, which was
countersigned by the apothecary Adam.

Some days after Easter, the bishop of Poitiers came to Loudun to
bring his own authority to the matter. He declared "that he had not
come to inquire into the truth of the possession but to see that it was
believed and to uncover the circle of men and women sorcerers."[22]
This was a significant new development. The demons had already
been asked to name Grandier's accomplices, though without result;
but with such an authoritative statement from Bishop de La Rocheposay, it became imperative to conduct a witch-hunt. Anyone who
continued to be a friend of Grandier was now liable to be accused
of being an accomplice. Meanwhile, the bishop was lodged with the
widow Barot (one of Mignon's aunts), who was already housing a
number of the possessed and two exorcists.[23] This was convenient
for the bishop, since he was able to see for himself the unhappy state
of the possessed young women, both the nuns and the laywomen,
and to observe how carefully they were being looked after.

Laubardemont's case was well constructed by this time. He had
the demons (whose words were now considered infallible) accusing
the priest, and he had the evidence he needed that Grandier was
marked by the insensitive points of the Devil. In the Gaufridy case,
the priest had been promised power over women in return for his
written pact with the Devil, so the next step for those guiding the
exorcisms was to find the pact that Grandier had made with the
Devil when he sold his soul. At the exorcism of 28 April 1634,
Laubardemont interrogated the demon Asmodée, who was one of
the seven in possession of Jeanne des Anges. At first, Asmodée
would not respond, but under heavy pressure he eventually promised to provide a copy of the pact which, he said, was kept safely
by his master Lucifer. The next day at the stated time, to the great
satisfaction of the commissioner and the exorcists, the demon produced it through Jeanne des Anges:

My Lord and Master, I acknowledge you as my God and I promise to
serve you as long as I live, and from this time I renounce all others

including Jesus Christ and Mary and all the saints in heaven and the Catholic and Apostolic Roman Church and all its benefits and prayers which might be offered in my favour. I promise to adore you and to pay homage to you at least three times a day and to do all the evil that I can and to draw to evil as many persons as I can, and with all my heart I renounce my anointing and baptism and all the merits of Jesus Christ, and … I give you my body, my soul and my life, as holding it from you, having given it over forever and irrevocably.

Signed by Urbain Grandier with his blood.[24]

This document was, apparently, vomited up by the mother superior during the public exorcism. It had to be done in public, or there would have been no point to it; and, of course, Jeanne des Anges must have been an active participant in producing the pact. She had an enormous capability for self-deception. It is not difficult to imagine her convincing herself that a pact must exist, for she too was a child of her times. She may even have considered it an act of religious virtue to create the evidence and thereby beat the Devil at his own game. There was also the fact that by this performance she had proved once again that the show could not go on without her.

The guilt of the mother superior is clear, and possibly the exorcist was guilty too. Which of them first suggested the miracle we do not know, though from what we do know of Jeanne des Anges' unbalanced mind and her ability to manipulate everybody around her, it seems unlikely that she would willingly have played a secondary role to the exorcist. Indeed, the priests may have had no part at all in any of the frauds, apart from the roles they unwittingly accepted under Jeanne's guidance. Week after week since October 1632, the various exorcists had been asking the nuns the questions laid down in the manual as they demanded information from the devils: names and numbers, the reason for possession, how they entered and when, and exactly how long they intended to stay. The procedures provided the nuns with a detailed menu of answers, role enactments, and expected reactions.[25] These leads in role enactment were probably conveyed outside the exorcisms as well, though often unintentionally. They would have included conversations in the possessed nuns' presence about their symptoms or the symptoms of others, their timing, and when they might terminate; and opportunities for one nun to observe the performance of others who were more accomplished or experienced. So although the exorcists may, on occasion, have coached some of the nuns with a view to getting a more convincing performance, they were not necessarily pulling all the strings. They may have been as much manipulated as anyone else.

Those who believed that the possessions were false have almost universally held that the evidence against Grandier that was revealed during the exorcisms was cleverly created by the exorcists, and Jean Mignon is the priest usually identified as the principal culprit. Grandier himself held Mignon to be the source of the fraud in the possessions. In his "Factum," which he wrote in his own defence shortly before his death, he stated:

One of the witnesses and parties to the first trial [the one before the bishop with all the lechery accusations] was the director of conscience to the said nuns and their ordinary confessor. This Mignon, with evil guile and by insinuations, soon began to hatch a plot against the said Grandier, by means of a new, detestable and calumnious accusation. Abusing the readiness of these young women to listen to his advice, he told them that they were possessed, taught them to make grimaces, to speak lasciviously, and to name Grandier in all their discourse during the exorcisms, which he held without following any proper procedure.

But was Mignon really the man behind it all? When it is recalled that a total of thirty officially appointed exorcists were involved, and not all together but in successive waves, it is clear that the sophistication and degree of conspiracy would have had to be extraordinary to be successful; all the exorcists would have had to be acting in concert over a period of years.

There are other inconsistencies too. For instance, the miracles went on after Grandier's death when a new exorcist was appointed in the form of the saintly Father Surin. And they changed in nature. They had originally been connected with the demons in the form of demonic instruments such as thorns and roses, and then with the production of pacts with the Devil and the exit of Asmodée; but later, as will be seen, they attained a saintly quality in the form of a holy unguent, a miraculous chemise, and holy names. Moreover, although the sceptics were sure that Barré, Mignon, Tranquille, and Lactance must at least have been implicated and may well have been responsible for the possessions, these suspicions were never raised against Surin. Those who have rejected the possessions have always held Jeanne des Anges responsible for the fraud of the miracles that occurred during Father Surin's watch. But they do not seem to have taken the next, and perhaps obvious, step of questioning whether she was also responsible for the earlier events. To be more precise, if Surin was an innocent dupe of Jeanne des Anges, were the earlier priests also perhaps merely her instruments and not her controllers?

In the mind-set of the time, nobody could imagine that it might be a woman who was responsible. The general view was that women were weak, inconsistent, inclined to whims, and without the wit or constancy to take charge of things. While it was believable that the nuns could be manipulated, it was inconceivable that one of them could do the manipulating. Yet throughout all the years of the possessions, the mother superior was the one person in a position to manipulate the nuns and, through them, the priests. She was the only person who was with the other nuns day and night for all those years, and she was their superior; they would follow her lead, whether she gave it in the full knowledge of what she was doing or in the semiknowledge of her sickness.

The whole picture becomes much simpler if one assumes that Jeanne did it all herself, without the knowledge of the priests. It was always her demons who promised to deliver something new and then did so. As we shall see, even after Grandier died, it was she who had the miraculous chemise, and it was her hands that were marked with the indelible sacred names. These were all things that she could accomplish without any collusion on the part of the exorcists.

She did much of it by suggestion, and the duplicity worked, at least on those who mattered. Her greatest coup was the pact with the Devil, for it was irrefutable proof of Grandier's sorcery; his signature proved this beyond any doubt. However, Laubardemont set out to prove for himself that the document had in fact been "signed" by Grandier with his own blood. The record shows that "Asmodée, having provided the pact on a small piece of paper spotted with blood, declared after some resistance that the blood which appeared on the paper came from the thumb of his master's right hand."[26] On hearing this, the commissioner went straight to the prison and had the doctors pay a visit to Grandier. They confirmed that there was indeed a small wound in his right thumb. Clearly, the pact had indeed been sealed with Grandier's blood. The unfortunate curé protested that he had cut himself when slicing bread with a knife that one of his guards had lent to him, but Laubardemont would hear nothing of it. But how could Jeanne des Anges have known about the cut thumb? She probably heard of it from Mme Bontemps, the jailer's wife, who visited her at the convent every day and reported on every detail of Grandier's actions.[27]

Laubardemont and the exorcists did not have it all their own way, however. Some of the sceptics were people of such high reputation that they had to be included in the circle of people who were allowed close to the exorcisms. Marc Duncan and Claude Quillet were two such men. Duncan was a Scottish Calvinist who had settled in Saumur, where he had gained considerable renown. He was principal of the Huguenot school/college of the city and taught philosophy there. Claude Quillet was a poet and doctor from Chinon. He had travelled widely and held important posts in the household of one of the great French nobles. These two Huguenots were already sceptical because of their religious beliefs, and their doubts were increased by what they witnessed at the exorcisms. Only a miracle could hope to convince such sceptics. Jeanne des Anges obligingly produced one. At the exorcism of the 19 May, her demon Asmodée brought out the following letter:

I promise to leave the body of this creature and to make on her a wound (*fante*) below the heart the length of a pin, as well through her clothing, which wound will be bloody, and this tomorrow, Sunday the twentieth of May at six o'clock in the afternoon, and promise as well that Grésil and Amand will also make their openings in the same manner although smaller in support of what Leviathan has promised to do with their companions on this register of the Church of Saint-Croix.

ASMODEE[28]

Since Laubardemont was confident that this miracle would indeed occur, he took every step necessary to attract to the spectacle Duncan and Quillet, along with the pastors and other notable Protestants of Loudun. He announced, "The evil spirits which are in possession of the bodies of the nuns have promised to leave them; to this end they are going to be forced by the exorcists tomorrow, Sunday, at five in the afternoon." In inviting the Protestants to be present on this extraordinary occasion, he promised to make sure that they would have excellent places reserved for them where they would be able to see and hear everything. He went on to say "that he knew of no work more agreeable to the king; that he, Laubardemont, had been charged to take care that His Majesty should hear exactly about their conduct on this occasion in order that he could render praise and gratitude if they rendered themselves worthy of it; but if the case were to the contrary, he would use his power to constrain them."[29]

The Huguenot pastors saw the trap that Laubardemont had set for them and replied "that they were the very humble and obedient servants of His Majesty, but that in a matter where their conscience, their duties, and their honour were involved they regretted that they could not promise to believe." When the commissioner pressed them further, they said "that the king, by article 6 of the Edict of Nantes, accorded liberty of conscience and the free exercise of their religion," and that they must follow where their consciences led them. Despite this pronouncement, Laubardemont was confident that even they would be persuaded when they saw the demons actually expelled.

On 20 May the mother superior was led with great pomp into the Sainte-Croix church. An immense crowd[30] had many hours earlier invaded the nave of the church and the choir, and was waiting impatiently. Nearly all the gentlemen from the surrounding countryside were given places on this solemn occasion. Among the doctors were Duncan and Quillet, along with others whom Laubardemont had charged to examine Jeanne des Anges. Although the examination was only superficial, the doctors declared publicly that the mother superior had no wounds on her. Laubardemont then ordered Lactance to begin the exorcism. At this point, Duncan stated loudly that the nun should have her hands and feet bound before the exorcism to avoid any suggestion of sleight of hand that might later be made. But Lactance evaded this by arguing that there were many present who had never seen the convulsions that fell upon the possessed and that it was appropriate for their benefit that the nun should be exorcized before being bound.

Lactance now recommenced his exorcisms and adjurations, and immediately the mother superior made

a contortion of her body which appeared quite unbelievable. After she recovered from this first convulsion she went into another. She stayed in the position for some time and then was heard to groan. Because the contortion caused her to lie balanced on her left arm and side, her right hand was in front of her chest. When she withdrew it from her breast it could be seen that her finger-tips were stained with blood. The three demons had just brought about their exit. And when Jeanne des Anges was examined again by the doctors, they discovered three wounds on her chest, just as had been foretold. The demons had been expelled through them. In her clothing they discovered the holes through which they had exited.

Unfortunately for the general effect, there was in the crowd "a gentleman audacious enough to say that there was no point in his being there, for in a loud voice he declared he had seen the iron implement that she had used to make the wounds on herself."[31] A great tumult ensued through the whole assembly. The Commandeur de la Porte, Richelieu's uncle, told Laubardemont that he was displeased with the proceedings, and the commissioner replied that "something was amiss."[32] Nevertheless, he later insisted that the doctors submit a report confirming the reality of the wounds.[33]

Duncan openly mocked the demons – to the extent that he found it necessary to return immediately to Saumur to avoid Laubardemont's anger. Once safely back there, he invoked the protection of the Marquis de Brézé, which was just as well because an order had been issued to have him arrested. Claude Quillet found himself in similar danger:

One day the devil during an exorcism promised to lift a disbeliever to the vaulted arch of the church if one would come forward. Quillet, who heard this, said nothing, but the next day at the appointed hour he offered himself in the church. In the presence of M. de Laubardemont and of a great assembly of people he challenged the devil to keep his word and mocked him to such a degree that the poor devil found himself totally crestfallen and all devilry quite beyond him. M. de Laubardemont was completely scandalized and found against Quillet ... who judged that neither Loudun nor France were any longer safe for him. He left and promptly went into Italy.[34]

The results of the miracle had clearly not been as startling as Laubardemont had hoped. But these adverse reactions were neither typical nor widely held. If there were two thousand people in the Church of Sainte-Croix, as Laubardemont estimated, it was so crowded that only a tiny proportion could have clearly seen and heard what went on. In any case, by this time what actually happened made little difference to people's view of the events. The many who were convinced that the possessions were genuine would have remained convinced. Those who already disbelieved would have seen and heard nothing that would make them change their minds. And as for those who did not really care one way or another but

L. Exorcisme.

Bishop de La Rocheposay exorcizing Jeanne des Anges.
Source: Musée Charbonneau-Lassay, Loudun

found the continuing theatrical offerings a wonderful change and a delightful source of gossip, they just hoped that it would never end, or at least that it would end on a high note.

GRANDIER'S TROUBLES ESCALATE

Although everything seemed to be going Laubardemont's way, it was not by any means smooth sailing. In early May, some two weeks before the mother superior's miracle, his plans had received a setback that was potentially very serious. The commissioner had been informed that René Grandier had left for Paris to make a new attempt to get the parlement to take over his brother's case. Laubardemont was furious. He was well aware that his procedures would not meet the standards of an objective examination by legal experts. Nor would the cardinal be at all pleased that Grandier's brother had been allowed to get away from Loudun, possibly to stir up anew the struggle between the king and the parlement over who had authority in this case. Laubardemont knew, too, that as the man on the spot, he would be held responsible for anything that went wrong. According to bureaucratic standards, he should have foreseen the possibility of René Grandier making trouble, and he should have forestalled it.

René Grandier carried with him every piece of information he had been able to collect on the commissioner's procedures – certainly enough to raise the hackles of the legal experts in the parlement. So the moment Laubardemont learned of his departure, he dispatched Thibault to pursue the lawyer and to inform the cardinal of whatever occurred. Richelieu lost no time in undertaking damage control. He ordered the chancellor, Pierre Séguier, to do whatever was necessary to help Thibault block René's efforts. Séguier responded on 7 May with the following note: "As to the brother of the curé of Loudun, as soon as Sieur Thibault makes known to me where the man is lodging, I will give the order to have him arrested."[35] The next day Thibault managed to discover the address, whereupon René Grandier was arrested, led under close guard to Loudun, and imprisoned in the same house as his brother.

Jean Grandier, Urbain's youngest brother, was next. Denounced by the demons as being an accomplice of Urbain, he too was arrested and imprisoned. Only François, the vicar of Saint-Pierre, was left at liberty. He was no doubt relieved to hear that the demon had declared that "he was neither a magician nor a sorcerer, but merely loved women and good wine."[36] Clearly, anyone who still actively supported the Grandier case was under threat of imprisonment. Whether the commissioner was actively involved in the demons' accusations we cannot say, but from this day on the curé's partisans were victims of a series of activities and accusations designed to involve them as Grandier's acolytes in sorcery.

Madeleine de Brou was the prime target. It started when the devils claimed that Grandier's books of magic were in her possession. Her home was invaded by her worst enemies, at the head of whom were Menuau and Adam. Everything was turned upside down. Not a thing was found, but the *avocat du roi* and the apothecary had got their pound of flesh. Madeleine could not go out of her house without being insulted by someone. One day Menuau stopped her in the street and loudly accused Grandier of having corrupted her and other women with his words and suggestions. Despite the danger that threatened anyone who spoke up for the priest, she boldly replied that "she had never heard issue from his mouth anything but words of edification and charity which had consoled and edified her." Another day it was le Mousnier who accosted her and told her that she would be excommunicated, but she replied "that she had no reason to fear these threats." Then Moussaut du Fresne's wife challenged her publicly in the Church of Saint-Pierre: "So you have nothing to say against this evildoer? We'll get the devil to say something to shame you!" And indeed, every day the devils who possessed Jeanne des Anges accused Madeleine as well as Grandier.[37]

There was also an attempt to implicate the *bailli*, Guillaume de Cerisay, and his lieutenant, Louis Chauvet (both of whom were relatives of Madeleine de Brou), and to establish them as accomplices of a plan to help Grandier escape. On 9 May 1634 a young woman in rags handed the *bailli* the following letter:

Monsieur, it is bruited abroad everywhere that you are a supporter of M. Grandier in his misfortunes. The accusations against him are so false that his enemies passionately want to see him condemned. But where there is such a feeling of violence, there is no room for justice. For that reason, it is time that his friends think about getting him out of there. I am writing to you so that under your protection I can undertake it, at peril of my life, provided that you assure me of your help in case of need, which will depend on the situation around the place where he is kept prisoner. I will await your news Thursday next at the Cheval Blanc at Chinon, by the bridge where I will have someone on my behalf. I have no wish that the carrier of this should appear at your home, fearing a thousand traitors who are there.

I remain, Monsieur, your very humble servant,

RATIGNY
9 May 1634[38]

Louis Chauvet received an identical letter. Both men immediately suspected a trap. If they did nothing and kept the letters secret, they left themselves open to being accused of plotting Grandier's escape and being his allies in crime, so they went immediately to Laubardemont and handed him the two letters, making sure that they were given a receipt for them. They then proceeded to conduct their own inquiry and found that their suspicions were sound. The person who had given the letter to the beggarwoman for delivery was Pierre Cherbonneau, the man who had first denounced Grandier to the bishop of Poitiers in 1629.

It was not long before rumours were flying that both de Cerisay and his wife were to be accused of sorcery. Fortunately for de

Cerisay, his reputation sheltered him from such nonsense. But by now there was a vicious atmosphere of mortal accusations, unsubstantiated rumours, and the settling of old scores. Loudun was a dangerous place for all who had enemies. Furthermore, many people believed that the Devil was truly roaming through the city. Even so, the crowds continued to arrive from ever more distant places in the hope of seeing an exorcism. As Legué writes, "Reason rebels at a recitation of the extravagances committed during the long months that this whole strange procedure endured. One has to read all the voluminous minutes of the proceedings, for the most part written in the hand of Laubardemont, to understand the reality of such acts. Anything the most deranged mind could invent would have difficulty in approaching the truth of what actually happened."[39] The public exorcisms were still spectacles of extraordinary contortions and changing facial expressions as different demons took over the persons of the nuns. Even more titillating were the lewd positions, obscene suggestions, and indecent cries made each day by these women. And to these orgies of sensual fury all were invited, including the young women of the town. They were often addressed directly by the demons, who teased them during the exorcisms, calling them "my dainty young misses" and declaring that there was nowhere where "chastity was so low as in the homes of the young women of Loudun."[40]

Most dramatic of all was the scene that took place in the Church of Sainte-Croix on 23 June in the presence of the bishop of Poitiers.[41] Laubardemont had decided to confront Grandier with the nuns for a second time, this time in public. To give full solemnity to the occasion, he had both the curé and the nuns conducted to the church in a stately religious procession. The cortège left at about two in the afternoon from the convent of the Ursulines. At the head of the procession were the possessed, eight in number, accompanied by all the personnel of the convent. Following them came the bishop dressed in his full episcopal robes, then the clergy of the town, then all the monks of the different orders, wearing their albs and stoles. Then came Laubardemont, robed in red, accompanied by the other magistrates and officers of the king, all in their uniforms. Between Bontemps, his jailer, and the clerk of the court walked Urbain Grandier, firm and upright. A body of armed guards brought up the rear. Meanwhile, every bell in the town was pealing at full volume. The crowd was so large that the procession took more than an hour to cover the distance between the Ursuline Convent and the Church of Sainte-Croix, though it was little more than one hundred and twenty paces by the most direct route. After the opening prayers, which were led by the bishop, the commissioner ordered the accused man to be presented with the different pacts that had been delivered up by the demons:

The first of ashes, of worms, hair and nails from a human body, delivered up by Asmodée in the exorcism of the 15th May.

The second composed of blood, of greyish matter which it was impossible to identify, and two morsels of something about the size of a hazelnut. (This pact was delivered on Sunday the 17th May by Leviathan.)

Finally the last pact, wrapped in paper was composed of three blood-stains which had the appearance of eight orange pips.[42]

In addition, the accused was presented with the stem of a feather quill, retrieved by Jeanne des Anges at the exorcism of 13 June, as well as a little bundle of five straws "found on her on the 30th April last." (Obviously, the written pact between Grandier and the Devil which Jeanne des Anges had vomited up at the public exorcism of 28 April had been only the first of a series of such performances.) The group of doctors chosen by Laubardemont were asked to give their opinion on these items, and after examining their composition at length they certified that it was truly the work of Satan.[43] Laubardemont then had a brazier brought in which the pacts were burned after they had been exorcized so that they could not cast spells on those who dealt with them. All of this was viewed by the hundreds of people present. They packed the church, which was lit by the candles carried by the priests and acolytes and clouded by the smoke of the incense that accompanied the prayers and incantations.

When this ceremony had been concluded, eight exorcists went in procession to lead in the possessed nuns, who had been held in the sacristy. There were eight of them. (The nuns who were less stricken were classified as obsessed rather than possessed.) The eight were led into the choir, which was raised above the body of the church by a few steps and was therefore visible to all (with a bit of craning perhaps from those behind the pillars). When the nuns were in position, prayers were recited asking for forgiveness for the past sins of the whole congregation. Then the bishop gave his benediction to the crowd.

The time had now come for the public exorcisms, which were to be led by Father Lactance. Unexpectedly, he told the bishop that he

had just had an inspiration from on high "to present to the said
Urbain Grandier the book of exorcisms and to pray him to exorcize
the said energumens."[44] The bishop consulted briefly with Laubardemont to see that there would be no objection on his part. It was
certainly an unusual procedure to have the supposed sorcerer
demand of his demon allies that they obey him under exorcism.
Laubardemont cautiously avoided any responsibility, telling the
bishop that he did not have the competence to make such a decision;
but he said that, in his opinion, the bishop was free to permit the
procedure if he thought it appropriate. Lactance then repeated his
request to La Rocheposay, promising "that it would result in an
extraordinary effect," and after some hesitation the bishop approved
the request.

Grandier was presented by Lactance with a stole, an item of
priestly vestment. Turning towards his bishop, he went through the
proper formalities. He "asked him if he was permitted to proceed,
to which he replied yes, and Grandier put the stole about his
neck."[45] Lactance then presented Grandier with a book containing
the prayers and ritual of exorcism. Grandier prostrated himself at
the feet of the bishop, lying flat on the floor, face down, with his
arms stretched out at the sides so that his body took the shape of
a cross. This was the way a priest publicly showed his humility on
the altar before God on a solemn occasion; it also declared his
submission to the authority of his bishop. La Rocheposay then gave
him his benediction, after which the hymn "Veni Creator Spiritus"
was chanted, calling on the Holy Spirit to fill everyone present with
a desire to do God's will.

Then Grandier stood up and asked the bishop, "Monseigneur,
whom should I exorcize?"

"These young women," the bishop replied curtly.

"Which young women?" asked Grandier.

"These young women who are possessed."

Grandier then said, "Monseigneur, I am obliged to believe in
possession. The church believes in it, thus I believe in it. But I
consider that a sorcerer cannot possess a Christian without his
consent." This raised a great clamour among the exorcists, for
Grandier was in fact saying that the nuns were not innocent parties
to this affair.[46] The exorcists shouted "that he was a heretic to
advance this belief." Grandier backtracked quickly and replied "that
he had not decided firmly upon the belief determined above, that it
was only his opinion; in any case, he submitted to the opinion of

the body [of the church as a whole], of whom he was but one member." He pointed out that "nobody was ever a heretic for having doubts, but only for having obstinately persevered."

After this incident, Lactance led him towards Sister Catherine de la Présentation. But as Grandier began to exorcize her, the other possessed nuns suddenly burst out with screams and yells. Jeanne des Anges and Claire de Sazilly were louder than all the others in the violence and crudity of their language. They all advanced on him, shrieking, shouting, and reproaching him for his blindness and obstinacy. Obviously, he had no hope of exorcizing them, but he continued to try.

After a while, the mother superior had a period of calm, and Grandier took advantage of it to ask if he was permitted to question her in Greek, to which her "demon" replied through her, "Ah but you really are very stupid! You know very well that it is one of the first conditions of the pact made between you and us that we will not respond in Greek." The bishop nevertheless authorized Grandier to use the language, provided that he first wrote down what he wanted to say. But before the nuns could be put to the test of whether their demons understood Greek, "all the possessed recommenced their cries and their fury, with unequalled desperation, and extraordinary convulsions, each one different."[47] They crowded around Grandier, shouting, screaming, and threatening to break his neck. Indeed, the spectators nearest to the nuns had to hold them back to prevent them from actually doing so. Meanwhile, Grandier stood his ground. With steady eye he looked at the screaming women and protested his innocence, praying to God to be his protector.

Then he turned and spoke to the bishop and Laubardemont, "imploring the royal and ecclesiastic authorities of which they were the ministers, to order these demons to break his neck or at least to make a visible mark on his forehead if he was the author of the crime of which he was accused, so that the glory of God might be manifested, the authority of the church exalted, and himself confounded, provided nevertheless that the women did not touch him with their hands." But La Rocheposay refused to be drawn. He replied "that he had no wish to expose the authority of the church to the ruses of devils who could have already made a pact with Grandier to this end." These words were in direct contradiction to the theories of the exorcists, who had affirmed in their sermons "that the devils could not resist the authority of the church." In the midst of all the drama and excitement, few were conscious of such a theological nuance. But Grandier was sharp enough to pick up on it, and he told the bishop, "If it ever existed, you can break that pact by virtue of the power that God has given to his church."

The bishop did not respond. Possibly, he did not even hear Grandier's reply. The possessed nuns had by now worked themselves up into a state of screaming fury. Roaring and howling, they were acting like drunkards, tearing their clothes to shreds, baring their breasts, assuming the most obscene postures, and furiously hurling themselves against their enemy. Through it all, Grandier remained calm, "as if he had a legion of angels to guard him." But eventually the nuns' attack became so forceful that he would undoubtedly have been torn limb from limb if the spectators had not surrounded him and helped him get out of the church. Even then the nuns did not stop their antics. Not until some time later did the exhausted women, gasping for breath, finally collapse at the feet of their exorcists.

The Trial

In spite of the gravity of the situation, there were some in Loudun who were prepared to treat the affair with humour. Every day posters were found attached to the walls of the churches making fun of the commissioner. One event during an exorcism in the Church of Sainte-Croix was particularly galling to him. When the devil who possessed one of the nuns was ordered by the priests to speak the truth, it proclaimed in a loud voice, "Monsieur de Laubardemont is a cuckold." The commissioner was absent at the time at another exorcism, so the clerk duly transcribed these irreverent words.[1] That evening, when he took the minutes to the commissioner to have them signed, Laubardemont did not bother to read them but simply wrote, as usual, "I confirm that this is a true record." This delightful story flew around the little city. It was the one occasion when the entire population was prepared to believe that what the devils said during the exorcisms was true. The minutes were suppressed!

Furious with the townspeople who had dared to attack him, Laubardemont determined to find out who they were. At the exorcisms, he asked the possessed nuns and their devils to name the authors of the placards attached every night to the door of the Church of Sainte-Croix. The demon named a Huguenot, two other people, and some young scholars. The commissioner had them arrested, but a few days later he was forced to release them for lack of evidence. Now more angry than ever, he placed a guard on duty day and night at the door of the church to prevent further placards, and he issued the following proclamation:

It is expressly forbidden to anybody of any rank or condition to speak disparagingly against the nuns and other persons of Loudun afflicted with evil spirits, their exorcists or anybody else connected, on pain of a penalty of ten thousand livres fine or more, and of corporal punishment if it be considered necessary. And to ensure that nobody may claim ignorance of this order it shall be read publicly from the pulpit of each parish church of the city and attached to the doors of each church and elsewhere as necessary.

Issued at Loudun this Sunday the second day of July 1634.

Jean-Martin de Laubardemont[2]

Having silenced the troublemakers, Laubardemont began to assemble the body of magistrates who, with him presiding, would sit as Grandier's judges. He chose prominent magistrates from Chinon, Châtellerault, La Flèche, Tours, Poitiers, and Orléans among other places. Laubardemont has been criticized for selecting a body of judges who were inimical to Grandier, and there is no doubt that he chose men who would recognize that the king and cardinal expected a guilty verdict. But these were not men who would pay only lip service to justice. They were all highly qualified and experienced magistrates. The mass of evidence against the priest was considerable both in terms of the number of witnesses who testified against him and in the weight of the testimony of the demons. These men were not theologians. Since the priests in Loudun had given their firm opinion that the devil under constraint of exorcism was bound to tell the truth, they as magistrates would accept the testimony from the exorcisms.[3]

The commission met for the first time on 26 July 1634. However, it was only on 28 July that Grandier learned the composition of the court that was charged with passing judgment on him. He promptly wrote to his mother asking her to have ready various documents necessary for his defence. He told her that he was accused of two things, immoral behaviour and sorcery:

As to the first, I was interrogated on the facts of the first accusation against me. [He is referring here to the accusations made against him to the bishop of Poitiers in 1629.] In response to which I said that I was cleared of that, and that this could be proved by a review of my four sentences of absolution; two from the présidial of Poitiers, and two others from the Archbishop of Bordeaux ...

The second accusation concerns magic and the sickness of the nuns. On this I have nothing to say except the constant truth that I am completely innocent and wrongly accused ... As to the rest, I leave everything to the providence of God, to the witness of my conscience, and to the equity of my judges, for whose enlightenment I continually pray to God.

It seems that he still did not realize that his fate was already sealed.

THE CASE AGAINST GRANDIER

Seventy-two witnesses appeared before the judges at Grandier's trial as Laubardemont built up his case to prove that the Ursuline nuns were indeed possessed (rather than being sick, charlatans, or the victims of manipulation) and that Grandier was the sorcerer responsible for their plight.[4] Much of the evidence collected over the previous months was now brought forward to prove him guilty of witchcraft. First there was his pact with the Devil. Under exorcism, the demons possessing Jeanne des Anges had been forced to give up their pacts, which contained material that was accepted as having originated with the accused priest. Then there was the evidence about the sabbath, and this is where Elisabeth Blanchard's evidence was so important. It will be recalled that she was one of the possessed seculars and a friend of Susanne Hammon (the sister of Marie de Medici's "shoemaker"). When Madeleine de Brou could not be proved to be Grandier's acolyte, Elisabeth had come forward and accused the priest not only of having had carnal relations with her but of inviting her to a sabbath with him – accusations which Susanne Hammon had confirmed.

It was known that a witch could take another form, the most common being a man in black or grey, a shadowy figure, or a black cat or dog. This ability to assume the appearance of a cat is what had made Mignon's exorcisms of the convent pet "rational" (if no less amusing). The very first spectre, the one seen by Sister Marthe, had been a shadowed man dressed in black – which was why she had been so frightened. Although the spectres seen by the nuns during the following weeks changed in appearance, they were all of a dark and shadowy nature and were recognized as demonic. This is why the nuns' accusations that the spectre was Grandier were so easily accepted as valid evidence against him at his trial.

Then there were the insensitive "devil's marks." Mannoury's procedure had been normal (even if his alleged fraud had been grievous), and Grandier's "insensitive" marks were taken as fully admissible evidence against him. Furthermore, Grandier was later found to possess the well-known ability of witches to resist the pain of torture. It was also known that witches could not cry tears (because they dreaded salt) and could not look on a crucifix.[5] Both of these "proofs" of guilt were ultimately laid against Grandier.[6]

As for proof that the nuns were indeed possessed, the testimony of the vast majority of participants at the various exorcisms was more than enough to persuade the judges that real demonic possession existed in Loudun; but what really convinced them was the extraordinary behaviour of these women of good family.[7] Here was a group of respectable women who had been known all their lives as perfectly normal "nice" young ladies, and suddenly they had begun to do things that were totally out of character and were increasingly horrific. Particularly terrifying were the many voices of the demons possessing the nuns, which changed as one demon took over from another. In the case of Françoise Fillatreau, "several voices were heard disputing with each other at the same time."[8]

Then there were the extraordinary contortions of the nuns:

Sometimes ... they passed their left foot over their shoulders to their cheeks. They also raised their feet up to their heads, until their big toes touched their nose. Others again were able to stretch their legs so far to the left and right that they sat on the ground, without any space being visible between their bodies and the floor. One, the Mother Superior, stretched her legs to such an extraordinary extent that, from toe to toe, the distance was seven feet, though she herself was but four feet high.[9]

Another description comes from a contemporary, named Deniau, who said that the nuns

struck their chests and backs with their heads, as if they had their necks broken, and with inconceivable rapidity ... Their faces became so frightful one could not bear to look at them; their eyes remained open without winking. Their tongues issued suddenly from their mouths, horribly swollen, black, hard, and covered with pimples ... They threw themselves back till their heads touched their feet, and walked in this position with wonderful rapidity, and for a long time. They uttered cries so horrible and loud that nothing like it was ever heard before.[10]

Another eyewitness recorded:

Asmodée made her face swell up in an instant, and it was so frightful that, without exaggeration, it was three times its normal size, and above all, her eyes instantaneously became as large as those of a horse; she held this posture for more than a quarter of an hour; and then suddenly, in an instant, returned to her natural state, which was that of a beautiful young woman. During the time she was so disfigured, the doctor from the Sorbonne tested her pulse and found it to be quite normal.[11]

One of the exorcists who spent months with the nuns left his own description:

I saw something which surprised me greatly, and which was common to all the Possessed: which is that being on their backs, their head came towards their feet, and they walked about that way with surprising speed and for a very long time …

Nearly all moved their heads with movements so violent that nobody could see it without saying that they were not human.

Their cries were strange beyond belief. It was the howling of damned souls, of enraged wolves, of horrible beasts. One cannot imagine the force with which they cried. There was nothing in it that could be called human.

The Mother Superior made a contortion twisting her arms at the shoulder joints, elbows, and wrists, and making a complete turn of each one of them … She rested her abdomen on the ground, joined her feet together, and turning her arms back, joined her hands and her feet. And to create this position, she made a complete turn of each joint of the wrist, elbow, and shoulder.

One thing that was common to all the possessed women was that all the travails and horrible agitations that they underwent during the exorcisms, and which were so violent that it sometimes took the strongest of people to restrain them, caused no increase in their pulse rate, which stayed as normal as if they were in their perfectly ordinary state.[12]

Reinforcing the certainty of most observers that the nuns were possessed was their unnatural indecency. They uttered blasphemies and obscenities and behaved with the greatest immodesty: "Sister Claire de Sazilly fell to the ground blaspheming, in convulsions, lifting up her petticoats and chemise, displaying her private parts without any shame and uttering filthy words. Her gestures became so indecent that the audience averted its eyes. She cried out again and again, abusing herself with her hands, 'Come on, then, f—

me!' Yet when she returned to her normal state, she had no recollection."[13]

Eroticism seems to have been a universal feature of those stricken. The official accounts of the trial record that "all the nuns, both those possessed and those who were free of it, as well as the Seculars, had a strong disordered love for the Accused; he was seen day and night in the Convent soliciting them to make love, over a period of four months."[14] The official records tell us that one of the nuns "was so strongly tempted to make love with her sweetheart, whom she said to be Grandier, that one day as the time approached to receive Holy Communion, she suddenly got up and went up to her bedroom, where, having been followed by one of the other nuns, she was seen with a crucifix in her hands which she was preparing to satisfy her evil desire, having already stuffed it under her skirt."[15] Gayot de Petaval gives an account of the same incident, identifying this nun as Claire de Sazilly.[16] He states that she "was one day overcome with desire to satisfy her passion, which she declared openly, and being unable to prevent herself she got up in church and went straight to her room, where she was seen like a person beside herself in violent and indecent movements which gave the suggestion of fires that she could not quench; this was given as a proof against the accused."[17]

This eroticism was contagious. At the trial, a number of respectable women gave evidence of their inexplicable infatuation with the accused priest. The official record states:

Three women came forward, of whom the first said that one day after having received communion from the Accused, who looked at her fixedly during that action, she was unwittingly surprised by a violent love for him, which began with a little tremor throughout her body ...

The [second woman] said that being stopped by him in the street he gave her his hand and that, unwittingly, she also was overcome by a strong passion for him. The [third woman] said that after having seen him at the door of the church of the Carmelites, where he entered with the Procession, she was so overcome by emotion and had such great bodily impulses that she willingly longed to make love with him ... She had no particular inclination towards him either before or after and was, besides, very virtuous and of very good reputation.[18]

Finally, there was the professional verdict of the doctors who had been called in to give an opinion. As mentioned earlier, most of them were from small towns around Loudun, and Grandier had complained about their quality as well as about the fact that some were friends or relatives of his enemies.[19] But four medical doctors from the Sorbonne had also been called in – men of the greatest authority, who were totally independent of local prejudice.[20] All these doctors had for months been in a position to observe and assess the nuns, and they found that "after having observed the agitations and movements of these young women, they consider them to be supernatural and to proceed from a cause where all the knowledge of their art can do little for their effects."[21] The certificates of their observations clearly established that they were faced with something that was not of this world. In this conclusion they reflected the medical knowledge of their time.

These facts go far to explain why so many people were ready to treat Grandier as a malevolent sorcerer. To Tranquille, Lactance, Barré, and even Laubardemont, he was a very dangerous criminal, armed with all the magic powers of the Devil. Much of the injustice inflicted on Grandier seemed totally justifiable, appropriate, and even righteous to those who believed him to be an agent of the Devil. Once the exorcists had become convinced of the truth of the possessions, it had been easy for them to believe that they saw the supernatural phenomena required by the church to prove demonic possession. These were the same proofs which the archbishop of Bordeaux had laid down a year and a half before: signs of levitation (the raising of the possessed person in the air without any means of suspension); the ability to know the secret thoughts of others; and the ability to speak and understand strange languages. They found all of these – or thought they did.

They thought the nuns could speak foreign languages that were unknown by them because they interpreted what they heard as being what they expected to hear. They found levitation in the case of the mother superior, who seemed to be floating in the air during one of her convulsions. (They ignored the person who lifted her long robes and saw that she was balanced on her toes and head, the classical "rainbow" position.) And they truly believed that Jeanne des Anges knew other people's secret thoughts. A well-known example of her capabilities occurred some months after Grandier's death. The new exorcist who had been brought in, Father Surin, was amazed when, on meeting Jeanne des Anges for the first time, she asked about a particular friend of his in a way that showed she knew the details of their friendship.[22] Since he came from far away, he thought it impossible that she could know about this relationship and that therefore she had the power to read his thoughts. He was unaware of her ability to manipulate people. Long after his death, Jeanne des Anges wrote that when Father Surin was coming, she found out as much about him as she could. Probably, she got the details of this friendship from one of his fellow Jesuits in Loudun.

Once the levitation and other phenomena were established, a detailed record of the occurrences was sent to the Sorbonne asking for confirmation that this was a case of true possession. Faced with such an impressive body of evidence, the Sorbonne supported the proposition. For Laubardemont and all the others concerned, the Sorbonne's approval made the case against Grandier watertight.[23] Most of all, it was the convulsions and the fact that the nuns were clearly not in possession of themselves that condemned Grandier. One or two individual cases might have been dismissed as an unknown sickness, but who could explain a whole convent as well as a number of cases in the town itself? There were too many afflicted. A handful of sceptics did attribute the events to some form of sickness, usually referred to as "melancholy," an expression that covered a number of mental disturbances and had little solid medical recognition, but for the great majority there could be only one reasonable explanation – possession.

Two hundred and fifty years later, the physician Jean-Martin Charcot and his disciple Paul Richer completed their landmark study of a considerable number of women who suffered from very similar symptoms as those evinced by the nuns in Loudun. It was Charcot and his disciples in the Salpêtrière of Paris who identified, classified, and detailed the medical condition now known as hysteria.[24] Here is a modern description of the symptoms of hysteria:

The essential traits are as follows. Imagine that after a period marked by rigidity extending to the whole body, and by gnashings of teeth so violent as to break them, there follows a phase of clownish movements, during which the convulsive patient expresses rage and fury, shouts, struggles, insults, blasphemes, curses, seems literally mad – and we still have only a faint image of what Charcot and Richer called the major demoniacal-hysterical crisis. One would really think that the person was suddenly transformed, that an alien influence was controlling him and providing him with strength, skill, daring and inventions, which his own nature could not provide.[25]

The typical convulsions found in the Salpêtrière were sketched by Richer and recorded for history. Some of the postures and behaviour exhibited during a hysterical attack show the modern reader a little of what was seen in Loudun.[26]

All the other characteristics evidenced by the afflicted nuns and seculars were found by Charcot in his patients, including the swallowing and regurgitation of objects (in Jeanne des Anges' case, the pacts), the awakening without memory of the "possession," and the unexpectedly normal pulse rate during the attack. Charcot and his team even discovered that the condition was contagious. Once one of the patients started to do something, others began to perform the same actions. In time, it became recognized that certain living conditions were conducive to the development of this contagious hysteria. These conditions were found in restricted communities – for example, convents, orphanages, and, in certain wartime conditions, military units – when under stress. Another finding echoes the events of the convent in Loudun: "Charcot, in every one of his lectures, insisted strongly on this: it is very difficult, in the account given of these subjects, to distinguish the false from the true, illusion from fact. Not that illusion can always be taken for pretence or voluntary lying; this may derive from a disturbance of judgment, a retreat of the mind into the state of childhood, which is known for its aptitude to create myths and inventions, void of foundation and perfectly disinterested."[27] So one of the keys to the puzzle of Loudun only became available centuries later – far too late to save Grandier.

CONDEMNATION

The records of the trial leading to Grandier's death, although succinct, consist of close to five thousand sheets of legal paper. The judges took eighteen full days, working six hours a day, to complete the trial.[28] Before even beginning, they had gone in procession from the Church of Saint-Pierre-du-Marché to the Carmelite convent[29] to celebrate High Mass. All the judges received communion, and Father Lactance preached a sermon "against those who did not believe in the possession or that the devils under exorcism must tell the truth." Then, addressing the judges, he compared them to "the cherubim whom God has placed at the gates of Paradise with a sword." He stressed that theirs was a "flaming" sword and that consequently they must be "flaming" in the work on which they were embarking.

He concluded by accusing Grandier of having committed all sorts of abominations.[30]

During their time in Loudun, the judges continued to attend mass every morning and to implore God's help in their task of serving justice. The Capuchins in their preaching continued to rail against Grandier and to state that the judges should have him burned, along with all heretics. On the other hand, the Cordeliers, though they had a long-standing rivalry with Grandier, refused to involve themselves, "not wishing," they said, "to wash their hands in the blood of this man." Besides, they held to the opinion that "devils even under exorcism are always liars." Clearly, not all theologians, even in Loudun, were in agreement with the doctrine on the devils preached by the Capuchins, which they claimed was supported by all the best authorities.[31]

This doctrine on the devils now became a matter of serious concern to the *bailli*, de Cerisay, as well as to a number of other leading citizens, for the Capuchins, led by Lactance and Tranquille, were openly preaching not only that Grandier ought to be burned but that other heretics, notably those who supported Grandier, should be burned too. The next development was predictable. The devils under exorcism started to name names. By the rules the Capuchins had laid down, to be named by the devils was to be guilty. Nobody was safe. Already some men whose only crime was to be courageous partisans of Grandier had been accused of the most heinous crimes. Two priests, Jean Buron[32] and Roger Frogier, had been denounced by one of the demoniacs under exorcism of having tried to violate her, and only with the greatest difficulty had they been able to prove their innocence.[33]

As always, it was Madeleine de Brou who was most viciously attacked. Through Jeanne des Anges, she was now accused of being a sorcerer. Laubardemont ordered her arrest, which took place at the Church of Sainte-Croix, where she was praying with a number of other young women.[34] She was led under armed guard to the house of an official who was given the task of guarding her. However, Laubardemont had not taken account of the fact that the de Brous were a powerful local family related to many nobles and notables. As a faction, they were as important in Loudun as Trincant and his extensive family compact. Thus, Laubardemont was immediately faced with the angry protests of Madeleine's many powerful relatives. He gave the order for her release two days later, though not without a warning that the matter was not finished with.

Some other young women, suspect through having taken up the defence of Grandier, became the butt of all sorts of allegations. One of the nuns, under possession, claimed that they had "magic pacts" on them. The commissioner found the women in the Church of Sainte-Croix and had them arrested and sent to the Capuchins for investigation. There was now a serious danger that what had happened in many other witchcraft scares was about to happen in Loudun. First, those associated with the accused sorcerer were accused of having been recruited. Then some, under torture, implicated others, naming whoever the exorcists suggested. This prospect became even more real when Tranquille, in the first days of August, published a resumé of the doctrine the Capuchins had been teaching since the beginning of the possession.[35] This, in a sense, changed their preaching into teaching. It gave the doctrine a formality that it had not had before.

Recognizing the danger, de Cerisay and his supporting officers called for a public assembly of Loudun's leading citizens. Trincant's allies and relatives, including Moussaut, Hervé, and Menuau, were summoned under the same proclamation as the others, though they tried in vain to prevent the meeting, claiming it was illegal. Most of the Loudun magistrates agreed that it was important to bring an end to the accusations of the demoniacs, and they decided to send a delegation to Paris to put their concerns before the king. The meeting selected the *bailli* and his lieutenant to carry out this delicate mission. Although this decision was recorded as being unanimous, it seems unlikely that it was. The magistracy of Loudun was by now split into two factions, one led by de Cerisay and the Chauvets, the other led by Moussaut, Hervé, and Menuau. Probably only a proportion, though a majority, approved of the action taken. In retrospect, this has all the appearances of a stacked meeting in which the *bailli*'s adherents were the majority. The document to be carried to the king began:

Sire, the officers and inhabitants of the town of Loudun find it necessary to have recourse to your Majesty, drawing to his attention very humbly that in the exorcisms being conducted in the said town on the nuns of Saint Ursula and on some other young women, said to be possessed by evil spirits, something very prejudicial to the public and to the tranquillity of your faithful subjects is being committed in that some of the exorcists are abusing their office and the authority of the church by asking questions in the exorcisms which tend to the defamation of the best families in the said town, and M. de Laubardemont the counsellor deputed by Your Majesty has already placed so much faith in the sayings and responses of these demons that on a false accusation made by them he entered the house of a lady with public show, followed by a considerable crowd, to seek for imagined books of Magic.[36]

The letter asked the king to refer the Capuchin doctrine on the devils to the doctors of the Sorbonne "so that they might judge and censure it, and so that the supplicants could protect themselves in the courts against the false accusations that were being made." De Cerisay and Louis Chauvet left for Paris the next day to deliver this document. De Cerisay also carried a long appeal that Grandier had written from his prison, begging for justice from Louis XIII.[37] With his usual verve, Grandier flayed Laubardemont and the exorcists. But the king had great faith in Laubardemont, a trusted and experienced man, and he was already satisfied of Grandier's guilt. Thus, he saw no need to receive the envoys of the town, despite the entreaties of d'Armagnac. Neither the magistrates nor Grandier received any reply. Meanwhile, the judicial commission issued an order annulling the meeting that had taken place at the town hall and forbidding any similar meeting under penalty of a fine of twenty thousand livres.[38]

By this time, the bishop of Poitiers had long since left Loudun. Having exercised his ecclesiastical functions – seen and questioned the nuns and been present at the exorcisms – it was appropriate that he should withdraw, leaving the secular authorities a clear field to hear the evidence and dispense justice. But the secular authorities had to have his episcopal confirmation that the possessions were valid, and on 10 August 1634 he sent them a decree from his chateau at Dissay stating that "the Ursuline nuns were truly tormented by demons and possessed by evil spirits." Grandier was immediately told about this document. It was a terrible setback for him, for it left him without any defence. He suffered a further blow when he learned of the document in which the theological doctors of the Sorbonne had given their opinion that there was a case of true possession here.[39]

Everything was now ready for the final act of the trial. The investigation was completed, and the commissioner had only to submit the findings to the judges. By virtue of the doctrine of the exorcists, all the depositions covering what the nuns and their demons had said under exorcism were admitted as the truth. However, there were several important pieces of evidence that had not been recorded. Some eight months earlier, around the beginning of 1634, Laubardemont had been approached by Jeanne des Anges:

After having made her deposition, while [Laubardemont was] receiving that of another nun, [the mother superior], dressed in her chemise, her head bare, with a rope around her neck and a candle in one hand, stood in the pouring rain in the courtyard for a period of two hours. And when the door of the parlour was opened to her, she threw herself on her knees in front of Sieur Laubardemont, declaring to him that she had come to admit the sin she had committed in accusing an innocent Grandier. Then when she withdrew; she tied the rope to a tree in the garden and would have strangled herself had the other nuns not run to her aid.[40]

Sister Agnes of Saint Jean, the "beautiful little devil" who was so sorely tried by sexual impulses, also attempted to confess to having falsely accused an innocent man. She sought on a number of occasions to declare that she was not possessed. And Sister Claire de Sazilly, on 5 and 7 July, with tears in her eyes, confessed that she was not possessed and that what she had said in the course of the previous two weeks had been a total calumny. On 7 July she suddenly took flight and tried to escape from the Church of Notre-Dame-du-Château where they were exorcizing her, but she was caught and brought back.[41] However, Laubardemont and the various priests placed no reliability on these confessions. They concluded that far from proving Grandier innocent, they proved him guilty, for they were an example of his powers. He could even make the nuns state that he was innocent and that they were the guilty parties.[42]

On 15, 16, and 17 August, Grandier was at last brought before the judges at the convent of the Carmelites. This was merely a formality, for he had no defence that would be acceptable. These sessions were held in secret, but thanks to the indiscretion of one of the judges, word leaked out that Grandier bore himself with dignity and replied with great presence of mind to the questions put to him. His lawyer read a document to the judges which the curé had written in his own defence. In a clear and logical argument, Grandier demonstrated all the weaknesses of the case brought against him and demolished piece by piece the scaffolding of proofs that Laubardemont had taken three months to build. Then he made his last plea, appealing for justice from these men. He did this in a written "Factum," which he had prepared in his cell.[43] It had no effect.[44]

Torture and Death

On the evening of 17 August, the judges held public prayers to implore God's aid in helping them search their consciences and do their duty. The following day, at five o'clock in the morning, they met at the Carmelite convent to give their judgment.[1] Without calling the curé of Saint-Pierre to the bar, the sentence was read out:

We declare the said Urbain Grandier duly guilty of the crime of sorcery, evil spells, and the possession visited upon some Ursuline nuns of this town of Loudun and of other laywomen mentioned at the trial, together with other crimes resulting from the above. For redress of these, he has been condemned and is condemned to make Honourable Amends with head bared, a rope around his neck, and holding in his hand a burning candle of two pounds weight, before the main doors of the churches of Saint-Pierre-du-Marché and Sainte-Ursule of this town of Loudun and there, devoutly kneeling, ask pardon of God, the King, and of Justice. He is to be taken to the Place of Sainte-Croix of this said town, to be tied to a post on a pile of faggots that is to be built in the said Place. There his body is to be burned alive together with the magic pacts and characters, and together with the manuscript book composed by him against the celibacy of the priesthood,[2] and his ashes are to be scattered to the winds. We have declared and now declare all and each of his goods confiscated to the King out of which shall be taken the sum of five hundred livres tournois to be employed on the purchase of a sheet of copper on which will be engraved this sentence and which will be placed in a prominent position in the said church of the Ursulines to stay there in perpetuity. Prior to proceeding with the execution of the said sentence, we order that the said Grandier be subjected to torture ordinary and extraordinary on the truth about his accomplices.

Issued at Loudun, 18 August 1634, and carried out the same day.

Grandier showed no surprise when this terrifying sentence was brought to him in his cell. He had expected no less. The attitude of the judges when he had appeared before them had clearly forecast what their decision was going to be. Moreover, on 15 August an officer close to the court had told him confidentially that the decision against him had already been made. That same day an Augustinian, Father Ambroise, had been permitted to see him; touched by the comforting words of this priest, Grandier had made a general confession of all his sins and had received communion from him. When Laubardemont heard this, he forbade Ambroise to visit the prisoner again. He did, however, authorize a Capuchin, Father Archange, to visit Grandier, but this monk gave no comfort. Two days before the sentence was pronounced, he informed Grandier that he was going to die. "God wishes to be glorified by my constancy," Grandier replied, "and if it is necessary that I should die, I pray God that it may serve as an expiation for my sins and my crimes." When Archange saw that Grandier accepted the news of his approaching torment with resignation, he broke off the interview.[3]

As soon as the sentence was passed, the first steps were taken to carry it out. On Laubardemont's orders, a surgeon named Fourneau was sent to Grandier's prison under the guard of two armed police officers. His task was to prepare Grandier for his torture and execution. On entering the room that served as a cell, Fourneau heard the curé railing against his old enemy, the surgeon Mannoury, who had arrived a few moments before: "Cruel butcher, have you come to finish it off? Unfeeling creature, you know the cruelties you have practised on my body, come on, finish it, kill me!"[4] Mannoury, who had probably been sent to work with Fourneau, was taken aback and left immediately. One of the officers present then told Fourneau that he would have to carry out the order by himself, "that is to say to shave Grandier and to remove from him all the hair from his head, his face, and from every part of his body." It was standard practice to do this to a witch because it was believed that the demons could hide in the hair of the head and body and thus might place spells on the magistrates, exorcists, torturers, and any other people present. Similarly, they avoided looking a witch straight in the eye, for this was another means by which a spell could be cast on them.

While Grandier was being shaved, Laubardemont arrived at the prison, and in a refinement of cruelty and to disfigure the victim completely, he ordered Fourneau to pull out Grandier's eyebrows and nails.[5] Fourneau objected – a dangerous thing to do with a man like Laubardemont – and even though Grandier assured him that he was ready for any suffering to be inflicted on him, Fourneau firmly refused to carry out this savage act. Indeed, with tears in his eyes, he begged Grandier to forgive him for putting his hands on him to shave him. Touched by his compassion, the curé said, "Monsieur, you are the only one who has had any pity for me," to which the surgeon replied, "Don't believe that, Monsieur, you don't see all the others."[6] Fourneau shaved all of Grandier's body and found "no marks other than natural ones except on his shoulder a little flat mark on his skin,[7] with another on his back which was slightly raised." These two places were very sensitive.[8]

It was about nine o'clock in the morning before these preparations were completed. Grandier was then made ready to be taken to the Palais de Loudun, where the death sentence that had been issued the previous day would be formally delivered to him. In place of his own clothes, he was given some sorry rags, and his hands were tied. Laubardemont did not even grant him shoes to wear; the prisoner had to make do with a pair of old worn slippers. At the door of his prison, as he bade farewell to the Bontemps couple who had been his jailers, he said, "You see how my enemies triumph over me. However, I forgive them all the evil they have done."[9]

Laubardemont had taken the precaution of sending his own closed coach to transport the curé, and Grandier climbed into it, accompanied by two officers of the law. Armed police escorted them, and there were guards all along the route. As the carriage made its way through the streets, it was surrounded by great crowds on this warm and sunny morning. But at the Palais de Loudun all was cool and quiet: cool because the heat of the August day had not yet warmed the stone of the building; quiet because precautions had been taken by the mayor of the town, Mesmin de Silly, not to allow anybody to enter the audience chamber except those authorized by the commissioner.

Even so, the hall was packed. The wives of the judges and numerous noble ladies of the district had been admitted into the enclosed tribunal area, where they occupied the seats normally reserved for the judges of the court. In the middle of this elegant group sat Laubardemont's wife, even though she was of lower rank than a number of others present. She was clearly bursting with pride at the exploits of her husband, but he bore himself with studied modesty; he sat in the place normally reserved for the court clerk, while the clerk himself stood before him. Near at hand in the body of the court (and below the ladies seated on the dais) were more guards, smart and polished. It was standing room only for the rest of the invited guests – the cream of Loudun society.

Before the ill-clothed and freshly shorn priest was brought before this illustrious audience, Fathers Lactance and Tranquille, armed with their holy water sprinklers, carefully exorcized him to force the devils to leave his person. Then, entering the chamber, they exorcized "the air, the earth and the other elements."[10] Meanwhile, Grandier was kept at the extreme end of the room so that the exorcisms would have time to take effect. After a short while, Laubardemont ordered him to be led into the tribunal enclosure and brought before the judges, who were ranged below the ladies. As Grandier approached, he humbly fell to his knees, but he could do nothing about uncovering his head because his hands were tied behind his back. However, the court clerk, perhaps with the aim of distinguishing himself, seized the condemned man's hat and skullcap and threw them at Laubardemont's feet saying, "Turn, wretch, and adore the crucifix which is above the judge." Grandier did everything he was ordered and stayed some time in mental prayer, quite motionless.

The clerk then began to read the sentence in a loud voice, which could easily be heard throughout the now silent chamber. This took some time, for it was quite long. Grandier listened with composure and then addressed himself to the judges: "Messieurs, I call on God the Father, the Son, and the Holy Ghost and the Virgin, my sole advocate, to witness that I have never been a sorcerer or committed sacrilege, or known any other magic except that of the Holy Scripture, which I have always preached. I acknowledge my Saviour and pray that the blood of His Passion may save me."[11] Then he pleaded with the judges to moderate the severity of his punishment and have pity on his soul. His great fear was that in the middle of the torments that awaited him he would be overcome with despair and cease to have hope in the mercy of God. He praised the martyrs who had endured their torments for the honour of Jesus Christ, and he expressed the hope that although he was not worthy to be compared to them, he might repay by his constancy and his bearing all the faults of his past life. These words were said with tears.

According to an eyewitness, this speech made a profound impression on the judges, and even more so on the ladies. Laubardemont now ordered the chamber to be cleared. Some authors give the impression that he did so because this sympathy for Grandier did not sit well with him. But it seems more likely that the hall was cleared because the public theatre of the staged reading of the sentence was now complete. The next act was to be a private one between the judges and the condemned man, in which he would be given an opportunity to name his accomplices in magic. This would be followed by the judicial torture designed to force from him the confession of his own guilt and the implication of his accomplices.

Laubardemont now approached Grandier and spoke to him in a low voice, with his mouth close to Grandier's ear so that nobody could hear what was being said. After a while, Grandier asked for paper, but he was refused. This exchange seems to have annoyed Laubardemont, for he now began to hector Grandier loudly. He told him that the best means of obtaining a reduction of his sentence would be to reveal the names of his accomplices. Grandier replied "that he was a great sinner, but that he had never committed the crime of which he was accused." Laubardemont then drew from his pocket a paper and ordered Grandier to sign it, confessing to his crimes. But Grandier remained adamant; he refused to put his signature to the paper. In an effort to get him to do so, the commissioner tried both promises and threats, as well as prayers and even tears. He reminded Grandier of the terrors that awaited him in the afterlife if he died without confessing his crimes, and entreated him not to lose his soul by remaining so obstinately silent.[12]

In similar circumstances, the priest Gaufridy had made a general confession of totally imaginary crimes from fear of the punishment that faced him. But Grandier was a different man. He refused to make a false confession even though the assembled magistrates impressed on him "that thirteen of them had sat as judges at his trial and that with one voice they had declared him duly guilty and convicted of crimes of magic, sorcery, etc., and that they were fully certain that he was a sorcerer."[13] Since he remained obdurate, the judges had only one recourse; they agreed that he should be subjected to the torture prescribed in his sentence. Accordingly, orders were given for Grandier to be taken to the torture chamber. Thus began the next act of the tragedy.

Grandier begged his judges to allow him to have present the Augustinian priest who had confessed him the previous Tuesday so that he might have his support during the torture. Laubardemont had no intention of allowing any priest who was not convinced of Grandier's guilt to get close to the condemned man. For justice to be served, Laubardemont had to exact from Grandier a confession of guilt to the judges, which would be followed by confession to a priest in order to save Grandier's soul. Grandier would be less likely to admit his guilt if he was supported by a sympathetic priest. Anyway, the Augustinian had already been given orders to leave Loudun. Grandier's request for Father Grillau, a staunch friend, was also refused. At this, Grandier said to the judges, "Messieurs, I see clearly now what you have in mind. Not only do you want to make a martyr of my body, but you want me to lose my soul by being thrown into despair.[14] One day you will have to settle your account with my Redeemer. At least give me a half hour so that I may confess to God, so that in these last moments I may beg him to give me the strength to face the pains you are preparing for me."[15]

Grandier was granted a quarter of an hour. As he prayed, one of the officers present copied down his words, and the prayer was later shown to others, despite Laubardemont's orders forbidding this. Grandier prayed:

Great God and sovereign judge, supporter of the oppressed, come to my aid and give me the strength to submit to the pains to which I am condemned. Receive my soul into the beatitude of the saints, forgive me all my sins and pardon me, the most vile and despicable of your servants.

Oh you, who are the sole judge of souls, you know that I am not in any way guilty of the crimes that I am accused of and that the fire that I will have to submit to is nothing other than a punishment for my concupiscence.

Grant pardon also, Redeemer of the human race, to my enemies and denouncers, but make them recognize their sins that they may show penitence to you.

Good Holy Virgin, protector of penitents, deign to admit my poor and unfortunate mother into your heavenly company, console her for the loss of her zealous son, who fears no other pains than those she will endure on this earth, from which he will soon be separated.

When Grandier's brief period of prayer was over, they started on the torture. They used the method called the *brodequins*, or "laced boots," which was the usual judicial torture in Loudun at that time; it was applied only to those condemned to death because many never survived it. First, the executioner and his assistants removed Grandier's clothes. Then they laid him on a wooden frame. They tied his arms "and along each side of each leg placed two boards, one inside and one outside, which they held tight against the leg by tying them firmly at the knee and above the ankle" in such a way that the cords that ran around the boards left enough space "to insert wedges." When each of the legs had been dealt with in this way, they were both tied together with heavy rope. While these preparations were going on, the two presiding priests, Tranquille and Lactance, were exorcizing the wedges, the mallets, and the cords.[16]

The chamber was small and crowded. The two exorcists[17] placed themselves at the head and foot of the torture frame, while the burly executioner and his assistants stood at one side of it. Between Grandier and the door were the officers of the court who had to be present as witnesses and those judges who wished to be present. There were not many of the latter after the first few minutes, for few had much stomach for this work. Outside in the corridor were those who were not important enough to gain entry to the chamber but who wanted to see and hear what was going on. Throughout the torture, the door was half open much of the time as officers and judges came and went.

On a signal given by Laubardemont, the hideous work began. The executioners inserted the first wedges – with blows from a mallet – between the middle planks "at knee level, and farther down at the level of the feet."[18] A horrible cracking sound was heard, for the bones had been broken with the blow to the wedge. The condemned man uttered a terrible cry of pain and fainted. They revived him as soon as they could, and when he was fully conscious, the judges and their officers demanded that he confess and that he name his accomplices. But Grandier would only plead his innocence. Accordingly, two more wedges were inserted. Lactance shouted to the executioner, "Hammer, hammer, hammer!" When Grandier heard these words, he said to the Recollet, "Oh, Father, where is the charity of Saint Francis?"[19]

Still they were only at the fourth wedge. Grandier's screams soon became so horrific that more people left the chamber, and in the corridor outside the audience melted away. Most of those who remained had to stay because their duty demanded it. Between each

The torture of the *brodequins*.
Source: A sketch, based on the records,
by Alex M. Johnston

blow of the mallet, the judges and priests demanded that Grandier confess. Sometimes their words were gentle, but more often they shouted in anger, especially Lactance. Meanwhile, Grandier lay in agony, his legs more and more fractured. From time to time he fainted only to be revived for further blows.

The executioner showed Grandier four more wedges as a promise of what was in store. Then the blows were redoubled. And still the curé would admit to nothing. "My God, do not abandon me!" he cried. "Don't let the torments I am suffering at this moment make me forget your holy name." At each cry of pain torn from the condemned man, Lactance yelled, "Tell! Tell!" He repeated the words with such rage that people afterwards referred to him as Father Tell.[20] Like virtually everyone in the chamber, Lactance genuinely believed that he was in the presence of a sorcerer and that the sorcery had to be rooted out and destroyed. Everyone knew that the devil's agents did not act alone, so it would not be enough to burn Grandier. The protection of all the people of the town demanded that the torture continue until his accomplices were named. That is why the priests and judges were so persistent.

When Lactance became exhausted, Tranquille took over, but with no better success. When pressed to confess, Grandier would only say, "Father, answer me on your own conscience, do you believe that any man is permitted to admit to a crime he has not committed in order to be delivered from even such pain as this?" Not only did Grandier continue to insist that he was neither a sorcerer nor sacrilegious, but three or four times during the torture he renounced the Devil and all his works. By the time the eighth wedge was about to be driven in, he had still, according to Legué, admitted only one thing, "that he had been too much a man, that he had loved women, but that since his sentence in Poitiers he had ceased and had done nothing scandalous."[21] Gayot de Petaval provides another detail, saying that "he admitted that he had delivered himself up of the pleasures of the flesh, but that he had composed his Treatise on Celibacy to overcome the scruples of a young woman with whom he had had relations for seven years ... He begged his judges not to make him reveal her name or specify the details of his sins."[22] Since the judges were desperate to know the names of Grandier's accomplices, it is interesting that they did not press him to reveal the name of this woman. One record says that Grandier had earlier revealed the name privately to Laubardemont.[23] Clearly, the woman was not Madeleine de Brou, or much would have been made of the fact. It was someone they wanted to protect, possibly Philippe Trincant.

What the priests and judges did repeatedly concentrate on was the case of Elisabeth Blanchard, one of the possessed laywomen.[24] It will be recalled that she had testified at Grandier's trial that he had had a carnal relationship with her and had promised to make her a princess of magicians if she would accompany him to a sabbath. Her testimony was, quite literally, damning. Here was the classic case of a magician recruiting an acolyte and taking her into the schools of magic. If they could only get him to admit the truth, both church and justice would be served. But he protested that he had never seen or met the woman.[25]

Laubardemont and the judges had not anticipated such strong resistance from Grandier. When all eight wedges had been used, the keeper of the torture instruments was sent to bring two more, of an even larger size. He returned with wedges the same size as the others. Laubardemont, who was under as much strain as everyone else in the chamber, lost his temper and threatened to punish the man if he did not bring bigger wedges, but the keeper pleaded that he had no larger ones.

Then followed a truly extraordinary scene. Since Grandier was still holding out, Lactance and Tranquille concluded that their exorcisms had not been effective enough. So they themselves seized the mallets and with frenzied blows drove in the last two wedges.[26] In the name of a religion of grace and pardon, these ordained priests struck again and again on the victim whose legs were split and whose bones were nearly crushed to pulp.[27] One author[28] says that at one point in his agony, Grandier allowed a confession of sorcery to escape but that he retracted it immediately, begging God's forgiveness for having denied him in this way. Moreover, it is said that Grandier even had words of charity and pardon for his executioners and that he went so far as to ask Lactance to give him the kiss of peace[29] – a symbolic action signifying mutual forgiveness and charity.

At last, after three-quarters of an hour, the torture was brought to an end, for Laubardemont had cause to fear that the condemned man would not last for the funeral pyre. By this time, Grandier's legs were totally shattered, with the marrow of the bones oozing out. Laubardemont ordered the curé to be carried into another chamber in the building. There he was laid on straw, and his legs were warmed to reanimate them, for he was freezing in spite of the warmth of the day. He fainted once more, and one of the officers gave him a glass of wine to bring him round.

Among those assembled in the room was an Augustinian priest. On seeing him, Grandier asked if he could be his confessor, but this was refused. Then he asked again if Father Grillau, his friend, could be allowed to come to him so that he could confess his sins, but that too was refused. Instead, he was put into the hands of two Capuchins, but he did not want them to hear his confession. When they withdrew, the room was cleared of all who had no need to be there, and for the next three or four hours Grandier was not seen by anybody except the clerk of the court, his Capuchin confessors,

and Laubardemont. The commissioner stayed with Grandier for
more than two hours in a final effort to try to get him to sign the
document admitting his guilt. During this time, Grandier asked
Laubardemont to have him strangled before being burned at the
stake. This was a common act of mercy. A cord was placed around
the condemned person's neck, and he was strangled as soon as the
fire was lit. But Laubardemont refused to agree unless Grandier
signed the confession.[30] Even so, Grandier would not sign it.

While these scenes of horror were taking place at the Palais de
Justice, another scene, hardly less moving, was taking place in the
Cordeliers' church. For some days Grandier's mother, Jeanne
d'Estièvre, had stayed there each day, praying to God to give her son
the strength to die. What drew her particularly to this church was
the statue of Our Lady of Pity that stood in the entrance. On this
last day of his life, she came early in the morning as usual to prostrate
herself at the feet of the Virgin. On her knees, she wept, "Holy
Mother of God, I beg you by the blood of your son, by your holy
tears to have pity on me, a poor mother, and to pray to my Saviour,
your son, for the salvation of my son." At this point, she fainted.

She revived on the arrival of Father Grillau, who led her into the
chapel of Our Lady of Loretto and, after comforting her as best he
could, he sang a High Mass of the Passion of Jesus Christ. He was
just finishing the mass when a friend arrived with the news that the
curé had submitted heroically to the torture and was now asking
for Father Grillau to come and confess him. But moments later,
another friend brought news that Laubardemont would not have
Father Grillau there at any price. Tearfully, Jeanne d'Estièvre begged
the monk to meet her son when he was on his way to the funeral
pyre and carry to him her last blessing. This he promised to do.[31]

Meanwhile, because Grandier had shown such great fortitude
under torture, the exorcists had begun to spread word that the Devil
had rendered him insensible to pain. Towards midday, he was
brought a little nourishment,[32] and at that time a Capuchin priest
entered the room. The condemned man was lying on a bench, his
legs covered with an old piece of green cloth. According to the story
that was later told, under pretext of verifying whether Grandier
really felt pain, this Capuchin roughly tore away the cloth and threw
it on the ground, and though this must have been agonizing for
Grandier, he had the courage not to cry out – whereupon the
Capuchin rushed out to tell his peers that it was perfectly correct,
"the magician is insensitive to pain."[33]

At two in the afternoon, the judges visited the condemned man. Some were no doubt troubled by the fact that he was quite ready to admit guilt for sins of the flesh yet still adamantly claimed to be innocent of sorcery. Some were not troubled at all. One of the leaders among them told Grandier "that he was totally convinced that he was a sorcerer, and based on this when Grandier spoke of God with respect, he meant the Devil, and when he said he detested the Devil, he meant that he detested God." Grandier did not reply.[34] Since he still refused to sign the confession Laubardemont had prepared, there was nothing more to be done. All that long hot day, the people had been massing in the streets, waiting for the condemned man to be brought out of the building and taken for execution. Now at last the time had come to satisfy the crowds.

DEATH

At four o'clock in the afternoon, Laubardemont ordered the executioners to clothe Grandier.[35] They dressed him in a shirt soaked in sulphur. A rope was put around his neck, a large candle placed in his hand, and he was carried on a wooden stretcher to the courtyard, where an open cart drawn by six mules was waiting to take him to his execution. The courtyard was hot and seemed very bright in the August sun. The building itself had been cool and relatively quiet, because only the officials had been allowed to enter. But as Grandier was brought to the door, he was faced by a great mass of people, who were shouting and shoving, and climbing up on every vantage point to get a glimpse of him. The sudden noise and dust, the cries to turn this way or that, and generally the ghoulish antics of the crowd all pounded in on him. As the clerk of the court approached him, there were cries for silence, and gradually the courtyard became quiet enough for those close by to hear what was said. The stretcher was tilted up so that Grandier could be seen and spoken to, and the clerk then read him the sentence of death in a loud voice.

For a few moments, Grandier looked around the courtyard in the hope of finding a friendly face. At least some eyes were fixed on him with compassion, and he heard murmurs of sympathy. Then, in a firm voice, first looking at the clerk and Laubardemont and the other officials near him, he lifted his head to the crowd, declared his innocence, and asked all who surrounded him to pray for him. At that, the shouting, the noise, and the pushing for a better view all started up again.

Grandier was placed in the tumbril, his face to the sky, to be taken to the places that had been selected for him to make amends for his crimes. The first of these was outside his own Church of Saint-Pierre-du-Marché; the last was to be the place of his execution. The commissioner and the judges were to accompany him throughout. They lined up behind the cart, surrounded by a sizable body of armed guards, who were there to ensure safe passage and prevent any attempt to release the priest. As the cortège moved off, all the bells throughout the city began to peal at full volume, announcing to the immense crowd (which had arrived from all points of the kingdom) that the execution was about to commence. At each corner and every crossroads a Capuchin or Recollet was stationed, forbidding the people to pray for the condemned man.[36]

Grandier's journey along the dusty, narrow streets was an excruciating ordeal as the cart pounded over the cobblestones. On the way to the Church of Saint-Pierre, he glimpsed at a window the lawyer who had defended him despite the risk of being accused as an accomplice in witchcraft. "Monsieur le curé," this courageous man called out to him, "keep God still in your heart and mind. Think or say nothing against him; this is how he knows those who are truly his own." Grandier called back, "I put all my hope in God; He will never forsake me."[37]

When the cortège arrived at the church, the crowd quietened a little in order to hear Laubardemont give the order for Grandier to be lifted down from the cart and placed on his knees. The order was carried out, but so great was Grandier's agony that as soon as he was left alone he fell heavily on the cobbles face down; his broken legs could not carry him. He lay without complaint waiting for someone to lift him up again, and when this was done he asked those around him to pray for him.[38]

At this moment, his friend Father Grillau came out of the church, and before anyone could stop him he threw himself weeping into Grandier's arms, whereupon Grandier cried, "Father, pray God for me. I commend myself to your prayers and to those of all the priests of your order."

Grillau, who seemed even more moved than the condemned man, answered, "My friend, in these last moments stay hand in hand with God whom you have always loved. Remember how, in the past, you yourself have consoled the afflicted and given strength to those who didn't know which way to turn. Think on these things. Your mother at this moment is praying to God for your consolation. She begs you to lose yourself in Jesus Christ and think only of dying as his man. Through me, she bids you farewell and sends you her blessing."

"Father, I thank you for your charity," replied Grandier, "and I pray God to have pity on my mother, to console her."[39]

While this exchange was taking place, the two were being roughly pulled apart by the guards. The sudden and unauthorized appearance of Father Grillau from inside the church had taken the authorities by surprise, and for the first few moments Grillau had had his chance to give Grandier words of comfort. But Laubardemont quickly ordered the guards to remove the offending Cordelier. They did this with such brutality that Grillau hardly had enough strength to drag himself back inside the church. It is said that a monk profited from this moment of tumult to dart forward and strike Grandier on the head with a stick while he was still on his knees.

Even this act of savagery did not draw a complaint from Grandier. He waited patiently while he was commanded to make, in a loud voice, the public statement required by his sentence. He then admitted that he was a great sinner before God. The clerk of the court then ordered him to beg pardon of the king and of justice, which he did with great humility, but he also strongly protested his innocence.[40] At this, the crowd again began to revile him noisily, though a few brave souls shouted words of support. During this stop at Saint-Pierre, there was a flock of pigeons fluttering around the church door. Among them was a white one, which flew so low that one of its feet touched Grandier's head as it passed.[41]

When this ceremony had been completed, the executioners put Grandier back on his stretcher and carried him to the cart. Their next stop was the Ursuline Convent. On the way there, Grandier spied Canon Lebrethon, with whom he had always had excellent relations, and called out to him, "Farewell, Monsieur Lebrethon, pray God for me." The canon was so overcome with tears that he could not answer.[42] On arrival at the Ursuline chapel, the same ceremony took place, but when the clerk of the court ordered Grandier to ask pardon of the Ursulines, he replied, "I have never offended against them,[43] but I pray God to pardon them." Then, just as the executioners were about to put him back on the cart, he saw an old enemy, Moussaut du Fresne, with his wife. "Farewell, Monsieur du Fresne," he said. "Let each of us forget all that has happened. I die your servant."[44] And he begged them to pardon him.

At last they arrived at the final stop on this long and agonizing journey, the Place Sainte-Croix. It was quite small and very irregular in shape, and on each of its sides scaffolding had been erected so that the enormous crowd could see the spectacle that was about to take place. On the scaffolds, on the roofs, on every point where people could climb and hold on, as well as at every window, on horseback, and on the ground, more than six thousand people were waiting to see the long-expected drama. So closely were they packed up the sides of the buildings that they looked like bunches of grapes enjoying the warmth of the summer sun. There was a holiday atmosphere about the scene. Although there was scarcely room to move, pies, cooked meats, and drinks were being sold and passed through the crowd, and favours and souvenirs were hawked. The pickpockets thrived, many of them children small enough to wriggle their way around legs and between feet. Meantime, their older sisters and sometimes their mothers bargained their bodies for later delivery. But the centrepoint of this event was not forgotten. On one side of the square, to the left of the Church of Sainte-Croix, the funeral pyre had been prepared. It was three feet square, in the form of a grill and composed of faggots, billets of wood, and straw. In the middle, planted in the ground, was a post about fifteen feet high, to which was attached an iron "stool of repentance."

When the cortège entered the Place Sainte-Croix, the guards had to force their way through the crowd to get to the church. There stood René Bernier, the curé of Trois Moutiers, one of Grandier's earliest enemies. Today he was overcome with remorse and had declared his intention of asking Grandier's pardon for any harm he had ever done him. Although Bernier had no official part to play in the execution, he was wearing his surplice and biretta[45] and had managed to get to the door of the church.

"Monsieur, we have quarrelled with each other in former times, and I testified against you," he said to Grandier. "I beg you for your forgiveness. Will you forgive me as you have forgiven all the others who gave testimony against you?"

"Yes Monsieur, I gladly pardon you just as I firmly believe that God will grant pardon to me and will receive me this day in Paradise," replied Grandier.[46] Bernier then offered to say a mass for the condemned man, and in thanks Grandier kissed his hands.[47] Turning to the priest who had accompanied him on his journey that day, Grandier then asked him to give him the kiss of peace.

After Grandier had made his public apology before the portal of Sainte-Croix, he was replaced on the cart and taken towards the funeral pyre, with much pushing and shoving as the guards forced a path through the crowd. And now Grandier realized the final indignity that had been prepared for him, for the funeral pyre was only a few feet from the window occupied by his most implacable enemy, the former *procureur du roi*. There sat Louis Trincant with Philippe and Louis Moussau, along with Mignon and Thibault. At other windows were the company of Laubardemont and the wives of the judges.[48] "He had been placed," said an eyewitness, "with his head turned towards Trincant's house to please Laubardemont's wife and the wives of the other judges, who were finding pleasure in seeing him die in the flames." At the sight of his worst enemies, Grandier lowered his eyes.

The officer in charge of the execution saw what had happened and understood Grandier's distress. As was often the custom, he begged the condemned man's forgiveness for having to put him to death. "You have done me nothing wrong," the curé replied. "You have only done your duty." Then Grandier requested a last kindness, the one he had asked of Laubardemont, that when the flames were lit he should be strangled before they reached him. Although Laubardemont had refused this customary act of mercy, the officer in charge of the execution could grant it. And not only did he agree to Grandier's request but he promised to allow him to address the crowd.

The Loudun executioner, a big strong man, lifted Grandier bodily from the cart, carried him onto the scaffold, and placed him on the iron seat that faced the windows where Trincant, Philippe, and the others were sitting.[49] As the executioner tied Grandier to the post to which the seat was attached, the crowd fell silent. Then the monks took over. First they exorcized the air and the wood of the pyre, and then they asked the condemned man yet again if he would recant. As usual, Grandier declared his innocence, and he asked them to let him die in peace. At this, the clerk of the court came forward and for the last time read out the dreadful sentence – in a full voice so that even those far back in the crowd could hear every word. He, too, asked Grandier if he persisted in the innocence he had claimed under torture. Grandier replied that he had nothing more to say and that all he had said was true. As this went on, the monks told the clerk to stop the questioning; they said he was giving Grandier too much opportunity to protest his innocence.

Things happened very quickly now. When Grandier began to address the crowd, the monks moved in to stop him. They threw such quantities of holy water in his face that his words could not be

Contemporary sketch of the execution of
Urbain Grandier.
Source: Originally published by René Allain,
Poitiers, 1634; later published in Legué,
Urbain Grandier et les possédées de Loudun

heard,[50] and they pushed their crucifixes at him so roughly that he was struck in the face.[51] Realizing that his last moments were at hand, Grandier begged them to grant him the kiss of peace. As before, they refused. But the people around the pyre began to murmur; they were indignant that such a wish should be denied. As the shouts from the crowd became louder and angrier, Father Lactance stepped forward and reluctantly embraced the man about to die. Then someone in the crowd called out, "Watch the kiss of Judas!"

This infuriated Lactance, and he totally lost control of himself. Grabbing a straw torch, he plunged it into the brazier that had been placed ready and held the flaming brand in front of Grandier's face. "Wretched man, recant and renounce the Devil!" he shouted.

"Father, God who is my witness knows that I have told you the truth," Grandier replied.

"Now is the time for you to confess to your crime, you have only a moment more to live," Lactance shouted back.

"Father, I have told the truth," Grandier repeated.

Then a monstrous thing happened. Lactance, mad with rage, took upon himself the office of executioner. Without waiting for the signal, he plunged the brand into the straw of the funeral pyre. The straw burst into flames immediately, setting the dry wood alight. In horror, Grandier called out to officer in charge, "This isn't what you promised me."[52] He cried it three or four times. The officer, furious with Lactance, shouted to the executioner, "Strangle him, Strangle him!" The crowd picked up the cry, and the executioner rushed to carry out the order, but already the fire was too hot to approach. Some said that the monks had knotted the rope around Grandier's neck to prevent his being strangled.

At this moment, the same flock of pigeons that had been seen before the portal of Saint-Pierre reappeared, fluttering above the head of the doomed man. Soon they disappeared into the clouds. The partisans of the possessions said that the birds were a band of demons come to carry away their master. Others claimed that these gentle doves had come to render witness to the innocence of the unfortunate curé.[53]

Soon the flames enveloped him from every side. As the ropes that bound him to the post burned through and broke, he fell, still alive, into the middle of the pit of fire. From the thick smoke could be heard his last words:

"Oh my God!"

Epilogue

When the fire had burned out, the executioner took some of the ashes and threw them to the four winds as the sentence required. Many of the spectators then rushed forward to get some small part of the victim's remains as a souvenir of the event.[1]

After the principal actor had gone from the stage, many of the cast also disappeared from view in that they lived out unrecorded and unremembered lives. But a surprising number left further traces of themselves.

LACTANCE, THE RECOLLET

On 18 September 1634, exactly one month after Grandier's execution and death at his hands, Lactance died in convulsions so terrible that many of his contemporaries were convinced it was a punishment from God. On the day after the execution, Lactance showed signs of losing his wits, and he became preoccupied and sunk in gloom. According to eyewitnesses, he was overcome by remorse at having refused Grandier a confessor. "God is punishing me, God is punishing me!" he cried. He fell sick with a fever, and in his delirium he sometimes addressed his victim, shouting, "Grandier, it wasn't I who put you to death!" In his delirium he bit the pillows, sheets, and curtains, tearing them to shreds. He died without any show of piety, making fun of the apothecary Adam, who was preparing the medicines, and hitting the attending priest so hard that he was felled.[2]

MANNOURY,
THE SURGEON

A short time later, Mannoury died without warning. One evening, about ten o'clock, he was returning from visiting a patient, accompanied by two other people, when suddenly, in the middle of the town, he stopped and cried, "Look, there's Grandier. What do you want with me?" Shaking with terror, he continued to talk to Grandier, imploring his pardon. He was carried to his home, where the terrors and delirium increased. After some days of excruciating agony of body and mind, he died. The "vision" stayed with him to the end.[3]

MADELEINE DE BROU

Madeleine was quick to feel Laubardemont's vengeance for having refused to testify against Grandier. On the day after the curé's death, Laubardemont ordered her immediate arrest wherever she might be found. Friends and relatives warned her and hid her, despite the danger to themselves. For some time she stayed out of Laubardemont's clutches, but on 3 September he discovered her whereabouts. She was arrested and imprisoned in Loudun, where she was treated as a common criminal.[4] She stayed there for a month. Meanwhile, her relatives intervened and threatened to take her case before the king. Faced with such a threat from powerful people who might jeopardize his career, Laubardemont allowed her to be released into the hands of her family. Even at that, he demanded and got an undertaking that she would be kept under strict supervision. This was probably given freely enough; however innocent, she was an embarrassment to her family. Within a short time she left Loudun for ever and entered a convent, where she remained for the rest of her life.

LOUIS CHAUVET,
THE LIEUTENANT-CIVIL

This honourable man was the next participant to suffer from the Grandier affair. He was one of the bravest men involved, for he had openly supported Grandier throughout. After the execution, he became very despondent, fearing that he would be accused of the same crime as Grandier and be treated as an accomplice because he had worked so hard to save the curé. Sadness and despair seemed to overwhelm him. He lost both sleep and appetite, began to have nightmares and delusions, and gradually became demented. Before long, he died.[5]

TRANQUILLE, THE EXORCIST

Another sufferer was Father Tranquille. Like some of the other exorcists, he began to show signs of mental disturbance. Before long, Laubardemont was writing to Richelieu to say that the priest was showing the same symptoms as the nuns he had exorcized. Despite this, Tranquille continued to carry out his role in the exorcisms for many months; he seems to have truly believed in the validity of the possessions. He died in May 1638, suffering from terrible convulsions. The sound of his agony could be heard in the street outside. "Ah, how I am suffering!" he cried. "I am suffering more than all the devils together and all the damned."[6]

RENÉ GRANDIER, URBAIN'S BROTHER

Grandier's lawyer brother, who had worked so hard in his legal defence, was another victim. Laubardemont had had him arrested and imprisoned in Loudun well before the priest's death. He was held there for nine months, during which he was continually in danger of being accused as an accomplice of his brother and threatened with the same bitter end. Happily for him, he had friends in the town who were prepared to risk themselves on his behalf. On 20 February 1635, with the aid of these friends, he was able to outwit his guards, lowering himself down the walls of his jail on sheets tied together to form a rope. His escape was proof that despite the criticisms that most authors have rained upon Laubardemont for his close imprisonment of Urbain, the commissioner had been wise to take such stringent measures.[7] Helped by his friends, René fled Loudun on horseback and was able to get far enough away to escape Laubardemont completely. He settled quietly at Doué-la-Fontaine, where his mother had taken up residence, and was permitted to stay there in peace. His descendants were still living there in the late eighteen hundreds.

DE CERISAY,
THE BAILLI

Little is known of this brave and constant friend, except that he had a stroke within a few months and was completely paralysed on the right side. He was forced to resign from his position and was not heard of further.

JEAN D'ARMAGNAC II,
THE GOVERNOR OF LOUDUN

After Grandier's death, Jean d'Armagnac lost any remaining influence he had at court. Not only was he no longer governor of a powerful walled city, but his association with the priest had not gone down well with Richelieu, nor did the king look on it favourably. Depressed at his loss of influence, d'Armagnac left the court and retired to his Paris house. There he refused to see anyone or have anything to do with Loudun – though he could not escape some contact with the town.

This was because of a man named Duluc, who had been employed as the governor's official representative during his absences from Loudun. Despite his position, he had been acting against the governor's interests and consorting with the enemy. As a result, d'Armagnac had refused to pay Duluc (who had since left his service) the three thousand livres which Duluc said was owing to him. Duluc lost his ensuing court case and was ruined by it. He went to Paris and begged d'Armagnac on bended knee to have pity on him, but d'Armagnac ordered his servants to eject the man from the house. Two days later, in the evening, Duluc returned, and when his pleas were again rejected, he drew a poignard from under his clothes and stabbed the governor repeatedly. D'Armagnac survived for three days, dying on 23 April 1635.

Duluc was sentenced three days later. His punishment was "to have his upper and lower arms and legs broken, together with his back, while still alive; this to be done on a scaffold to be erected in the open place at the crossroads of the Croix du Tirouer." The execution was carried out on 3 May. The only result of his appeals for a reduction of the punishment was that the executioner received instructions to strangle him secretly before the first blow was struck.[8]

JEAN MIGNON,
CONFESSOR TO THE URSULINES

This implacable enemy of Grandier was not without redeeming features. He was a constant spiritual and financial supporter of the nuns, especially when they fell on hard times. In later life, he used his considerable fortune to found and support a home for the poor, which still existed centuries after his death.

BARRÉ,
THE EXORCIST FROM CHINON

This priest continued to discover possessed women, whom he exorcized and publicized; when the events in Loudun had finally settled down, Barré was still in full operation in his parish at Chinon. There was considerable unease within the local population, for the fears of a witch-hunt had simply been transferred from one town to another. Nobody felt safe. Nor were the church authorities pleased with this development. There were already enough questions being raised about the Grandier case without a further series of possessions. It was feared that if Barré was not stopped, he would fan the flames of possession in every town in the kingdom; already it was said of him that for lack of anything better, he would have exorcized stones.

In December 1634 an inquiry was held by four suspicious bishops, who called Barré and his possessed women before them. When asked questions, the women stayed silent, and when Barré was asked why they would not or could not speak, he declared that there was a pact of silence between the demons who possessed them and the author of the possessions. This kind of response had worked well in the highly excited circus that had been the scene at Loudun but these bishops were less than impressed. "Do you not see," one of them, a cardinal, asked, "that although these women are not truly possessed, they believe themselves to be so on your word? It is based as much on their own sickness as on the high opinion that they have of you."

Another of the bishops remarked that if Barré had been under his jurisdiction, he would have him punished. The group concluded that he was a serious public danger and informed both the king and Barré's own archbishop of Tours of their conclusion. But Barré's archbishop believed in the demons and supported his priest. Nevertheless, he did have him warned to be circumspect, and from that time there was a certain lessening in the number and severity of the possessions. For a long time nothing of note happened. But some years later, Barré's obsession with demons gave birth to an affair that ultimately ruined him. This was in 1640.

One of the "possessed" women whom Barré was treating was named La Beloquin. Early one the morning, she entered Barré's parish church of Saint-Jacques as if to make her devotions, but she had come for another purpose. As soon as she saw that she was alone, she approached the altar with a vial full of blood and emptied it onto the altar cloth. When Barré came in and saw the blood, he took steps to find out where it came from. This led him to question the woman's demon, who declared that the blood was hers. He said that a local curé, Giloire (a priest of good reputation), had, by magic arts, encountered the woman early in the morning and that just as she was finishing her devotions, he had violated her on the altar.

This made a neighbour of La Beloquin think back. This woman had bought a chicken, which she, a friend, and La Beloquin had eaten together. She recalled that La Beloquin, after bleeding the chicken, had saved its blood in a vial. Eventually this story came to the ears of the local authorities, and an inquiry was set in motion. On hearing of this, La Beloquin complained of being under a spell, and while continuing to accuse the curé Giloire, she asked to be taken before the archbishop of Tours. She was given her wish, supported by Barré and other exorcists, but the archbishop was absent that day, and she found herself in front of his coadjutor, a severe and down-to-earth man, who soon uncovered her fraud. He had her arrested and taken to Chinon's prison. He then went to the town to pursue the inquiry, calling on the magistrates of Richelieu and Chinon to judge Barré and his "possessed" woman. The sentence handed down deprived Barré of all his positions and income. He was banished from the diocese of Tours and exiled to Le Mans, where he was imprisoned in a monastery until the end of his life. The many women he had exorcized, who had made false accusations over the years, also were confined for the rest of their lives.[9]

LAUBARDEMONT

For a long time Laubardemont seemed to go from strength to strength. First, Richelieu appointed him absolute master of Loudun in order to ensure that the town and its Huguenots were kept quiet and peaceful. Then, as a fuller reward for his services to king and cardinal, he was appointed intendant, the king's personal representative, for the provinces of Maine, Anjou, and Touraine (including Loudun and its surrounding countryside). Laubardemont continued to enjoy the full confidence of Richelieu, for he could be relied on to do any task required of him, regardless of public opprobrium. For this reason, he was called from time to time to perform special, and unpleasant, work for Richelieu. He played a major part in two famous interrogations and state trials, both of which were regarded by many as disgraceful affairs.[10]

But Laubardemont's power rested on his close personal association with Richelieu, and the cardinal was dying. He survived the famous trials by only three months. After Richelieu's death, Laubardemont gradually slid into obscurity. His wife and children died before him. The last of his sons left home and died as a robber, killed in a fracas while attacking a coach. Only later was it discovered that the young man's father was the infamous official who had put so many to death. Laubardemont lived out his last days by himself in his Paris mansion. He died in 1653 after a long period of deep depression.[11]

Did Laubardemont truly believe in the possessions or was he simply carrying out Richelieu's orders? We shall never know for certain. I incline to the view that he did believe. True, he was a cynic and a creature of Richelieu, but it was he who triggered Richelieu to action, not the other way round. When he first went to the convent to see his relatives and heard their story, he became convinced, and he later went to Paris to convince his master. I think his actions were quite consistent with belief, though others may come to a different conclusion.

THE NUNS

Religious communities, like military units aloof from the surrounding world, are expected to live up to high ideals. The individual members under normal human stresses and temptations draw strength from their community, often sublimating their own difficulties to achieve a higher good. Occasionally, though, the organism becomes diseased; its members, still in concert, act according to a corrupted standard that is totally inimical to its natural state. The very fact that the enclosed community is set apart from the "normal" world facilitates the spread of this corruption if it is not stopped at the outset. When this happens, respected military units run amok, reputable institutions can become affected with physical and sexual abuses, and respected convents can act like the Ursulines of Loudun.

The unwitting causes of the whole affair, the Ursulines remained under regular exorcism and treatment for months and in some cases years. On Laubardemont's orders, the city was forced to pay for the lodging of a substantial number of exorcists. Between twelve and fifteen houses were expropriated for this purpose. This was very unpopular, particularly with the Huguenots. In the meantime, the nuns' financial situation grew increasingly desperate. For months, they had had no money coming in. Their school was closed. Families did not want to send their daughters to their boarding school, let alone have them enter the convent as nuns. Their reputation affected other Ursuline convents. The Ursulines of Chinon, just a few miles away, where Barré's parish was situated, wrote: "At the time when the possession of Loudun was bruited about the world, our reputation was confused with theirs and all the scorn of their misconduct fell unjustly upon us."[12]

Laubardemont decided that only much grander quarters and official public support would change their status. He assumed the responsibility of seeing that they were suitably housed, and he had just the place in mind. The Huguenots had a *collège,* a school of higher learning, of which they were justly proud. Laubardemont confiscated it and gave it to the nuns. This was a far better property than they had had before. The Huguenots protested vigorously, and Laubardemont had to bring in eight hundred troops from Poitiers before they would accept the expropriation. Meanwhile, the exorcisms continued, though they were no longer public events after 1634. The last exorcism was conducted in 1638. During these years, the attitude towards the nuns and the possessions changed. At Grandier's trial, both church and state had officially recognized that the nuns had been possessed through no fault or weakness of their own, but gradually people began to think that they had been selected to suffer for the glory of the church. The possessions became almost a blessed visitation.

People came from afar to see for themselves the extraordinary possessions which the nuns were suffering. The most important of these visitors was the king's brother.[13] While some left Loudun believing that much of what was going on was trickery, others were convinced by what they had seen, and they spread the details throughout France. The nuns thus acquired a new respectability. In time, the convent thrived once again, and the possessions became a proud event. The nuns owed much to their mother superior for this happy change in circumstance.

THE SECULAR WOMEN
WHO WERE POSSESSED

This changed view of those who were possessed applied to the seculars also. A word picture has been handed down. The little procession of women was seen at regular hours going for their exorcisms. When they were asked if they were still possessed, they replied, "Yes, thank God." They were always accompanied by a group of devoted helpers. When these helpers were asked if they too were possessed, they answered that they were not so fortunate, that God did not love them enough for that.[14]

JEANNE DES ANGES,
THE MOTHER SUPERIOR

The person who survived the events with the greatest reputation was Jeanne des Anges.[15] For months she continued under exorcism, yet the external signs of her possession continued. Although the saintly Father Surin was brought in especially to deal with her possession, she eventually became so weak that she was expected to die before the night was out. But the next morning, when the doctor returned, he was amazed to find her apparently completely cured. In the night Saint Joseph had appeared to her, she said, and had given her some ointment with a beautiful smell. Her guardian angel had put the ointment on her, and she had immediately recovered from her sickness. As evidence of this, she showed the doctor her chemise, which had five drops of this marvellous remedy still visibly marking it. (It just so happened that Jeanne des Anges excelled in the creation of fine-smelling oils and unguents!)

This became the starting point for a whole series of wonderful cures connected with Jeanne des Anges and her miraculous chemise. The first to benefit from the oil of Saint Joseph was Laubardemont's wife, who was in Tours suffering from a mass of symptoms – nausea, violent headaches, loss of sight, and bloating. The doctors could do nothing for her, and they feared for her life. As soon as Laubardemont heard of the cure effected by Saint Joseph on Jeanne des Anges, he arranged for the miraculous chemise to be taken to his wife. The bishop's right-hand man was sent personally to bring it. Nobody was disappointed. The cloth arrived at Laubardemont's house at eight in the evening and was immediately placed on the sick woman, who was suddenly seized with pain. A few moments later she had a miscarriage, producing a foetus that must have been dead for some time. From then on, she quickly recovered her health. News of the miracle spread like wildfire, and soon pregnant women were making pilgrimages to Loudun to touch the miraculous garment, firm in belief that it would protect them. As the name of Jeanne des Anges became as well known as her miraculous chemise, the reports of her virtue spread too. To those who believed, it seemed clear that she had been afflicted by the Devil not because she was weak and sinful but because she was a prey worthy of all his powers. The miracle of the chemise was followed by another. Upon her hand appeared the names of Jesus, Joseph, and Mary. Beneath them was that of Saint François de Sales, her patron saint. This was taken as a further proof that she had been chosen for special things.

Jeanne des Anges was by now sufficiently recovered to make a pilgrimage to the tomb of Saint François de Sales. To get there, she had to go through Paris, where she stayed at the Laubardemont mansion. Richelieu invited her to visit him at his palace and gave her a donation of five hundred écus. She visited other noble persons in and about Paris, and when the king and queen heard she was in the city, they too were anxious to meet her. The queen was pregnant at the time and was most anxious that Jeanne should return to Paris bringing the miraculous chemise. Jeanne arrived back just in time, and the queen asked to be clothed in the garment, since she was nearing the end of her confinement. Shortly afterwards she gave birth safely.

With such attentions from royalty, Jeanne des Anges had now reached the height of any ambition she could have had for this world; and since her convent was recognized as a place of sanctified events, it was attracting increasing numbers of nuns from the best families (after she returned to the convent, there was no revival of the possessions). The high esteem in which Jeanne was held can be seen from a letter written by a contemporary, Marie de l'Incarnation, who was an Ursuline nun at the convent in Tours:

At that time, the Mother Prior of the Ursulines of Loudun [Jeanne des Anges] went to Anessi [Annecy] by order of Monseigneur the Bishop of Poitiers to make her vows at the sepulchre of Blessed François de Salles.

She passed by our Monastery of Tours,[16] carrying with her the holy unction
with which Saint Joseph had cured her of a mortal illness when she was
in agony. This unction gave forth an odour which was not of this world,
and it bore a miraculous and totally heavenly virtue. The Community
kissed it [the chemise] and smelled the sweetness of its odour, and at the
same time felt its effects to the depth of our souls.[17]

Jeanne des Anges continued to have apparitions of Saint Joseph
and also of the Virgin Mary and the infant Jesus.[18] During Holy
Week, the week before Easter each year, the names marked on her
hand became notably brighter, glowing red, and many people came
to the grille of the Ursuline parlour to wonder at this proof of her
sanctity.

Jeanne des Anges died on 29 January 1665, having been paralysed
on one side for the last two years of her life. Not surprisingly, her
death was treated as that of a saint. Her head was preserved in a
reliquary and became the subject of veneration, and the miraculous
chemise continued to draw pilgrims to the convent. The convent
itself was closed in 1772. By then, more then a century after these
events, it was in financial straits like many other religious houses.
The remaining nuns and all the properties and possessions of the
convent were divided between two other convents. The relics and
the miraculous chemise were seen no more.

THE TRINCANTS

It had taken Louis Trincant five years to get his revenge, yet even
Grandier's death did not satisfy him. He had to blacken the curé's
character too, creating a Grandier from whom no woman was safe,
a priest who used his confessional to lure them to sin. In pursuing
this aim, Trincant brought about his own loss of honour and
position as well as Grandier's death. Trincant devoted his last years
to private studies and died in 1644.

And what of Trincant's daughter Philippe, whose seduction had
started the whole affair? We know little of her life afterwards except
that she had six children between 1630 and 1641[19] and died in 1661,
being buried on 30 November.[20] In addition, there is an oral legend
that is still told in Loudun. The story goes that after Grandier's
burning she was asked what she thought about it. "It was all right,"
she is said to have replied, "but I found the smell disagreeable."[21]

Appendices

Appendix One

Grandier through the Ages

Over the centuries since Grandier's death, dozens of books and hundreds of articles have been written on the subject, and there have also been plays, films, and an opera. The views expressed and conclusions drawn have changed over the years, answering some old questions but raising new ones. Some of the main books and other documents are summarized below to show the principal outlines of these changes. (The full references of these works can be found in the bibliography.)

Urbain Grandier, "Factum pour Maistre Urbain Grandier" (1634)
   This is the earliest defence of Grandier, written by himself and designed to save his life. Composed shortly before his death, it contains all his arguments in support of his innocence, including those that bolster his assertion that the Ursulines were not possessed, that it was all trickery. His main thrust throughout the document is that Trincant, Hervé, Mignon, "and others in their cabal" had plotted since 1629 to bring about his ruin; he follows all the steps they took against him since that time. The person whom he finds directly responsible for the accusations against him is Mignon who, according to Grandier, told the nuns that they were possessed "and taught them to make grimaces and say lascivious words," naming Grandier as responsible. This document should be read in conjunction with his "Lettre au Roi," in which he emphasizes that he does not believe the nuns to be possessed and that if they are, he is not responsible. These brief documents are well worth reading; what he said in 1634 in his defence is largely held to be correct today.

Rev. Fr. Tranquille, *Véritable relation des justes procédures observées au fait de la possession des Ursulines de Loudun, et au procès de Grandier* (1634)

This was written by the exorcist Tranquille shortly after Grandier's death. From the document, it is clear that there were already enough people questioning the validity of the possessions to make Tranquille feel the need to "prove" that the nuns were possessed and that Grandier was responsible. "Those who call the possessions a hoax sin against reason or against conscience," he writes. "I ask you, how is it possible that a number of nuns, to say nothing of seculars, all of good birth, who have been painstakingly nourished and brought up to honesty and piety could become cheats from one day to the next? ... In your opinion, to what end could they have planned to play such a strange comedy, and what fruits could they hope to have harvested from their supposed cheating? Who was the charlatan who taught them everything in so little time to make such frightful contortions that more than thirty doctors judged them beyond nature, and in what school of atheists and libertines did they learn to vomit forth such horrible blasphemies and to spit out such vileness?" Tranquille puts forward his best case – that the behaviour of the nuns was so extraordinary that only possession could explain it.

Abbé Hédelin, "Relation de M. Hédelin, abbé d'Aubignac, touchant les possédées de Loudun" (1637)

By 1637 "people of quality" were visiting the nuns to see for themselves the extraordinary things that were happening during the exorcisms. One such visitor was a Catholic priest, the Abbé D'Aubignac, who was both a good theologian and a sensible and no-nonsense person. He stayed in Loudun for a week and during that time saw many of the exorcisms, along with the exorcists and possessed women, sometimes without warning. He claims to have been of an open mind when he arrived, though a careful reading suggests that he was already sceptical. By the time he left, he was satisfied that the practices of the exorcisms failed to follow the proper rituals of the church, that the nuns could not understand foreign languages or read other people's secret thoughts, and that the "supernatural" convulsions could be covered by natural explanations. Furthermore, he believed that the names on Jeanne's hand were a fraud. If anything, D'Aubignac was too ready to put everything down to chicanery, but he was the first and one of the very few Catholic clergy to express doubts about the possessions.

Sœur Jeanne des Anges, *Autobiographie d'une hystérique possédée* ([c 1644], annotated edition, ed. Legué and Tourette)

This is the printed version of the autobiography of Sœur Jeanne des Anges, together with additional notes and comments by later authors. Jeanne's original manuscript was written some ten years after Grandier's death, and Grandier is hardly mentioned. The book concentrates on the possessions and on Jeanne des Anges herself. From her writing, it is clear that she was an erotic woman with terrifying urges for a nun. Her principal weaknesses, once beyond her control, become ascribed to external person-alities – real persons though supernatural – each with his own name and characteristic sins. The story until her final release from the last of these demons is one of a gradual struggle to rise from the depths of possession. In the final stages, there are voices from heaven and visions of angels. From being a possessed nun she becomes a mystic, an instrument of God.

Much of Jeanne's manuscript has a ring of truth in that, whatever chicanery she practised, she believed herself to be possessed. Jeanne describes, in the context and mind-set of her century, what happened to her while she was possessed. Even though we now accept the miraculous names on her hands as a hoax, we do not know for certain how they were done; they were tested time and again in her day, and we should not be too quick to dismiss as fools those who believed. In the end, she reveals the real target of the exorcisms, the Huguenots: "They could not stand what was evident; that is, the power of the Catholic Church over the demons."

Rev. J.J. Surin, *Histoire abrégée de la possession des Ursulines de Loudun et des peines du Père Surin* ([late 1640s], published 1828)

This was written by Father Surin about ten years after he left Loudun, although there are occasional later insertions; these were almost certainly the work of nuns in the Ursuline Convent, as evidenced by the description of Jeanne des Anges' life and death, written probably in 1665. The book is divided into four parts: (1) the nature of demons and demonic posses-sion; (2) his experiences as Jeanne's exorcist; (3) The terrible events of his own possession, which started while he was Jeanne's exorcist; and (4) his description and praise of his relationship with God.

Surin was clearly a saintly man, though by our standards naive and credulous. Like most of his contemporaries, he believed in demons and the reality of possessions, and he believed that Jeanne des Anges was truly possessed. His own experience of being possessed as a result of the exorcisms

he conducted could only have confirmed this belief. To us, the most interesting part of the volume is his description of the possessions and exorcisms
of the mother superior. These are the same events that she describes in her
autobiography. Although written in different times and places, the two
accounts are remarkably consistent. Together they seem to prove that what
was described was true – that the contortions and blasphemies really did
take place. Furthermore, Jeanne's experiences are validated by Surin's. There
is more to the case than chicanery, hoaxes, and the so-called miracles, but
it is difficult for us to say exactly what. For Surin, as for most Catholics of
his time, the only explanation was diabolic possession. He never had any
doubt of that, and nobody reading his book can doubt his honesty.

Nicolas Aubin, *Histoire des diables de Loudun* (1693)

The revocation of the Edict of Nantes in 1685 caused thousands of
French Huguenots to leave France in a search of religious freedom. One
who left was Aubin, a Huguenot minister from Loudun who had been a
young man at the time of Grandier's death. Living in Amsterdam, he was
free to publish the truth as he saw it about "the malice and the long and
deadly intrigues of a convent of nuns and a great number of Ecclesiastics,
supported by a body of magistrates, of habitants of the town, and favourites of the court," all of which he said was done with the aim of damaging
the Huguenots. Nowhere does Aubin doubt the existence of demonic
possession; he simply does not believe it existed in this case.

According to Aubin, Grandier was innocent of any crime of sorcery and
the accusations of extreme lechery were also false; the nuns, supported by
the priests, were imposters rather than possessed victims. Aubin regards
Mignon as the central figure in the plot and accuses him of telling the nuns
that they would draw great advantage from the affair – that it would
confound the Huguenots, finish off the debauched curé, give glory to God
and the church, and acquire for their convent an extraordinary reputation,
with gifts and alms. Whereas Tranquille put forward what became the
orthodox Catholic position on the possessions for the next two centuries,
Aubin, equally biased, was the initiator of the standard Protestant view. His
book was widely read. From this point on, the battle lines were drawn.

François Gayot de Petaval, *Histoire d'Urbain Grandier, condamné comme
magicien et comme auteur de la possession des religieuses Ursulines de
Loudun* (1735)

By this date, it was widely recognized that Grandier had had nothing
to do with the possessions. This was Gayot's position: "If it is true that

Urbain Grandier was innocent of the crime of magic, as the sane part of the world alleges ... what opinion should we have of the nuns of Loudun who were said to be possessed?" Grandier is no longer the issue. The battle is now between the orthodox Catholics, who make it a point of faith that the nuns were possessed, and the disbelievers, some of them Catholics, who usually claim chicanery. Gayot accepts that possession can occur and that the exorcisms and ceremonies of the church are perfectly valid and respectable, but he sees "no convincing proof of possession" in this case, and like Aubin he thinks that Mignon "created" the whole affair.

While his story is almost totally based on Aubin, he presents a great deal of fascinating additional information on the possessions. Moreover, although he argues that the convulsions were in fact taught to the nuns, he suggests that some of their behaviour might be put down to hysteria or nymphomania. This is the first solid recognition that sickness may have played an important part.

Abbé Jean-Baptiste de La Menardaye, *Examen et discussion critique de l'histoire des diables de Loudun* (1747)

This is a response to Aubin's book. "Few works of this type have been as much read as this one," states La Menardaye, and "few have been given so much credence," but "the alleged history is a most unworthy calumny against the whole Catholic Church ... full of contradictions, the greatest impostures, and palpable absurdities." The *Examen* is written as a series of discussions between an uncle and his nephew. The nephew has read Aubin and was impressed, but the uncle convinces him, step by step, that Aubin is wrong. According to La Menardaye, the nuns, exorcists, Laubardemont, and judges were all people of the highest probity; the witnesses who came forward to testify produced a solid body of evidence against Grandier; Richelieu was concerned with moral standards and public order, not personal vengeance; the doctors did indeed find the devil's marks on Grandier; and the nuns' convulsions, levitation, and knowledge of foreign languages and secret thoughts were all valid.

La Menardaye's arguments, in the light of his times, were not without substance. All of his contentions were backed by the evidence at Grandier's trial, whereas Aubin and his supporters could produce no proof that the convulsions, for instance, were staged. Nor could they put forward a convincing reason why the nuns acted as they did. By this time, each side had to prove the other wrong because its prestige was at stake. This is a long book but well argued, and it gives the orthodox Catholic position of its day – one that had already been held for a century and would hold constant for more than another hundred years.

Pierre Ambroise Leriche, *Etudes sur les possessions en général et sur celles de Loudun en particulier* (1859)

"It is a matter of faith that the rebel angels, called demons by Holy Scripture, can, to sate the rage and age-old jealousies which torment them, tempt men in their mind, even possess their bodies, but only with the special permission of the Divinity; consequently, whoever doubts this truth, who believes himself permitted to discuss it rationally, should be rejected from the bosom of the Church and viewed as blasphemous."

With these words Leriche opens his defence of the truth of the possessions. He admits that "There can be imposture on the part of those who say that they are possessed" and states that, when found, these people should be cured by proper remedies, not by exorcism; but without hesitation he accepts the validity of the Loudun possessions, along with the records of the exorcists and the trial, and he blames the occurrences squarely on Grandier. There is nothing really new in Leriche. The importance of this work is that it was written during a period of anti-Catholic sentiment in France; its purpose was as much to defend the church as to oppose Grandier and his nineteenth-century adherents. For researchers of the subject, it offers a useful list of books and documents both for and against Grandier, dating from 1634 to 1859.

Louis Figuier, *Histoire du merveilleux dans les temps modernes: Les diables de Loudun*, vol. 1 (1860)

Figuier asks the question, Were the nuns in Loudun truly possessed or not? He objectively assesses the facts presented by Aubin, setting aside Aubin's conclusion that the possessions were all faked. While Figuier concentrates on the possession descriptions provided by Aubin, he adds details of the exorcisms that have not been covered by other authors, details presumably recorded in the original records of the exorcisms (now in Paris). His whole focus is on the exorcists, the exorcisms, and Jeanne des Anges. He presents nothing new on Grandier, except (and it is a significant exception) to suggest that Laubardemont may have recorded exactly what he saw and heard, and that he had no designs against Grandier.

Figuier's conclusion is that the nuns suffered from a disease of the nerves – "a convulsive hysteria with diverse complications." He does not believe that they were possessed, nor does he believe that they were simulating. Further, he considers that their problems were compounded by the exorcists, who reinforced their conviction that they were indeed possessed.

Figuier's analysis is valuable. It precedes Legué's by twenty years but is well on the way to arriving at the same conclusion. But although Figuier disagrees with Aubin, arguing for a mistaken diagnosis, he perhaps goes too far in the other direction by excluding chicanery altogether.

Alphonse Bleau, *Précis d'histoire sur la ville et les possédées de Loudun* (1877)

"Urbain Grandier died innocent, he died the victim of a judicial assassination." With these words, Bleau states his main thesis in a book that is unemotional, objective, and well argued. "We can find him innocent in his death without approving of his life," he states. His conclusions are based on three principal findings: (1) that Grandier's conviction was based solely on the depositions of the possessed nuns and five or six secular women, all of whom were in the same state of intellectual and organic disorder (he is somewhat disingenuous in this contention, for in fact it was based on the evidence of seventy-two witnesses and on a great deal of physical evidence that was acceptable to witchcraft trials); (2) that it was ridiculous to assert that the Devil, the author of lies, could be accepted as telling the truth and that anybody could be convicted on his word; and (3) that the judges were swayed by the prejudices of their time and the pressure of public opinion, by the milieu in which they lived, and by Grandier's reputation for immorality. After a good analysis of the possibilities, Bleau's final suggestion is that "in the case of the Ursulines, there were both sickness and possession together; there was a complete union of a natural and a supernatural cause."

The book is valuable for two reasons. It is well argued and balanced, and it takes a considerable step forward in arguing for sickness as a factor. It is worth noting that Legué's *Histoire médicale* was published in 1874, so Bleau had access to that work in forming his ideas.

Gabriel Legué, *Urbain Grandier et les possédées de Loudun* (1880)

Legué tells Grandier's story in a much fuller manner than anyone had done previously, and he uses a great deal of original material from the Bibliothèque nationale and various archives to support his case. His principal arguments are that Grandier was innocent, that he was the victim of a concerted plot, and that the nuns were sick, not possessed. To support this last claim, Legué uses the findings of Charcot, a precursor of modern psychiatry, who had wide experience in the mental hospital of the Salpêtrière in Paris. Like all writers to this day, Legué presents Grandier as being a lecher and libertine from the time of his arrival in Loudun, and he establishes who his enemies were, and why: the Carmelites and Capuchins because he had little time for them and attacked them; other priests, whom he despised; Richelieu, whom he had insulted and whose policies he later threatened in Loudun; and above all the extended Trincant family, whom he had shamed by seducing Louis Trincant's daughter.

Like all authors in the case, Legué shows biases, in this case anti-Catholic, and he is often too ready to accept rumours as facts, for instance, with the "marriage" of Madeleine de Brou and Grandier. Nevertheless, his contribution to the Grandier case is so considerable that every work on the subject ever since has used him as an essential source. This book is a "must" for any inquiry into Grandier.

Henri Brémond, "Surin et Jeanne des Anges," in *Histoire littéraire du sentiment religieux en France, depuis la fin des guerres de religion jusqu'à nos jours,* vol. 5 (1920)

Brémond was a Catholic religious historian of considerable reputation, a priest, a pioneer of modern Catholic intellectual and spiritual history, and a man of the twentieth century in his thought, even though he was somewhat conservative by modern standards. To him, there was no doubt of the facts: Grandier was not guilty of causing possession. Some nuns may have been possessed, some sick, some both, but in no case did Grandier have anything to do with it. Brémond's major criticism is of the exorcists. He holds that they were very much in error in the way they conducted the exorcisms; their procedures were bad; they should not have conducted public exorcisms; and they were far too ready to believe what they wanted to believe. If they had followed the rules of the church, either of Brémond's time or as laid out by Archbishop de Sourdis, this travesty of justice would not have happened.

Brémond points out that many of the exorcists and the four bishops who encouraged them by their presence (and even took part) went wrong because they were so eager to convert the Huguenots and prove the power of the Roman Catholic Church over the Devil. Once entered on this path, all their actions were directed to proving the possessions valid and finding Grandier guilty of causing them; and once this path had been taken by them, many subsequent Catholic authors did their utmost to convince their readers that the events of 1634 were valid. Brémond's eminent position in French Catholic historiography made it respectable and fully acceptable, from this time forward, to be openly critical of the exorcists and the possessions.

Aldous Huxley, *The Devils of Loudun* (1952)

This book is readable although inaccurate in some details and subject at times to imagined conversations and events. Inevitably, it is dated in much of its background on witchcraft, which has been extensively studied since Huxley's time. As far as Grandier's story is concerned, Huxley bases his work almost totally on Legué. One significant contribution of this book is that it was the first major work on Grandier published in English; and since Huxley was a well-established author, it gained a wide circulation that has lasted to this day. Another contribution of significance is Huxley's concentration on Surin and his experiences with Jeanne des Anges. Huxley had a deep interest in mysticism, and when he writes about Surin, the whole style changes; it is serious, understanding of mystic experience, and complex, whereas the sections on Grandier tend to be cynical and are essentially repeating Legué.

Huxley's book was written during the McCarthy era in the United States. Without actually stating the comparison, he draws a picture of the same guilt by accusation, the same dangers of demagoguery and crowd manipulation. This was an important step forward in the history of the Grandier case – a recognition that many situations in our own time are repetitions of similar attitudes in different circumstances in earlier times and that witch-hunts can happen under many guises. Another point of interest is that although there had been many works on witchcraft before Huxley, there had been very few on witch-hunts. Since then, it has become a major field of study by historians.

Michel de Certeau, *La possession de Loudun* (1970)

This is a beautifully written book and another significant step forward in analysing the complexities of the Grandier case, for de Certeau points out that "possession becomes a great public trial ... it is a theatrical performance, which draws the curious from throughout France and virtually the whole of Europe." The pattern of this theatrical performance was set by the possessions in Aix en Provence in 1611, which involved Madeleine Demandolx, her exorcists, and Louis Gaufridy, Grandier's priestly parallel. That case was so famous that during the possessions of Loudun, all the actors knew their parts; thus, all the main events had to be repeated, down to Grandier's death. Even the purpose of the performance was the same as in Aix – to convince the Huguenots that the possessions were real and that the true church had the power to expel demons.

One of the interesting features of this work is that de Certeau has gone back to original source material, making extensive use of the enormous mass of records at the Bibliothèque nationale in Paris. Thus he quotes from material that is not readily available to people who are unable to spend the necessary time in Paris. Like Legué, therefore, he is a valuable source of original information. It should be noted, however, that this book assumes that the reader knows the main events of the Grandier story, and it should therefore be taken up after reading one of the more general works.

Roland Villeneuve, *La mystérieuse affaire Grandier: Le diable à Loudun* (1980)

This book is a repetition of earlier works, but the historical setting and background information provide a backdrop to the story, making it more understandable to the contemporary reader. One of the things that has fascinated readers for the last three and a half centuries is that there are so many plausible interpretations of why Grandier was killed and who should be held responsible. Villeneuve is somewhat ambiguous in his views. At one point he lays the blame on Richelieu and Father Joseph: "There is no doubt that Grandier was the victim of a cabal led by the Capuchins, on the tab of Father Joseph and Laubardemont, the damned soul of Richelieu seeking to avenge the honour of the cardinal, who had been offended so many times by the curé of Loudun." Elsewhere he states that "many hold that heresy was the preponderant cause of the loss of Grandier" and that it was Grandier's treatise on celibacy that condemned him, for heresy was unpardonable in a priest. But then he argues, "The ulterior search for marks and a diabolic pact, the allusions made in the records about the accused being unable to cry, and the pressure of infernal creatures around his execution prove, it seems to us, from the evidence, that sorcery prevailed as the issue in the mind of the judges." The main contribution of this book is that it retells the story for a general and modern audience. Its principal drawback is that it has a strong anti-Catholic bias, which colours many events.

Michel Carmona, *Les diables de Loudun: Sorcellerie et politique sous Richelieu* (1985)

About half this book is devoted to the internal French politics of the period, concentrating on Richelieu and providing the background to the events in Loudun. The other half is devoted to the Grandier case and its aftermath until the final expulsion of the demons from the nuns in 1638. The Grandier story itself is almost completely based on Legué and includes Legué's repetitions of old rumours as facts.

There is one area that Carmona covers well, namely, his analysis of the different theories about why Grandier was executed: that he was a free-thinker out of his time; that he defended the walls of Loudun against the new town of Richelieu; that he was a leader of the anticardinalist party in Loudun; that he was arrogant and created enemies who took advantage of his fall; that "spiritual incest" was the cause, as it had been for the curé of Beaugé; and so on. Unfortunately, he covers this only briefly. Nevertheless, it is a valuable addition to the catalogue of possible explanations.

Even today, there are still uncertainties about the story. Most of the open questions about Grandier have now been resolved, although even there the degree of his concupiscence is in doubt. As for Laubardemont, we still do not know whether or not he really believed the nuns to be possessed, and Jeanne des Anges is still much of a puzzle. We can see clear evidence of sickness and hysteria, but for all our psychiatric advances, we cannot be sure how much she was in control of events and how much she was subject to them. We can see aspects of repressed memories and other terms we recognize today. We can see how she took advantage of events to create her sanctity and occupy a respected, indeed commanding, position in her world. What is less apparent is that in a man's world which had little respect for a woman's intellect, she manipulated men to the point where she was respected and admired and could talk publicly in a way few other women could. How much of this did she direct? How much was she merely taking day-to-day advantage of the opportunities presented to her by gullible, manipulable men – Mignon, Surin, Richelieu, the king?

In our modern society, it is a virtual given that true possession by the Devil could not have occurred because the Devil of the horns and the tail, in whom the people of Loudun believed, does not exist. Yet if evil ever existed, it was in Loudun, and to some extent it manifested itself in all the participants through their weaknesses and hatreds. Nor is this limited to seventeenth-century Loudun. The same witch-hunt that killed Grandier can be found in every situation where to be accused is to be held guilty by society.

Appendix Two
Blood Is Thicker than Water

There is an assertion throughout this book that Grandier was the prey of Louis Trincant and his family from the time the priest seduced Philippe Trincant. This was a family compact. There is no doubt that Grandier's constant enemies were all related to Trincant by blood or marriage. In proof of this, some of the main relationships are noted below, together with a reliable source for each.

Louis and Philippe Trincant, father and daughter (Archives municipales de Loudun, record of baptisms, GG10)

Louis Moussaut, father of Philippe Trincant's husband (who was also named Louis Moussaut). The older Louis married Rachel Mesmin, Mesmin de Silly's sister. Thus, the Moussauts and Mesmins were directly connected (S. Rohaut, "Réflections sur Urbain Grandier," *La Gazette du Loudunais*, July/August 1995, 2)

Louis Moussaut, Philippe Trincant's husband (Archives municipales de Loudun, GG10)

Jean Mignon, Louis Trincant's nephew and Philippe's cousin (Grandier's "Factum")

Barot, Trincant's relative (exact relationship unknown), Jean Mignon's uncle (Aubin, *Histoire des diables de Loudun*, 10; Legué, *Urbain Grandier et les possédées de Loudun*, 55, 204)

René Hervé, Trincant's relative and Mesmin's son-in-law (Legué, *Urbain Grandier et les possédées de Loudun*, 13); Claire de Sazilly was his sister-in-law.

Pierre Adam, Louis Trincant's nephew, Philippe's cousin, and Mignon's cousin (Figuier, *Histoire du merveilleux*, 139), and Mesmin de Silly's nephew (ibid., 140)

René Mannoury, Louis Trincant's cousin (Legué, *Urbain Grandier et les possédées de Loudun*, 30)

Richard the lawyer, Louis Trincant's relative (relationship unknown) (ibid., 87)

Pierre Fournier the lawyer, Richard's son-in-law (ibid., 200)

Jacques de Thibault, a "distant" relative (according to Burckardt, *Richelieu and His Age*, 265, and Hanotaux, *Histoire du Cardinal de Richelieu*, 252)

Pierre Menuau, Mignon's and Adam's cousin (Grandier's "Factum"), and Madeleine de Brou's early admirer, who became her bitter enemy when he was rejected (Legué, *Urbain Grandier et les possédées de Loudun*, 39)

Paul Aubin, Sieur de Bourgneuf was married to Mesmin's de Silly's daughter (who was a cousin of Louis Moussaut, the husband of Philippe Trincant). It was his brother who arrested Grandier (see S. Rohaut, "Réflections sur Urbain Grandier," *La Gazette du Loudunais*, July/August 1995, 2). He had earlier been an active enemy of the priest (Legué, *Urbain Grandier et les possédées de Loudun*, 159, 189).

Notes

ABBREVIATIONS

AM Archives municipales
AN Archives nationales
B Bibliothèque
BM Bibliothèque municipale
BN Bibliothèque nationale

PROLOGUE

1 All translations are by the author.

TWELVE GOOD YEARS

1 Various authors give figures ranging from twelve thousand to twenty or even twenty-five thousand as the population of Loudun. The most recent work is currently being done by Edwin Bezzina at the University of Toronto. In a personal note to the author, he suggests a figure of less than ten thousand, though he has not yet completed his estimates. Given what we know of town sizes at the time and taking into account all the uncertainties, fourteen thousand would seem to be a maximum figure for the population of Loudun in the early sixteen hundreds, with perhaps ten thousand or a little less as a lower probability. This would still make it a sizable provincial town by the standards of the times. For a description of the town and its defences, see Trincant, *Abrégé des antiquités de Loudun et pays de loudunois*.

2 Archives municipales (AM) de Loudun, GG9. The signature of Urbain
  Grandier appears for the first time in Loudun on 4 August 1617,
  when he baptized a child.

3 We cannot with certainty presuppose that a seventeenth-century
  twenty-seven year old felt and thought the same as one would
  today. Still, it seems more likely than not that Urbain Grandier's
  reactions to his first entry into Loudun were much as I have
  described them. For simplicity I have written this passage assuming
  that his reactions would be like ours.

4 Priests had the reputation of being far too accessible to women in
  the early seventeenth century. Dulong (*La vie quotidienne des
  femmes au grand siècle*) notes that in the diocese of Chartres, in the
  years 1630–40, 8 per cent of priests lived in concubinage or committed fornication on occasion. The church at this time was becoming
  much more demanding on the subject of celibacy, but there was still
  a long way to go in France. Grandier, however, was Jesuit trained.
  He certainly would have been taught not only to be unavailable to
  women but to convey the impression of inaccessibility.

5 The characters in this story lived in a world in which heaven and
  hell were very real and very close. What they thought about this
  world and the next is beautifully portrayed in Dante's *Divine Comedy*. Although it was written more than three hundred years earlier,
  Catholic theology had not changed; Dante's heaven, hell, and purgatory were as real as ever, though by the seventeenth century, hell
  had become the pre-eminent concern. To understand that world better, Dorothy Sayer's translation and particularly her commentary, are
  highly recommended.

6 Urbain Grandier was born in 1590 at Bouère in Mayenne. Neither
  he nor his family had any connection with Loudun until his arrival
  there in 1617. His father was a royal notary, a legal officer of some
  local importance, and a successful provincial lawyer.

7 Jeanne d'Estièvre, Grandier's mother, is usually described as the
  daughter of minor but distinguished nobility, though there is some
  doubt about this. The suggestion that she was not of noble birth
  comes from Ledru, *Urbain Grandier*. See Archives départementales,
  Sarthe AA 216. What cannot be doubted is that she was a woman
  of great character and of great fortitude in adversity.

8 Ledru, *Urbain Grandier*. Ledru says that he does not know the ages
  of all the brothers and sisters or their order in the family. He does
  tell us that François was born in 1605 and René in 1608, so these
  two were much younger than Urbain and would have been twelve

and nine years old, respectively, when Urbain went to Loudun. With such a big age gap between Urbain and François, it is likely that Jean and the two girls were born between 1590 and 1605. Grandier's parents may have had other children in between who died, for the rate of child mortality at the time was about 50 per cent.

9 For an easily read background history of France at this period, see the first half of Briggs, *Early Modern France, 1560–1715*.

10 For an overview of Catholicism in France at the time, see Delumeau, *Catholicism between Luther and Voltaire*.

11 Calvin was born in 1509, was chased from Paris in 1533, and wrote his *Institutes* in 1535.

12 On the number and distribution of Huguenots in France, see Baird, *The Huguenots and the Revocation of the Edict of Nantes*, 1–5. This is the best book in English that I have found. It is an excellent and easily absorbed story of the Huguenots and Huguenot wars. Written more than a hundred years ago, and openly biased in their favour, it nevertheless shows the fears and dilemmas which they faced in a largely hostile environment.

13 For a more detailed picture of Catholic/Huguenot fears in Loudun, see Dumoustier de La Fond, *Essais sur l'histoire de la ville de Loudun*. This book also gives background information on much of the other material relating to Loudun contained in this chapter. See also Moreau de la Ronde's *Les châteaux de Loudun*.

14 See Barbier, *Jean d'Armagnac II*, 178. On 29 July 1621 d'Armagnac took an oath that indicated he had changed his religion and was now a Catholic.

15 The full complexities of a Catholic/Huguenot community are far beyond this book. For an insight into these relationships in two other communities, see Hanlon, *Confession and Community in Seventeenth-Century France*, and Cassan, *Le temps des guerres de religion*. Even more directly significant, Edwin Bezzina is preparing his doctoral thesis at the University of Toronto entitled "The Protestant and Catholic Families of Loudun, 1595–1685: A Case Study in the Social History of 'Religious Toleration' in Seventeenth-Century France." When completed, it will provide valuable additional background.

16 We will return to the fortifications of Loudun in chapter 4.

17 Saint Vincent de Paul, beginning in 1616, was the outstanding leader in encouraging women to become actively involved in all types of social work. During this same period, many young women were also acting on their own initiative, both in social work and in

teaching, often supported and advised by priests. This social change was still in its early stages, not yet a full reality but in the air. In 1634 a group of religious young women were supporters of Grandier in his darkest days. Given that many of his ideas were in advance of his time, it is quite likely that he had encouraged women to be active in his parish from the start.

18 There is no record of his installation, but in the circumstances, this is probably a fair description.

19 Brief biographies of Scévole de Sainte-Marthe and his two sons can be found in Lerosey, *Histoire civile*, 435–40.

20 Louis Trincant was born in 1571. At the time of Grandier's arrival at the age of twenty-seven, Trincant was forty-six. He was exactly the same age as the two sons of Scévole de Sainte-Marthe and was treated by them like a brother; their fathers had known each other all their lives and were close friends. "From the time of our youth," Trincant wrote, "we lived together, studied under the same masters ... and when finally separated we always maintained our sincere friendship with close and frequent letters, and we went on like that for more than fifty-two years." See Bibliothèque nationale (hereafter BN), Collection Duchesne, 67, cited in Legué, *Urbain Grandier*, 23.

21 For precise information on offices such as *procureur du roi, lieutenant-criminel, bailli*, and other terms mentioned in this book, see Mousnier, *The Institutions of France*. For specific information on these offices in Loudun, see Lerosey, *Histoire civile*, 42–59.

22 Jean d'Armagnac II was born and brought up a Huguenot. His father fought for Henry IV before Henry became king, was rewarded with the king's friendship, and became a member of the royal household. When Louis XIII was a child, d'Armagnac was one of his favourites, and when Louis took over the reins of power, d'Armagnac received the same privileges and friendship that his father had enjoyed. D'Armagnac obtained the office of *bailli* of the Loudunais in July 1614 (Barbier, *Jean d'Armagnac II*, 76, 177) and was named governor of the town and château in letters patent on 18 December 1617 (ibid., 177).

23 D'Armagnac's letters to Grandier give strong hints of the priest's friendly associations with leading Huguenots (see, for example, ibid., 83, letter dated 18 January 1630).

24 Precedence was a matter of enormous social importance. The whole structure of society was largely based on honour, privilege, and precedence. These were fundamental concepts to a "gentleman" of the time. Personal and family honour were things that one would fight

to the death to preserve. Every man of standing (and it was particularly true of those of the noble class, who set the pattern) was constantly on the watch for the least slur on his honour or on that of a friend or patron. D'Artagnan and his three musketeers are the perfect example of this attitude.

25 There seems to be no contemporary account of this event, and the first written record appears to be about fifty years after the death of Grandier. We cannot be certain that it actually happened, but the probability is that it did. All the authors refer to it.

26 For more on this fascinating and influential man, see one or more of the following: Tapié, *The France of Louis XIII and Richelieu* (a translation of the original French text, recognized as an authoritative account of Richelieu's life); Burckhardt, *Richelieu and His Age* (a translation from the original German and also very readable); Mousnier, *L'homme rouge* (a comprehensive work on the subject by one of France's great modern historians – and his last book before his death); Hildesheimer, *Richelieu* (a much shorter work than either of the two above, but very readable and with useful lists of further reading at the end of each chapter); Carmona, *La France de Richelieu*, which surveys the social background of this period (a useful book to read in order to get a wider view of the world within which the possessions of Loudun took place).

27 La Rocheposay has been described as "a prelate with a totally feudal outlook. At the beginning of his episcopate he went about his diocese armed in breast plate, lance in hand, supported by twelve horsemen, pistols by their saddles, and some forty foot-soldiers, each with a carbine ... Later he calmed down somewhat" (Jovy, *Trois documents*, 16).

28 BN, fonds français, MS 7618, cited in Legué, *Urbain Grandier*, 16–18.

29 Aubin, *Histoire*, 9.

30 The Bernier story is in BN, fonds français, MS 7618, and is cited in Legué, *Urbain Grandier*, 18–19.

31 See appendix 2.

32 Legué (*Urbain Grandier*, 13) refers to this incident as taking place in 1618; de Certeau (*La possession*, 87) talks of an incident in 1621. Whether or not there was more than one incident, this early enmity is clearly established.

33 Legué, *Urbain Grandier*, 13.

34 Carmona, *Les diables de Loudun*, 74.

35 For information on this man, who was to play such a significant part in Grandier's future, see Mémin, *René Mesmin de Silly*.

36 Legué, *Urbain Grandier*, 10.

37 In the late Middle Ages the miraculous had been accepted largely without question, but by the sixteenth century the humanists were already bringing a spirit of inquiry into such matters as miracles and relics; the Reformation was based in part on exactly this kind of scepticism. Ideas took time to filter down from the intellectuals to ordinary people in provincial towns and villages, and in France during the early 1600s many provincial and rural priests and laymen still had great faith in miracles, without asking too many questions. Highly trained men like Grandier, with inquiring minds, would still be unusual in a place such as Loudun. On this matter, as on a number of others, he seems to have been closer to many Protestants than to a large number of Catholics.

38 This reduced the income for the two orders at a time when the Carmelites, in particular, were suffering from a competing miraculous statue in a nearby town.

DISASTER

1 There is no record of the formal entry of the Ursulines into Loudun. There are, however, a number of descriptions of the arrival in other towns of new convents of teaching nuns about that same date. The description in the text is based on one of these: the entry of the teaching nuns of the Congregation of Notre Dame into the town of Provins in 1629. Provins was roughly the same size as Loudun. See Bibliothèque municipale (hereafter BM) de Provins, MS 251. For the letters patent from the king confirming the establishment of the Ursulines in Loudun, see Barbier, *Jean d'Armagnac II*, 198–202.

2 Tranquille, in his "Véritable relation des justes procedures," states clearly that Grandier had never seen the nuns. He was one of Grandier's enemies and was in a position to speak with authority, as we shall see.

3 Tapié, *La France de Louis XIII*, quoted in *Lexique historique de la France d'Ancien Régime* by Cabourdin and Viard, 60.

4 For a detailed picture of all the events leading to the fall of the walls, see Moreau de la Ronde's *Les châteaux de Loudun*. He also provides a useful picture of the principal players in the events leading up to the razing of the walls.

5 The Huguenots from throughout France held a number of important political assemblies in Loudun at various times, most notably the

assembly of 1619–20. Though the latter was held with royal authority, it behaved in a very independent fashion, at times ignoring directions from the crown. This independence, and the implied long-term threat to the central government, may have influenced Richelieu, who at the time was at the queen mother's right hand. He may have concluded that the fortifications would have to be razed because the city would always be vulnerable to a Huguenot coup.

6 The model town exists today, with all the sanitized appearance that one would expect of centralized planning, yet it remains a remarkable tribute to the "modernness" of those men of the early seventeenth century. A good outline of Richelieu's steps to increase the importance of the town of Richelieu at the expense of Loudun is in Moreau de la Ronde's *Les châteaux de Loudun*. See also Mémin, *René Mesmin de Silly*.

7 Philippe Trincant was born in October 1603. She was about twenty-five when the seduction took place and was about thirteen years younger than Grandier. Her birth record is held at Loudun, but she was born at Thouars, about fifteen miles from there. I am grateful to Mme Sylviane Rohaut for this item. Mme Rohaut, archivist for the municipality of Loudun, gave unstinting help in tracing these and other events in the municipal archives.

8 The most precise of these was La Menardaye's *Examen de l'histoire des diables de Loudun*. He argues in great detail all the issues that Aubin raised, but not the seduction.

9 (1) We know for certain from baptismal records in the Archives municipales (hereafter AM) de Loudun, GG10, that Philippe Trincant was godmother to a child in October 1628. This is also noted in Rohaut, "Réflections sur Urbain Grandier." Philippe could not have been obviously pregnant by that date. So allowing that she could have been less than three months pregnant at the time and still not showing it, the earliest possible date of conception would be about June or July 1628. (2) Philippe was married in early June 1629. If the marriage took place quickly, before her pregnancy showed, she might have been three or four months pregnant, not much more. So the latest possible date would be February or March 1629. (3) In September 1629 Trincant wrote a letter to his great friends the Sainte-Marthe brothers, saying that Grandier's once good reputation had been destroyed some eight months earlier, which indicates that the conception took place around that time, i.e., between January and March 1629.

10 Marriage records of Saint-Pierre-du-Marché (AM Loudun, GG11).

11 AM Loudun, GG10. My thanks to Mme Rohaut for this information. I am also grateful to Edwin Bezzina, who provided me with the actual text during his doctoral studies in Loudun.

12 This may indeed have been the second baptism of the child. The infant mortality rate was so high that babies were baptized within a day or two of being born, for only a baptized child could enter heaven if it died. So there was probably a first secret baptism performed somewhere, which was followed by the second, public, baptism by Meschin.

13 Louis Trincant resigned as *procureur du roi* in 1631, and Louis Moussaut inherited the position. Aubin (*Histoire*) tells us this, and it is confirmed by the fact that Moussaut is shown in the 1632 baptismal record of his second son as being the *procureur du roi*. Like many offices of the time, it was paid for and could be sold again or handed on to another.

14 Aubin, *Histoire*, 10–11.

15 It was quite common for mothers to hand their children over in this way for the first two or three years.

16 AM Loudun, GG10, and Rohaut, "Réflections sur Urbain Grandier," 2. These baptisms took place in 1625, 1627, and September 1628. Trincant and Marthe were still clearly friends at the time, which would indicate that Philippe was not yet known to be pregnant.

17 Information received from Mme Rohaut, archivist of Loudun. Marthe was married to Pierre Delahaye, and their daughter Madeleine is recorded as being baptized on 1 November 1633.

18 France at that date was a very legalistic society. If something was done formally and legally, that was the end of it. Once Philippe was married and the baby was shown to be Moussaut's, all society had to accept this as a fact not to be argued with. It could only be questioned (at peril) before the law, and to a large degree Trincant was the law in Loudun. No matter what people privately thought or whispered, from this time forward Philippe was legally innocent and untouched.

19 Trincant and Richelieu knew each other well; they had both been representatives at the Estates General in 1614 to 1615 and had worked closely together. See Carmona, *Les diables de Loudun*, 66.

20 Legué, *Urbain Grandier*, 56.

21 Grandier had won a legal battle against Father Mignon some years earlier over the ownership of a house, so there was probably already

dislike between them. Most authors mention this (see, for instance, Gayot, *Histoire*, 12–13).

22 Legué and La Tourette, *Sœur Jeanne des Anges*, 61–4.

23 For a brief review of La Rocheposay, see Formon, "Henri Louis Chastenier."

24 The Moussaut family was extensive, and the name appears in many different forms in the records: Moussau, Moussaut, Mousseau, Moussault. For simplicity, I have used the spelling "Moussaut" throughout, except when the name appears in a quotation.

25 Father Moussaut is referred to in Grandier's "Factum" as Louis Moussaut's uncle.

26 Legué (*Urbain Grandier*, 57) says that he was a squire, seigneur of Chasseignes and one of the king's two hundred light horse. Aubin (*Histoire*, 12) describes him as a rich man of great credit. Burckhardt (*Richelieu and His Age*, 265) describes de Thibault as "a member of the local gentry and a distant relative of the seduced girl." Hanotaux (*Histoire du cardinal*, 252) also describes him as "vaguely related" to the Trincant family.

27 The Marquis du Bellai (or Bellay). See Aubin, *Histoire*, 12, or Legué *Urbain Grandier*, 56.

28 Ibid., 57.

29 BM Poitiers, A2, MS 303.

30 The Parlement of Paris was a law court, not a legislative body. Although similar in name to the English Parliament, it had little similarity in its functions or powers. Its principal power was to register the king's decrees or, more importantly, to refuse to register them until certain changes were made. This was a source of continuing contention between the king and the parlement.

31 There were two parishes in Loudun, but the leading families all seem to have belonged to Grandier's.

32 See Mousnier, *The Institutions of France*, for further information on the functions of a *bailli*.

33 For the significance of these local jealousies in the Grandier case, see Lerosey, *Histoire civile*, 215.

34 The *bailli* was a strong and true supporter of the governor, although he personally was in favour of razing the walls.

35 We have met him before. He was the priest who had baptized the Trincant-Moussaut baby.

36 Legué, *Urbain Grandier*, 64.

37 BN, fonds français, MS 7618, quoted in ibid., 65.

38 Ibid., 68.

GRANDIER AND HIS BISHOP

1 Record of the arrest of Urbain Grandier in the Bibliothèque munici-pale (BM) de Poitiers, A2, MS303.

2 All the correspondence between Grandier and La Rocheposay in this chapter can be found in Legué, *Urbain Grandier*, chap. 6. The origi-nal records are in the Bibliothèque nationale (BN), Collection Barbier.

3 Legué, *Urbain Grandier*, 76.

4 Grandier was apparently also accused of "holding the doctrine of Théophile." This was Théophile de Viau, a man of Protestant origin who had been condemned to death for publishing libertine ideas and immoral writings. See Jovy, *Trois documents*, 14. On Théophile, see Michaud, *Biographie universelle*, 45: 366–48.

5 BN, Collection Barbier, quoted in Legué, *Urbain Grandier*, 82.

6 The case of the curé of Beaugé is described in Livonnière, *Cous-tumes d'Anjou*, 2:994. The curé was accused of adultery with one of his parishioners (or, more significantly, with the wife of one of his important parishioners) and of "spiritual incest" with her because she had "a spiritual affinity" to him, contracted through the sacra-ments of baptism and confirmation. The parallels with Grandier in Loudun are obvious.

7 The record of this address to the court is quoted in Legué, *Histoire*, 86. He cites the original as being in BN, fonds français, 520.

8 Barbier, *Jean d'Armagnac II*, 95, letter of 14 December 1630.

9 In contemporary terminology, this was the *lieutenant-criminel* and his staff, but for the modern reader it seems appropriate to refer to them as the police, even though this is not precisely correct.

10 The hours were a particular set of prayers that priests were obliged to say at set times of the day, and they were contained in a book called the breviary. Failure to say the hours was a serious sacrile-gious offence for a priest.

11 BM Poitiers, A2, MS 303, quoted in full in Legué, *Urbain Grandier*, 91–2, and in Aubin, *Histoire*, 18–20.

12 Archives nationales (AN), U832.11799f and K114A.1.1. Adam appealed his sentence but was found guilty.

13 Barbier, *Jean d'Armagnac II*, 83, letter of 18 January 1630. Gou-geon and Le Blanc often appear in the d'Armagnac correspondence. They were leading Protestants and friends of both Grandier and the governor.

14 See Legué, *Urbain Grandier*, 97, for the complete record of the deci-sion. He notes that the original of the "sentence of absolution" used

to be in the Bibliothèque de Poitiers but disappeared long ago, together with a number of other items concerning the Grandier trial.

15 Boulliau, "Lettre à Gassendi."

16 Aubin (*Histoire*, 23–4) says that the respectable people of Loudun were scandalized by this immodest conduct, that Grandier's enemies were beside themselves with anger, and his own friends disapproved.

17 See Legué, *Urbain Grandier*, 99.

18 BN, Fonds français, MS 7618, quoted in full, with signatories, in ibid., 100. This letter was written in mid-1631. Since Grandier did not get his final absolution from the archbishop of Bordeaux until November 1631, it would seem that the archbishop must have given him a temporary restitution during the year, pending his final decision.

19 See the baptismal entry for the child Pierre Moussaut, dated 16 July 1631 (AM Loudun, GG10).

20 Barbier, *Jean d'Armagnac II*, 144–7, letter of 7 March 1632.

21 Ibid., 161–2, letter of 11 April 1633. (In this letter, his annoyance with Grandier for pursuing this and another legal case to the limits is clearly apparent.)

22 Ibid.

DESTRUCTION AND PLAGUE

1 For the interesting story of the donjon up to modern times, see Crozet and Bouzon, *Le donjon cylindre de Loudun*.

2 We cannot be sure that Laubardemont found as many as a hundred witches in Béarn. It was not uncommon for witch-hunters and their supporters to exaggerate their claims. Nevertheless, Laubardemont's work certainly involved many burnings and was widely known. For a brief biography of Laubardemont, see the article on him in Michaud, *Biographie universelle*, vol. 23.

3 See Barbier, *Jean d'Armagnac II*, 103–5, 114–17, letters of 25 September and 29 October 1631.

4 Ibid., 103–5, 105–6, 110–13, letters from D'Armagnac to Grandier, 25 September, [undated] October, and 19 October 1631.

5 Ibid., 105–6, letter from d'Armagnac to Grandier, undated but probably October 1631 from the internal evidence.

6 Ibid., 110–13, letter from d'Armagnac to Grandier, 19 October 1631.

7 Legué, *Urbain Grandier*, 156.

8 Ibid., 162.

9 Bibliothèque nationale (BN), MS 7618, and Legué, *Urbain Grandier*, 165. This took place on 6 June 1632.

10 Many of the events in this chapter are covered in Moreau de la Ronde's, *Les châteaux de Loudun.*

11 This and the following quotations come from Legué, *Urbain Grandier,* 34–9.

12 De Certeau (*La possession,* 89–96), examines the treatise from a theological viewpoint.

13 Grandier, "Traité du célibat des prêtres," BN, fonds français, Collection Dupuy, 571, 66 ff. It was printed in 1866 by Luzarche, Paris.

14 She was born on the 22 December 1594. See Archives municipales (AM) de Loudun, GG5.

15 See Legué, *Urbain Grandier,* 38.

16 Ibid., 93, quoting the Archives nationales (AN) Registres du Parlement. Legué gives no date.

17 Legué was wrong when he said, in a footnote, that Grandier admitted composing it for Madeleine de Brou.

18 Legué, *Urbain Grandier,* 38.

19 The plague has been the subject of an enormous number of books. Many of these focus on the Black Death of 1346–52, which for its magnitude and virulence can truly be described as a European catastrophe. The disease returned again and again over the centuries, the last major European assault being in Marseille and Provence between 1720 and 1722. One of its most deadly onslaughts occurred in 1628–32, and it was during this outbreak that Loudun was devastated. To suggest books on the subject for further reading carries the risk that many equally useful books will be left out. Nevertheless, I offer the following, which contain a mass of information relevant to this chapter; they were the principal works I used as background reading.

The most directly relevant book is Delaroche, *Une épidémie de peste à Loudun,* which resulted from Delaroche's doctoral thesis as a medical doctor. He identifies the plague in Loudun from its recorded symptoms and describes the plans prepared by the town in the years before the event to deal with an attack. He covers the steps which the authorities, led by the *bailli,* took during the plague to try to prevent the spread of infection, and he covers the course of the epidemic in Loudun, with a valuable account from the records. In a conversation with the author in 1994, Dr Delaroche explained that over the years he had arrived at the opinion that the plague played a greater part in the possessions than had ever been recognized.

Hildesheimer's *La terreur et la pitié* provides a more general coverage of the plague in France over the centuries. It is well worth reading. It has a useful bibliography but suffers from the fact that there are no footnotes to identify the source of particular items. Nohl's *The Black Death* covers all the different aspects well, including both the diabolical and the erotic elements. An excellent recreation of the terrors of the disease, based on first-hand accounts, is to be found in Defoe's *Journal of the Plague Year*, which deals with the plague in London that killed 100,000 people in 1665. Although this was a different outbreak of the disease, it was close enough in time to be directly relevant to the 1630s epidemic in France. Brossollet and Mollaret, in *Pourquoi la peste?*, give a good history of the plague from the earliest times. The outstanding feature is its mass of illustrations. Nobody interested in the plague should miss this book. Lucenet's *Les grandes pestes en France* follows the plague there from the Black Death to modern times, dealing with all its aspects: social life, religious effects, medical facts. This book has a good bibliography. Cipolla's *Faith, Reason, and the Plague in Seventeenth-Century Tuscany* covers the same European epidemic that afflicted Loudun. Working on a base of especially rich documentation, Cipolla describes the effects of the plague on a sizable village in Tuscany in 1630–31. Boccaccio's *Decameron* was written shortly after the Black Death, which he had personally experienced. In his introduction, he describes very precisely the attitudes of his contemporaries towards each other and towards the plague itself. Delumeau's *La peur en occident* is well worth reading for its many facets. One sizable part of it deals with the plague, and the way Delumeau connects it to the general mood of anxiety of the time is most interesting. This book should be read by anybody interested in knowing more about the plague and its effect on Western society.

20 The figure of 3,700 is the one commonly used, and if the population was about 14,000, as some think, then the number of deaths would have been one-quarter or one-fifth of that. We cannot be sure of the accuracy of either figure, be we do know with certainty that the death rate in Loudun from the plague was terrifying.

21 Petrarch (1304–74).

22 This terrible onslaught of the plague was not limited to Loudun or even to France; it swept through Europe, lasting from about 1628 to 1642. In France alone, 271 towns were afflicted and about 2 million people died. See Hildesheimer, *La terreur et la pitié*, 14.

23 Delaroche, *Une épidémie de peste à Loudun*, 46. All the information in this chapter specifically about the plague in Loudun has come from this book.

24 Henri d'Effiat, Marquis de Saint-Mars; quoted in ibid., 44.

25 For a horrific eyewitness description of a city under the plague and the effect by the epidemic on the citizens, see Boccaccio's introduction to his *Decameron*.

26 The search for witches and other heretics, which accompanied attacks of the plague, has been noted by many authors. For an example, see "Peste et sorcellerie: Deux épidémies parallèles?" in Hildesheimer, *La terreur et la pitié*, 134–8.

27 This reaction has many parallels in modern times: for example, those who label AIDS a punishment for homosexuality; the communist witch-hunts of the McCarthy era in the United States; and the Holocaust in Germany. Each generation creates its own witches and its own witch-hunts. Only the labels change.

28 Hildesheimer, *La terreur et la pitié*, 24.

29 There are many good descriptions of the preparations made to deal with a plague attack on a town and the rules that were published by the authorities. For example, Delaroche deals specifically with Loudun; Hildesheimer (19–24) briefly describes the same plague in Agen; and Defoe reports at length in his *Journal of the Plague Year*.

30 Legué, *Urbain Grandier*, 104–5; Delaroche *Une épidémie de peste à Loudun*, 48.

31 See Nohl, *The Black Death*, 127–33, Brossolet and Mollaret, *Pourquoi la peste?*, 74–5; or Hildesheimer, *La terreur et la pitié*, 130, for the loose behaviour of previously moral people after the passing of the plague.

32 The details of Jeanne des Anges' condition are noted in the record left by her doctor, Daniel Rogier, and by the master surgeon, René Mannoury (BN, fonds français, MS 7619, cited in Legué, *Urbain Grandier*, 108).

33 Legué says that Moussaut died in 1631, but this seems to be a printer's error because he is also quite specific that the priest's death took place only weeks before September 1632 (*Urbain Grandier*, 108). Gayot (*Causes célèbres*, 7) says that Moussaut died in 1632. Madame Rohaut was kind enough to search the archives in Loudun for a record of Moussaut's death, but the death records were not maintained during the plague; presumably, such matters were the least of their problems at the time.

34 See Jeanne des Anges' autobiography for her own admissions (BM Tours, MS 1197).

POSSESSION

1 Young women entered a convent for many different reasons, which included the ones given in the text, but only in a minority of cases. For a picture of the creation and growth of teaching convents in the sixteen hundreds, see Elizabeth Rapley, *The Dévotes*; and for why women chose to be nuns, see Rapley's "Women and the Religious Vocation in Seventeenth-Century France."

2 In the first half of the seventeenth century the cities and towns of France experienced what has been called "a fantastic conventual invasion" (Bardet, *Rouen*, 1:90).

3 For the names, ages, and family connections of these nuns, see de Certeau, *La possession*, 136–8. Surin, *Correspondance*, 248, gives additional details.

4 The nuns were so young because the house was new and thus attracted young women. This was common with the new teaching-order convents at the time. Once they were filled, the nuns grew older together. The average age in a mature convent was about forty-three, and the superior was normally an experienced nun of fifty or sixty who had worked her way up through the ranks in a variety of lesser posts.

5 For more details on her early life, see Surin, *Correspondance*, 1721–7.

6 Jeanne des Anges, autobiography, BM Tours, MS 1197, confirms these statements.

7 The principal records of all the events relating to the possessions are held in the Bibliothèque nationale. Michel de Certeau's extracts and comments about the possessions have been used extensively because he is both accurate in his selections and historical in his analysis. This particular document comes from BN, MS 7619, and is quoted in his *La possession*, 26–8.

8 The thorns were described as being *de la longueur d'une épingle et de la grosseur d'une aiguille à coudre en caneux*; ("the length of a pin and the thickness of a needle for sewing canvas.") See BM Tours, MS 1197.

9 BN, fonds français, MS 7619, Barré and Mignon's minutes, quoted by de Certeau in *La possession*, 28–9; Legué in *Urbain Grandier*, 114; Gayot in *Histoire*, 26–30.

10 BM Tours, MS 1134.

11 De Certeau, *La possession*, 24.

12 BM Tours, MS 1134.

13 Legué, *Documents pour servir à l'histoire médicale*, 42, taken from Mercure François, vol. 20.

14 Figuier, *Histoire du merveilleux*, 93.

15 Ibid., 86–94, 104–22, is particularly valuable because it gives more detail on the early exorcisms, including who was present at some of them.

16 In the records, Jeanne des Anges was sometimes referred to as the mother superior and sometimes as the prioress. The terms were interchangeable.

17 Bibliothèque nationale (BN), fonds français, MS 7619, quoted in de Certeau, *La possession*, 30–1.

18 It was always accepted by the church authorities that the Devil could only act with the permission of God. If he were able to act at will on his own against God, he would be as powerful as God. This dualism was recognized as the basis of Manichaean heresy.

GRANDIER THE ACCUSED

1 For an authoritative coverage of French law and magistrates and of religious courts in witchcraft cases, see Mandrou, *Magistrats et sorciers*.

2 As noted earlier, the apparition that first plagued the nuns was that of Father Mousseau, but after a few days it developed into Grandier. However, the first official accusation against him as the source of the possessions was made on 11 October in the exorcists' official record.

3 BN, fonds français, MS 7619, cited in de Certeau, *La possession*, 32.

4 Bibliothèque municipale (BM) Tours, MS 1134.

5 Bibliothèque (B) arsenal, MS 4824, 39v, quoted by de Certeau, *La possession*, 50. All this occurred on the same day that Sister Agnès, who became known as the "beautiful little devil," made her profession; that is, became a fully fledged nun after her two years of training. It was she who first became afflicted on this particular occasion.

6 BM Tours, MS 1134, quoted in Legué and La Tourette, *Sœur Jeanne des Anges*, 67–9.

7 Legué (*Urbain Grandier*, 108) quotes this as a recorded description of the actual solicitations but does not give a source.

8 BN, fonds français, MS 7619, quoted in ibid., 109. Legué provides the following footnote: "In her memoirs, Mme. de Belciel [i.e., Jeanne des Anges] claims that God gave her the power to resist; but the Minutes left by Laubardemont say absolutely the opposite."

9 Asmodée was the demon of lechery and lust. Robbins, *The Encyclopaedia of Witchcraft and Demonolgy*, describes each of the demons and their "specialties."

10 Quoted in Surin, *Histoire abrégée*, 95.

11 "Extrait des Preuves" (BM Poitiers, A2, MS 303).

12 Minutes of the *bailli* of 11 October (BN, Collection Barbier, quoted in Legué, *Urbain Grandier*, 117–18).

13 Ibid., 119. See also Gayot, *Histoire*, 30; Aubin, *Histoire*, 32–3.

14 Michaelis the exorcist wrote a contemporary account, but the commonly used and very readable modern account of the Gaufridy affair is Lorédan, *Un grand procès de sorcellerie*.

15 This fascinating confession can be found in full as an appendix to Lorédan's *Un grand procès de sorcellerie* under the title "Aveux de Gaufridy aux capucins d'Aix."

16 Madeleine Demandolx, Gaufridy's reputed partner in the sabbath and his proclaimed lover, spent the rest of her life in self-imposed poverty doing menial work, constantly harried from place to place, feared as a sorcerer herself. In 1653 she was formally accused of sorcery and was tried and sentenced, but she was permitted to live out the rest of her life in seclusion. She died in the home of a kind widowed relative in 1670, aged about seventy-seven.

17 "During this century alone the witch-hunt has been attributed, in whole or in large part, to the Reformation, the Counter-Reformation, the Inquisition, the use of judicial torture, the wars of religion, the religious zeal of the clergy, the rise of the modern state, the development of capitalism, the widespread use of narcotics, changes in medical thought, social and cultural conflict, an attempt to wipe out paganism, the need of the ruling class to distract the masses, opposition to birth control, the spread of syphilis, and hatred of women" (Levack, *The Witch-Hunt in Early Modern Europe*). With so many points of view, there are clearly a great many books available on this subject, but I found the following particularly useful. Each has its own bibliography that will lead to a much deeper study for those who wish it. I have placed the more general ones at the beginning and those that deal with more detailed issues at the end:

Levack, *The Witch-Hunt in Early Modern Europe*. This book is designed to "fill the need for a one-volume study of the entire

European witch-hunt," and it does it well. It "does not pretend to be a comprehensive history of European witchcraft" but concentrates on the period between about 1450 and 1750. For both its writing and its treatment of the subject, it is an excellent book to read for an initial overview.

Scarre, *Witchcraft and Magic in Sixteenth and Seventeenth Century Europe*. This short book (68 pages) is an excellent introduction to the subject. The work is well written, easily read, and has a good introductory bibliography for further reading.

Briggs, *Witches and Neighbours*. As valuable to the reader entering the field of witchcraft studies as it is to the specialist, this book covers the whole area of witchcraft studies, acquainting us with the many questions answered over the last thirty years or more and the many fascinating problems that still challenge historians.

Trevor-Roper, *The European Witch Craze of the Sixteenth and Seventeenth Centuries*. Many books have been written since this one appeared, so it is somewhat dated, but it is a good first book to read on witchcraft, being both brief and comprehensive.

Mandrou, *Magistrats et sorciers en France au dix-septième siècle*. A landmark contribution to the history of witchcraft in France in the seventeenth century (1580–1700), it identifies how the judicial authorities shaped the course of the witch craze. When their certainty faltered, the pace of witch-hunting faltered too. This book provides a valuable background to the Grandier case.

Robbins, *The Encyclopaedia of Witchcraft and Demonology*. There are a few witchcraft encyclopaedias available, and although this one is a little dated, the text is easily read and it is comprehensive. The terminology is well covered and there are plenty of illustrations; interesting for the browsing reader.

Levack, ed., *Articles on Witchcraft, Magic, and Demonology*. A twelve-volume collection that contains an extensive variety of articles on virtually every aspect of witchcraft. Valuable for browsing.

Cohn, *Europe's Inner Demons*. A history of demons and demonology, of heretics and – ultimately – witches. The early modern idea of Satan was the product of a centuries-long development of thought. The demon, who in earlier times was the minor player on the human stage, had, by the time of the witch-hunts, become a tremendous and horrific presence.

Walker, *Unclean Spirits*. A book about possession and exorcism in France and England in the late sixteenth and early seventeenth centuries, this is particularly valuable in its coverage of exorcisms and Catholic/Protestant differences on possession and exorcisms.

Delumeau, *La peur en Occident*. This great work extends far beyond witchcraft, though it covers the subject at length. Delumeau's argument is that by the time of the Renaissance, fear had replaced stability and certainty in the Western mind – fear of heresy, of women, of death, of the Devil, of the end of the world and the Last Judgment – and that out of this pervading anguish came destructive behaviour, including the witch craze. This book provides a valuable insight into the mind-set of the seventeenth-century world.

Roper, *Oedipus and the Devil: Witchcraft, Sexuality, and Religion in Early Modern Europe*. In this delightfully written book, Roper argues that the early written sources were nearly all written by men. In witchcraft experiences, on the other hand, a woman translated her own life experiences into the language of the diabolic, performing her own diabolic theatre. When the actions of the Loudun nuns are viewed in this light, it can tell us new things about some aspects of the world of nuns in France in the 1630s; for instance, the stresses of young women in adjusting to convent life.

Kraemer and Sprenger, *Malleus maleficarum*. This work, first published in 1487, was reprinted thirteen times before 1520. At bottom, it is a compendium for judges on the techniques of seeking, recognizing, judging, and punishing witches. The work is outstandingly misogynistic, and many of its case studies of witchcraft are ludicrous to modern eyes. In its day, however, it made a significant contribution to the European witch craze. It should be looked at if only because it tells much about the mind-set of the times.

Ankarloo and Henningsen, *Early Modern European Witchcraft*. Before this book was published, much had been written about witchcraft in "mainland" Europe but very little on witch-hunting in Scandinavia and the other peripheries. This collection of essays is a study of periphery witchcraft. It holds that "some of the questions in the current debate are simply wrong or have to be redefined because they were raised from an oblique Anglo-Saxon angle." This is a good book for those already well versed in witchcraft studies.

Brauner, *Fearless Wives and Frightened Shrews*. This book seeks to establish, in depth, the nature of the society that hunted women as witches. In particular, it is an analysis of how women were viewed in that society in different contexts. "Brauner was fascinated by such

gender-based figures as the nun, the witch, the virgin and the proper
housewife," says her friend and colleague Robert H. Brown in the
introduction, which was written after her untimely death. The particular contribution of this book lies precisely in its concentration on
woman as witch: "I argue," says Brauner, "that the concept of
modern witchcraft is linked to changing notions of female gender,"
that is, not biological sex but socially constructed gender.

Barstow, *Witchcraze: A New History of the European Witch
Hunts*. "Any woman who challenges the patriarchal order may be
suspect." In her prologue, Barstow argues that this is the situation
today, and it was the situation at the time of the witchcraze. This
book asks and answers the question, "Why Women?" – in other
words, what was it that made women the principal victims of the
witch-hunts? The book is well researched and documented. It has
good value as a feminist analysis and is particularly valuable as a
summary of much of the modern writing on the witch craze.

Muchembled, *Le roi et la sorcière*. This book looks at sorcery not
as a phenomenon in itself but as an aspect of social and religious
life in the seventeenth-century state. Muchembled argues that "witchcraft was situated in the heart of the modernization of Europe" –
the state – and that "the justice which pursued witches ... was a
direct expression of political power in the course of renovation."
This is a useful book with a good analysis of some of the modern
works on witchcraft in the first chapter.

In addition to the many books, there are thousands of articles on
the subject. Again, selection of authors is not a matter of saying
"these are the best" but rather "these are some whom I have found
useful and whose bibliographies can extend the reading." I recom-
mend articles by Robert Muchembled, Lucien Febvre, Alfred Soman,
Jonathan Pearl, Robin Briggs, H. Eric Midelfort, Stephen Greenblatt,
and George Rosen.

18 Goubert, *Louis XIV and Twenty Million Frenchmen*, 21.
19 Briggs, *Witches as Neighbours*, 237.
20 Ibid., 292.
21 The French Revolution owed its immediate spark to a disastrous
   crop and the consequent shortage and high price of food in Paris.
22 See Delumeau, *La peur en Occident*.
23 For further information on Satan throughout the ages, see McKenzie, *Dictionary of the Bible*, 774–5. More generally, see Russell,
   Prince of Darkness. Russell has also written a number of more
   detailed works, which he has listed in the above book.

24 BM Tours, MS 1134, quoted in Legué and La Tourette, *Sœur Jeanne des Anges*, 69–74.

25 The words "demons" and "devils" are often used interchangeably.

26 One of the seven deadly sins: pride, avarice, envy, lust, sloth, greed, and anger.

27 Briggs, *Witches and Neighbours*, 260.

28 Robbins has a useful entry on confessions in his *Encyclopaedia of Witchcraft and Demonology*, 100–8.

29 For example, when Gaufridy was tortured at Aix, his torturers were demanding the names of his accomplices and searching for details of the sabbath(s) that he and Madeleine were thought to have attended.

30 Nearly every book on seventeenth-century witchcraft refers to sabbaths. For a brief exposition, see Briggs, *Witches and Neighbours*, 31–59. For a thorough analysis, see Jacques-Chaquin and Préaud, eds., *Le sabbat des sorciers*. This is the record of an international colloquium held in 1992.

31 This is a quotation from a noted witch-hunter of the first quarter of the seventeenth century in France, De Lancre. See Palou, *La sorcellerie*, 27.

32 We can see this clearly in Gaufridy's case. He took up the book of magic his uncle had left him and the Devil appeared, offering him the power of seduction at will. There was a pact between Gaufridy and the Devil, and Gaufridy was marked by the Devil's marks.

33 There were those who argued against belief in witchcraft and the power of witches. The most famous was probably Johann Weyer, author of *De praestigiis daemonum* (1563); see Mora et al., eds., *Witches, Devils, and Doctors in the Renaissance*. A few others doubted, and increasingly so in the seventeenth century in France; see Levack, *The Witch-Hunt in Early Modern Europe*, 239–46. These were often early thinkers in the Enlightenment, some of them judges, particularly in the Parlement of Paris. The church authorities regarded them as dangerous: "Catholic demonologists were convinced that learned incredulity was widespread and very dangerous ... Demons were part of orthodox faith just as angels were ... Their main function was to punish the immortal souls of the departed. To question their existence was to question belief in heaven and hell and indeed in the crucial doctrine of the immortality of the soul ... The demonist theologians ... made constant reference to 'atheists,' 'sceptics,' and 'libertines.'" (Pearl, "French Catholic Demonologists").

34 Protestant demonologists took a somewhat different theological view from Catholic ones. See Clark, "Protestant Demonology," 45–82.

35 For instance, see Levack, *The Witch-Hunt in Early Modern Europe*, 33: "The Devil's possession of individuals could and eventually did play a part in witchcraft, since the possession could take place as a result of the witch's actions. The witch could, in other words, command the Devil to possess a victim as part of the pact that the witch had concluded with the Devil."

36 See Briggs, *Witches and Neighbours*, 80. Exorcism, at least as it was practised at the local level, as in Loudun, raised increasing doubts at the upper levels of the Catholic hierarchy. The reaction of the archbishop of Bordeaux is an example.

37 For brief coverage of exorcism and how it was performed, see Robbins, *The Encyclopaedia of Witchcraft and Demonology*, 180–9.

38 See Pearl, "A School for the Rebel Soul," 286–306.

39 These are the reasons why public exorcisms were held in the Gaufridy case. That part of France contained strong Protestant areas, and the public exorcisms were directed at them.

40 Figuier, *Histoire du merveilleux*, 90.

41 The petition is in BN, Collection Barbier, and is quoted in full in Legué, *Urbain Grandier*, 120–1. Grandier later noted in his "Factum": "Mignon was recognized as one of the principal authors of another calumnious accusation from which the petitioner emerged innocent a year ago." This is probably a reference to the case that had been judged by the bishop and overturned by the archbishop.

42 See de Certeau (*La possession de Loudun*), who highlights the fact that possessions and exorcisms by now followed a pattern. Once they had begun, all those directly involved knew, from past cases, the part they were supposed to play. It became theatre, with the participants the actors and actresses.

43 The minutes were signed by Guillaume de Cerisay, Louis Chauvet, Irenée de Sainte-Marthe, and a man named Thibaut, the clerk.

44 Minutes of the *bailli*, quoted in Legué, *Urbain Grandier*, 122.

45 The chimneys of the time were very large and wide and quite big enough to allow a man to climb up.

46 See Lorédan, *Un grand procès de sorcellerie*.

47 The events described here and below come from the *bailli*'s minutes of 13 October 1632 and are quoted in Legué, *Urbain Grandier*, chap. 9. The *bailli*'s minutes are recorded more extensively in Legué, *Documents pour servir à l'histoire médicale*. The originals are in BN, Collection Barbier.

BISHOP VERSUS ARCHBISHOP

1 Minutes of the *bailli*, Monday, 23 October 1632. These are in the Bibliothèque nationale (BN), Collection Barbier, and are quoted in Legué, *Urbain Grandier*, 124.

2 Ibid.

3 Ibid.

4 Minutes of the *bailli*, Thursday, 26 October 1632, quoted in Legué, *Urbain Grandier*, 125.

5 Aubin, *Histoire*, and Legué, *Urbain Grandier*, both cover the events in this chapter. Legué quotes a number of original documents, but Aubin gives more details of daily events.

6 Certificate of Daniel Roger and René Mannoury (BN, fonds français, 7618, cited in Legué, *Urbain Grandier*, 126).

7 There were numerous controversies at the time about the use of antimony as a medicament in therapy. Some doctors swore by it, while others considered it the cause of all evils. This was apparently the opinion of the practitioners of Loudun on this occasion. They seem to have thought that the use of antimony was, at least in part, the cause of the nuns' condition. There have been suggestions from time to time that Adam deliberately gave the nuns antimony in order to produce the convulsions, but in fact it was a perfectly recognized treatment, even though a disputed one.

8 Although on this occasion the doctors did not support the subject of possession, the majority did so later, as will be seen. Mannoury signed this first report of the doctors along with the others. Most doctors later arrived at the conclusion that the things they had seen the nuns do were so extraordinary that there could be no natural explanation. It would take medical science about another two hundred and fifty years to recognize what was seen as being symptoms of a classifiable medical condition. For an excellent assessment of the doctors' involvement in the case, see Ballu. "Du rôle des médecins dans le procès d'Urbain Grandier."

9 Grandier petitions (BN, Collection Barbier, cited in Legué, *Urbain Grandier*, 127).

10 We do not know whether the bishop ever did turn up. There is no further reference in the records to a visit at this time, and the *bailli*'s minutes do not refer to any meeting with him. It is just possible that the bishop came into town and made a quiet visit to the convent and purposely avoided meeting the *bailli*, since that might have given the *bailli* status in the work of the exorcisms.

11 Minutes of the *bailli*, 23 November 1632, quoted in Legué, *Urbain Grandier*, 129.

12 Gabrielle de l'Incarnation, thirty-five years old, obsessed by three demons (Certeau, *La possession*, 138).

13 BN, Collection Barbier. Grandier's petition is quoted in full in Legué, *Urbain Grandier*, 130–1.

14 The original minutes prepared by Hervé are in BN, fonds français, MS 7618, cited in ibid., 131.

15 This letter is in the Bibliothèque nationale. The cousin he was referring to was almost certainly Isobelle Barot. She is probably the same nun whom de Certeau identifies in his book on p. 138 as Elisabeth de la Croix, née Bastad (signatures were no easier to decipher then than now). She was exorcized on 17 August at the grille of the parlour of the convent: "She did not do much beyond barking like a dog" (Lerosey, *Histoire civile*).

16 BN, fonds français, MS 7618. The full letter is quoted in Legué, *Urbain Grandier*, 133–4.

17 The letter to the bishop was followed by one sent to one of the bishop's right-hand men, which also received no reply. The letter is given in full in ibid., 135–6.

18 BN, Collection Barbier, MS 7618, 19, quoted in ibid., 138.

19 Order of 27 December 1632 (BN, Collection Barbier, cited in ibid., 139).

20 BN, MS, 7618, reproduced completely in Aubin, *Histoire*, 91–4.

21 Letter of 30 December 1632 (BN, fonds français, MS 7618).

22 BM Tours, MS 1197.

23 BN, Collection Barbier, MS 7618, 21.

ARREST

1 Barbier, *Jean d'Armagnac II*, 163–4, letter of 7 September 1633.

2 Bibliothèque nationale (BN), fonds français, MS 7618, cited in Legué, *Urbain Grandier*, 169.

3 Bibliothèque municipale (BM) Poitiers, A2, MS 303, "Déclaration de Moussault, proc. du roi à Loudun, sur ce qui se passa le jour de la Fête Dieu."

4 Champion left behind him an interesting manuscript of memoirs on Urbain Grandier, "Discours sur l'histoire de la diablerie de Loudun" (BN, fonds français, MS 24380; BM Poitiers, A2, MS 303).

5 Anne de Saint-Agnes, daughter of Jean, Marquis de La Motte-Brassé.

6 Another daughter, Susanne, was left with them in Loudun. Years later she became one of the secular women who were possessed and one of the most ardent accusers of Grandier.

7 This does not necessarily mean that she made the queen's shoes. It was an office in the queen's personal retinue with its own title. Very likely her official function was to take care of everything to do with the queen's shoes.

8 Quoted in Legué, *Urbain Grandier*, 176.

9 See Champion, "Discours sur l'histoire."

10 Unfortunately for Grandier, he had a copy of this libel in his home. It was discovered when he was arrested, though whether it was planted is unknown.

11 See Legué, *Urbain Grandier*, 99, and Aubin, *Histoire*, 182. Their stories vary slightly in detail, but the essence of both is the same.

12 The Capuchins in Aix had been deeply involved in the Gaufridy affair also and had largely been responsible for pressing the accusations against him.

13 During his stay in Loudun, Laubardemont invited Grandier to his table on a number of occasions (BM Tours, MS 1134).

14 BN, fonds français, MS 7618, cited in Legué, *Urbain Grandier*, 183.

15 Tapié, *The France of Louis XIII and Richelieu*, 135.

16 These documents are from "Extrait des registres de la commission ordonnée par le roy, pour le jugement du procès criminel fait à l'encontre de Maistre Urbain Grandier et ses complices," quoted in Legué, *Urbain Grandier*, 189.

APPEAL OF INNOCENCE

1 Legué, *Urbain Grandier*, 192.

2 Ibid., 39.

3 The exact phrase in French was *quant à présent*.

4 Possession meant that the body of the person was taken over by a demon. Obsession was a state in which the person was clearly travailed by one or more sins but was in control of her own body.

5 Surin. *Correspondance*, 248.

6 Legué, *Urbain Grandier* 195.

7 See de Certeau, *La possession*, 138–40, and Surin, *Correspondance*, 249, for the names, ages, and families of both the nuns and the seculars.

8 "Extrait des registres de la commission." See Legué, *Urbain Grandier*, 195–7, where the letter is given in full.

9 "Extrait des registres de la commission," cited in ibid., 197.
10 Quoted in ibid., 198–9.
11 Quoted in ibid., 202.

THE EXORCISMS

1 For an objective assessment of the doctors, their competence, and their role, see Ballu, "Du rôle des médecins dans le procès d'Urbain Grandier." Ballu suggests that the problem lay not with the competence of the doctors but with the state of medical knowledge at that time.
2 Legué, *Urbain Grandier*, 206; Gayot, *Histoire*, 82–4; Aubin, *Histoire*, 124–5.
3 Bibliothèque municipale (BM) Tours, MS 1134.
4 Father Joseph came to Loudun incognito to install his colleagues but did not involve himself personally with the exorcisms (Legué, *Urbain Grandier*, 208; Aubin, *Histoire*, 117; Gayot, *Histoire*, 85).
5 For a brief but illuminating review of exorcism and its use for religious propaganda, see Walker, *Unclean Spirits*, 4–10.
6 Most authors – and all modern theologians – find this assertion of the Loudun exorcists to be ludicrous. But in its day it had a certain logic to it, however specious. In 1620, however, some of the doctors of the Sorbonne had issued a clear statement that no faith could ever be placed in anything the Devil said (see Aubin, *Histoire*, 250–2). Consequently, if the matter had been dealt with properly, there should have been a reference from Loudun to the Sorbonne on this issue in 1634.
7 At least according to Laubardemont, who declared that the cardinal had approved this doctrine *par lettres closes à luy escrites* (Bibliothèque nationale (BN), fonds français, MS 7618, quoted in Legué, *Urbain Grandier*, 209).
8 Tapié, *The France of Louis XIII and Richelieu*, 135.
9 He is referring Brother Sansïn Birette's *Réfutation de l'erreur du vulgaire touchant les réponses des diables exorcisés* (Rouen: Jacques Besogne 1618).
10 Legué, *Urbain Grandier*, 209.
11 "Manuscrit d'un habitant de Loudun" (BN, Collection Barbier, quoted in ibid., 210).
12 BM Poitiers, A2 MS 303. *Lèse-majesté* was a form of treason.
13 Much of the material in this section comes from Aubin's *Histoire* and is quoted word for word by Legué, Gayot, and others. Each

gives small additional details, Aubin and Legué together being the most valuable.

14 Brémond, *Histoire litéraire*, 184.

15 Bracketed remarks have been added to this section to make the meaning clearer.

16 The ciborium is a sacred vessel used to store the consecrated host.

17 Manuscript of Jacques Boutreux, Sieur d'Etiau (BN, Collection Dupuy, 576, quoted in Legué, *Urbain Grandier*, 211).

18 This took much longer than anybody expected. Jeanne des Anges was not cured until the end of 1638, more than six years after the onset of the possessions.

19 For the popular conception of witches and their characteristics, see Kraemer and Sprenger, *Malleus maleficarum*. The *Malleus* was written about 150 years before the Loudun case, but this modern translation conveys an excellent idea of the theories and fantasies surrounding witchcraft at the period.

20 BN, fonds français, MS 7619, quoted in Legué, *Urbain Grandier*, 212; Gayot, *Histoire*, 87; Aubin *Histoire*, 129.

21 Aubin, *Histoire*, 130; Legué, *Urbain Grandier*, 212; Gayot, *Histoire*, 87.

22 Legué, *Urbain Grandier*, 213.

23 Barot was an old enemy of Grandier. He was Mignon's uncle, important in the town, rich and without children, "and consequently," says Aubin, "highly considered and well beloved by those who would inherit." At some time (we do not know when) Grandier had insulted him and thus made enemies of the whole connected family (Aubin, *Histoire*, 10).

24 Aubin, *Histoire*, 130; Legué, *Urbain Grandier*, 214.

25 This idea of unwitting direction of exorcists to demoniacs comes from Spanos and Gottlieb, "Demonic Possession." I have modified the wording for my own needs, but they were the source.

26 "Extrait des Preuves." (BN, fonds français, 24163, quoted in Legué, *Urbain Grandier*, 214).

27 Legué, *Urbain Grandier*, 215.

28 BN, fonds français, MS 7618, quoted in Legué, *Urbain Grandier*, 216. This is an extraordinary document because the demon signed his name. There is an even more surprising example in the same BN file. In that case, the official record of an exorcism was signed by the appropriate priests and civil officials. Among their names appears Asmodée's signature confirming with the others that this was a true record of the exorcism. Cooperation indeed!

29 Ibid., 217.

30 Laubardemont in his record estimated the number to have been two thousand.

31 Record of an eyewitness (BN, Collection Barbier, MS 7618, quoted in Legué, *Urbain Grandier*, 218). Gayot (*Histoire*, 94–6) gives a number of details not included in Legué.

32 An expression Laubardemont used in the minutes he maintained.

33 Legué published this report in his *Documents pour servir à l'histoire médicale des possédées de Loudun.*

34 Sorberina, article on Quillet, quoted in Legué, *Urbain Grandier*, 219.

35 Letter of Chancellor Séguier to Cardinal Richelieu, 7 May 1634, cited in Legué, *Urbain Grandier*, 220. Legué notes: "We are obliged to the late M. Gabriel Charavay for this letter. It proves the extent of the interest that Richelieu took in this matter when he did not refrain from personally involving the chancellor to have him give orders for the arrest of a person of such minor importance as René Grandier."

36 Laubardemont's minutes (BN, fonds français, MS 7619, quoted in ibid., 220).

37 "Manuscrit d'un habitant de Loudun" (BN, Collection Barbier). The quotations referring to Madeleine de Brou are from Legué, *Urbain Grandier*, 221.

38 Laubardemont's papers (BN, fonds français, MS 7619, quoted in ibid., 221–2).

39 Ibid., 223.

40 Laubardemont's minutes (BN, fonds français, MS 7619, quoted in ibid., 223).

41 For the official record of the events of this day, see "Interrogatoire de maistre Urbain Grandier, prestre, curé de Saint-Pierre-du-Marché de Loudun, et l'un des chanoines de Sainte-Croix dudit lieu." This appears as an appendix in Villeneuve, *La mystérieuse affaire Grandier*. The original source is BN, Receuil Morel de Thoisy, réserve no. 92, folios 377–82. The bishop was present at a number of the exorcisms at this time, though only one is described here. See Jovy, *Trois documents*, 18.

42 Minutes of the proceedings of 23 June 1634, quoted in Legué, *Urbain Grandier*, 224.

43 Report of the doctors on the pacts presented at the exorcism of 23 June 1634. (BN, fonds français, Collection Barbier, cited in ibid., 225).

44 Minutes of 23 June 1634 (BN, fonds français, MS 7618, cited in ibid., 225).

45 Related by Irenée de Sainte-Marthe, sieur des Humeaux. See ibid., 225.

46 This was another argument among theologians. Many held that a possessed person was partly responsible for the possession. Others held that this person had no responsibility.

47 Related by Irénée de Sainte-Marthe (ibid., 237).

THE TRIAL

1 Legué, *Urbain Grandier*, 230.

2 Ibid., 231.

3 For a detailed analysis of the testimony that convicted Grandier, see Gayot, *Histoire*, 154–68.

4 Ibid., 126. Gayot notes that there were seventy-two witnesses and gives interesting details on the trial of Grandier and the accusations against him.

5 Bodin, an expert on witchcraft, said, "Sorcerers have a horror of salt and they cannot cry" (*La démonomanie des sorciers*, 1580). This book is available in an English translation by Scott and Pearl, *On the Demon-mania of Witches*.

6 Aubin, *Histoire*, 245. He states that it was alleged that when Grandier received word of his sentence, he did not look at a crucifix, he spoke only of how to have his sentence reduced, and he refused prayers when they were offered to him. All of these were taken as evidence that he was an adherent of the Devil. Aubin details the accusations against Grandier one by one and offers his criticisms of them (219–52).

7 Ibid., 287. Aubin, no friend to the priests or the Catholic Church, says of the exorcists who later suffered similar "possession" symptoms to those of the nuns: "One cannot avoid declaring here that all the memoirs agree that Fathers Lactance, Tranquille, and Surin, after Grandier's death, were agitated by the Demons, and that all Persons, Huguenot or Papist, who were involved with these affairs ... have declared that they do not believe that the abominable things that they have seen and heard could have been produced by the power of nature alone, or by fraud alone, but the Demons must have been involved in it, and that they did in actual fact possess these supposed exorcists." It was a reflection of the way women

were viewed that Aubin would accept possession in the case of the priests but would reject it for the nuns, believing their possessions to have been fraud or manipulation. This quotation is also interesting to the reader of today because it indicates that a Huguenot minister had no doubt about the existence of diabolical possession; he only doubted its reality in the case of the nuns.

8 See Bizouard, *Des rapports de l'homme avec le démon*, 593–5 Françoise Fillatreau (or Fillastreau) was one of the possessed seculars.

9 Quoted from L'hermitte, *Vrais et faux possédés*, 41.

10 Quoted in Robbins, *Encyclopaedia of Witchcraft and Demonology*, 316–17.

11 Mandrou, in *Magistrats et sorciers*, 214, quoting from a letter in B arsenal, MS 4824 fol 24.

12 The observations of the exorcist Father Surin, quoted from La Menardaye, *Examen et discussion critique*. 349–51. Father Tranquille gives additional information, telling us that in the intervals between demonic attacks, they went back to all their normal behaviour, that they never discontinued their religious observances, and that they were sensible, modest, doing their work, and taking pleasure in hearing talk about God and learning the means of serving him better (Tranquille, *Véritable relation*, 207).

13 Robbins, *The Encyclopaedia of Witchcraft and Demonology*, 316.

14 Aubin, *Histoire*, 229.

15 Bibliothèque municipale (BM) Poitiers, A2, MS 303.

16 Other than Jeanne des Anges, Claire de Sazilly was the most affected of the possessed women. Like Jeanne, she had seven demons. Although Claire de Sazilly played a minor part to Jeanne des Anges, it seems clear that she was her rival for attention. Like Jeanne, the evidence of her possession was exceptional. At the same time, it seems to tell us something about the characteristics of hysteria that the specific behaviour of these two women reflected their own characters. Jeanne was obsessed by controlling her surroundings; Claire was clearly obsessed by sex. This rivalry between the two also has an interesting parallel with the Gaufridy case. There, Madeleine Demandolx de la Palud had a rival, a much more open one even than that of Jeanne des Anges. Madeleine's rival was Louise Capeau, and Louise fought hard to gain pre-eminence in the degree of her possession. See Lorédan, *Un grand procès*.

17 Gayot, *Histoire*, 130.

18 Aubin, *Histoire*, 225, who is quoting from "Extrait des Preuves," (a copy of which can be found in BM Poitiers, A2, MS 303).

19 See Ballu, "Du rôle des médecins dans le procès d'Urbain Grandier,"
   2–3.
20 Ballu (ibid.) gives their names.
21 Bibliothèque nationale (BN), fonds français, MS 24163; La Ménar-
   daye, *Examen et discussion critique*, 210; Ballu, "Du rôle des
   médecins dans le procès d'Urbain Grandier," 8.
22 Much depended throughout this affair on the ability of the nuns,
   and particularly Jeanne des Anges, to surprise observers by how
   much they appeared to know of what other people wanted or were
   thinking. A more recent case throws light on the kind of thing that
   may have been happening in the convent at Loudun. The greatest
   prisoner-of-war escape story of the First World War was based on
   the ability of two prisoners to claim the powers of the supernatural
   to know what others were thinking and to find buried treasure. To
   find how they did it, see Jones, *The Road to En-Dor*.
23 The opinion of these theological doctors of the Sorbonne can be
   found in BN, fonds français, MS 7619.
24 The term "hysteria" has been widely used since that time. More
   recently, other terms have been created to avoid giving the sense
   that this is a condition associated with female patients. For simplicity, I have used the one that is still most common, i.e., hysteria.
   There is an extensive literature on hysteria. By far the most relevant
   to this case is Evans, *Fits and Starts*. It covers the history of hysteria
   from earliest times, concentrating on France. It is very readable and
   makes a complex subject both fascinating and understandable to the
   lay person. It includes a good bibliography for further reading.
   Other books that I found valuable were:
      Veith, *Hysteria*. "Hysteria is an extraordinarily interesting disease,
   and a strange one. It is encountered in the earliest pages of recorded
   medicine and is dealt with in current psychiatric literature." These
   opening words of Veith's book convey the scope of her work, which
   is to trace the history of the disease at different times and in different cultures. It is well worth reading.
      David-Ménard, *Hysteria from Freud to Lacan*. "The hysteric feels
   an intense pleasure, an improper pleasure, that cannot properly
   speaking be allowed into experience." This book is an analysis of
   this phenomenon.
      Didi-Huberman, *Invention de l'hystérie*. This is a photographic
   recollection of the scenes and patients in the Salpêtrière at the time
   when Charcot was at the height of his prestige. The text is excellent
   and the pictures are revealing.

Krohn, *Hysteria, the Elusive Neurosis.* The author says, "My central task is to study a set of psychopathological and personality types called hysteria, conversion hysteria, anxiety hysteria, hysterical character, hysterical personality, hysteroid personality, etc. These terms are used by everyday clinicians. At best they are defined imprecisely, and at worst completely arbitrarily." His purpose is to set guidelines on how to do correct diagnosis.

Shorter, *From Paralysis to Fatigue.* This is a history of psychosomatic illness in the modern era, "beginning with such notions as hysteria in the eighteenth century, and continuing into our own time ... an account of how historical eras shaped their own symptoms of illness." It is an interesting survey of the changing nature and identification of hysteria. Shorter deals at some length with Charcot, though he considers the value of his work to have been transitory.

25 Lhermitte, *Vrais et faux possédés,* 69.

26 Charcot and Richer, *Les démoniaques dans l'art* and *Nouvelle iconographie.*

27 Lhermitte, *Vrais et faux possédés,* 44.

28 BM Tours, MS 1197, 61.

29 In English, we commonly use the word "convent" to describe a female religious house and "monastery" to describe a male religious house. In fact, nonmonastic orders such as Capuchins, Carmelites, and Cordeliers lived in houses that are properly termed convents.

30 "Manuscrit d'un habitant de Loudun," quoted in Legué, *Urbain Grandier,* 234.

31 Ibid., 235.

32 It is worth noting that Jean Buron has appeared briefly in this story already. When Grandier went to Dissay to try to see Bishop de La Rocheposay and was fobbed off on the major-domo on 22 October 1632, he was accompanied by "a priest named Jean Buron, a staunch and devoted friend" (ibid., 124). Here is another example that by this time to be a friend to Grandier was to risk one's life.

33 BN, fonds français, MS 7619, cited in ibid., 235.

34 BN, fonds français, MS 7618, cited in ibid., 235; see also Gayot, *Histoire,* 117.

35 BN, fonds français, "Receuil Morel de Thoissy," 92, cited in Legué, *Urbain Grandier,* 236.

36 BN, fonds français, MS 7619, quoted in full in Aubin, *Histoire,* 182–6; Legué, *Urbain Grandier,* 237–9. The woman mentioned was Madeleine de Brou. The letter continued:

"Further, other ladies have been arrested in the church and the doors locked in order to seek some alleged magic pacts, also imagined. Since this unhappy and recent event, so much has been made of these denunciations, accusations, and indications of these said demons that today a booklet has been published and circulated in the said town which is designed to establish in the minds of the judges: 'that demons, under exorcism, are bound always to tell the truth and that one can place on their depositions a sound belief and that according to the truths of the faith and the demonstrations of the sciences one may believe their words with certainty, and one may place faith in the fact that the words of the devil, when duly adjured, are not those of the father of lies but the words of the church, which has the power to force devils to tell the truth.'

"And to establish this doctrine even more powerfully in the town, two sermons have been preached in the presence of M. de Laubardemont which assert these propositions. Following which the said M. de Laubardemont has again a short time ago ordered arrested a daughter of one of the best families in the town, held her for two days in the house of a widower gentleman [this was Jacques de Thibault], and then released her into the care of close relatives."

The letter went on to say that to teach that devils under exorcism are bound to tell the truth is against the teachings of the fathers of the church and has been specifically rejected by the famous and celebrated doctors of the Sorbonne since 1620. Further, to preach this false doctrine would mean that anybody could be falsely accused, no matter how virtuous, and nobody could consider himself safe. Thus, they asked the king to forbid this abuse and profanation of the exorcisms which were daily taking place in Loudun.

37 Grandier, "Requête d'Urbain Grandier."
38 "Extrait des registres de la commission," quoted in full in Aubin, *Histoire*, 186–90.
39 BN, fonds français, MS 7619. It must be noted that the doctors giving the opinion had not seen the nuns. They had been provided with a full description of the nuns' convulsions and of the "miraculous" levitations, speaking in foreign tongues, and similar supernatural events, and were asked if these proved possession (see Legué, *Urbain Grandier*, 242).
40 Aubin, *Histoire*, 232.
41 Carmona (*Les diables*, 233–4) tells of these events. Grandier also refers to these retractions in his "Remarques et Considérations,"

adding to his "Factum." See Villeneuve, *La mystérieuse affaire Grandier*, 234–5, for this document.

42 This kind of logic was not confined to the seventeenth century. A similar mental attitude on the part of judges and authorities can be found in modern "witchcraft" trials – in Soviet Russia during party purge trials, in fascist Germany against enemies of the state, and in the democratic United States in the McCarthy hearings, to name just a few. It was the "witch-hunt" mentality of McCarthyism that aroused Huxley to write his book *The Devils of Loudun*.

43 Grandier, "Factum pour Maistre Urbain Grandier." A copy can be found in the municipal archives in Loudun.

44 For a summary of the proof used at the trial to condemn Grandier, see "Extrait des preuves qui sont au procès d'Urbain Grandier" (BN, fonds français, MS 24163; or BM Poitiers, A2, MS 303). Aubin (*Histoire*, 219–52) provides the same proof, with criticisms.

TORTURE AND DEATH

1 Legué's and Aubin's descriptions of this day are so compelling that I have drawn on them heavily.

2 So much attention is usually given to Grandier's alleged crimes of sorcery and lechery that little notice is paid to his treatise on the celibacy of the priesthood. But in the eyes of the judges, it was as important as the pacts with the Devil. Its contents were so heretical in the eyes of the Catholic Church that it alone would likely have been sufficient cause for the most severe punishment.

3 Bibliothèque nationale (BN), fonds français, MS 24163. Legué (*Urbain Grandier*, 247) says in a footnote that this comes from a statement made by Father Archange to the bishop of Nîmes on 4 September 1634.

4 "Mémoire de ce qui s'est passé à l'exécution de l'arrest contre Me. Urbain Grandier, prestre," quoted in Aubin, *Histoire*, 204, and in Legué, *Urbain Grandier*, 247.

5 Legué (ibid.) says that it was Laubardemont who raised this issue. Aubin (*Histoire*, 204) and Gayot (*Histoire*, 136) say only that it was "one of the magistrates." I have used the Legué version while recognizing that Laubardemont was so disliked that base acts might well have been attributed to him that were done by others.

6 "Récit d'un habitant de Loudun" (BN, Collection Barbier, cited in Legué, *Urbain Grandier*, 248). See also Aubin, *Histoire*, 205.

7 The texts of the early seventeenth century sometimes contained spell-ings or words that are not used today. The original word *cyn* was probably meant to be *sein*. Gayot interprets this as "stains," i.e., some skin discoloration.

8 Bibliothèque municipale (BM) Poitiers, A2, MS 303, See also Aubin, *Histoire*, 205.

9 "Relation véritable de ce qui s'est passé," cited in Legué, *Urbain Grandier*, 248.

10 "Mémoire de ce qui s'est passé," quoted in ibid., 249.

11 BN, Collection Barbier, quoted in Aubin, *Histoire*, 107.

12 Father Tranquille recounts that Laubardemont wished to save Gran-dier and that he cried over the (eternal) destiny of his victim.

13 Minutes of the torture and death of Grandier (Legué, *Documents pour servir à l'histoire médicale des possédées de Loudun*).

14 Despair in God was a mortal sin and, as such, his eternal life would have been forfeited.

15 "Relation véritable de ce qui s'est passé," quoted in Legué, *Urbain Grandier*, 252.

16 Boulliau, "Lettre à Gassendi."

17 There were other exorcists there besides the two main ones. See Gayot, *Histoire*, 142.

18 Four wedges were used for the "ordinary" question, or torture, and eight for the "extraordinary." See Gayot, *Histoire*, 141.

19 BN, Collection Barbier, quoted in Legué, *Urbain Grandier*, 253. Both the Recollets and the Capuchins were followers of the gentle Saint Francis of Assisi.

20 "Mémoire de ce qui s'est passé," quoted in ibid., 254.

21 Boulliau, "Lettre à Gassendi."

22 Gayot, *Histoire*, 143, quoting "Relation véritable de ce qui s'est passé."

23 "Relation véritable de ce qui s'est passé" (BN, fonds français, n.a. 6764).

24 Aubin, *Histoire*, 255.

25 Although Elizabeth Blanchard had confessed to being Grandier's aco-lyte, she was not held responsible and prosecuted (just as Madeleine de La Palud had not been held responsible in the Gaufridy case).

26 Grandier never uttered a word against his judges or against the Capuchins ("Mémoire au vray de ce qui s'est passé," cited in Legué, *Urbain Grandier*, 255, footnote).

27 This was as shocking at its time as it would be today. Churchmen were not permitted personally to shed blood or inflict torture.

28 Figuier, *Histoire du merveilleux*, 181, using as his source "Relation véritable de ce qui s'est passé."

29 "Minutes of the Questioning under Torture," cited in Legué, *Urbain Grandier*, 255.

30 BN, Collection Barbier.

31 Legué, *Urbain Grandier*, 257.

32 "Minutes of the Questioning under Torture," ibid. "Sieur Grisard ... told us that yesterday, prior to Grandier's execution, he dined with him and there seemed about him in his countenance or words no fear of death, he ate well ... and drank three times." This statement is ambiguous. Does it apply to the day that Grandier was tortured and executed or to the previous day? The latter seems more likely.

33 BN, fonds français, MS 24163, cited in Legué, *Urbain Grandier*, 258, footnote.

34 "Minutes of the Questioning under Torture," cited in ibid.

35 "Relation véritable de ce qui s'est passé" (BN, fonds français, n.a. 6764).

36 "Manuscrit d'un habitant de Loudun." I have used the description given by Legué, *Urbain Grandier*, 259–60. Aubin, *Histoire*, 211–12, adds a few minor details; de Certeau, *La possession*, 251–60, provides views of this day as seen by different participants, principally Laubardemont.

37 B arsenal, quoted in Legué, *Urbain Grandier*, 260.

38 The authors always talk about Grandier making his "amends" on his knees. But this hardly seems possible, given the condition of his legs. Although this detail may not be correct, it is repeated here in the form it has always been told.

39 "Manuscrit d'un habitant de Loudun." I have quoted Father Grillau's words as given by Legué, *Urbain Grandier*, 260. The "Relation véritable de ce qui s'est passé" gives a much shorter conversation between Grillau and Grandier. In the circumstances, it seems more likely that the "Relation" is closer to what happened.

40 "Mémoire au vray de ce qui s'est passé," quoted in Legué, *Urbain Grandier*, 261.

41 Quoted in ibid., 261.

42 "Manuscrit d'un habitant de Loudun," quotd in ibid., 261.

43 "Relation véritable de ce qui s'est passé" (BN, fonds français, n.a. 6764).

44 Aubin, *Histoire*, 213, and Gayot, *Histoire*, 147. This man was an enemy of Grandier, supposedly because he believed Grandier had seduced his wife. See Legué, *Urbain Grandier*, 12–13.

45 A particular form of hat worn by priests of the day when performing some religious service.
46 Boulliau, "Lettre à Gassendi."
47 "Manuscrit d'un habitant de Loudun," quoted in Legué, *Urbain
   Grandier*, 264.
48 Ibid., 265.
49 Ibid., 264; Aubin, *Histoire*, 214. Legué gives the original source as
   "Denede's manuscript."
50 Aubin, *Histoire*, 216; Gayot, *Histoire*, 151.
51 Aubin, *Histoire*, 110; Legué, *Urbain Grandier*, 265; and Gayot, *Histoire*, 151. This may or may not be precisely correct. It can well be
   imagined that with the press of the crowd, he may have been hit in
   the face accidentally if they put a crucifix to his mouth to kiss.
52 Different authors give slightly different versions of what was said by
   Grandier over these last hours; although the specific words may
   vary, the same thoughts are generally reflected. For instance, his very
   last words are recorded differently in Boulliau's letter to Gassendi
   and in the "Relation véritable de ce qui s'est passé," though in each
   case it was a prayer. I have used the version to be found in an eyewitness report in B arsenal, MS 4824, f27, quoted by de Certeau, *La
   possession*, 260. To me, these seem his most likely last words.
53 Legué, *Urbain Grandier*, 267.

EPILOGUE

1 In the Archives municipales de Loudun there is a small vial, said to
   contain fragments of bone and ashes, the remains of Urbain Grandier.
2 "Manuscrit d'un habitant de Loudun," cited in Legué, *Urbain
   Grandier*, 272–3.
3 Ibid., 273–4.
4 Bibliothèque nationale (BN), "Mémoire pour Madeleine de Brou,"
   Collection Barbier, cited in ibid., 274–5.
5 Aubin, *Histoire*, 267–8; Legué, *Urbain Grandier*, 275–7.
6 For the death of Tranquille, see Legué, *Urbain Grandier*, 298. Tranquille wrote about the possessions in his "Véritable relation" of
   1634. There seems to be little doubt that he believed what he
   described as having happened.
7 BN, fonds français, MS 7619, cited in Legué, *Urbain Grandier*, 298.
8 For these events, see ibid., 284–5.
9 A more complete version of the history of Barré's downfall can be
   found in Figuier, *Histoire du merveilleux*, 1:216ff. A few related

details can be found in an article on François Duclos, one of the
doctors in Grandier's trial, in *Le Journal de Loudun*, 30 August
1894.

10 He led the famous interrogations of the *solitaires* at Port-Royal as a
part of the suppression of the Jansenists there. Later he acted as
Richelieu's agent in the interrogation and trial of the Marquis de
Cinq-Mars and François de Thou in the "Cinq-Mars affair." It was
Laubardemont who could truly be credited with their execution.

11 For a brief history of Laubardemont, see the entry on him in
Michaud, *Biographie universelle*, vol. 23.

12 B Sorbonne, MS 769, f. 256.

13 Legué, *Urbain Grandier*, 288, 292.

14 See Gayot, *Histoire*, 184–5.

15 See her autobiography in Legué and La Tourette, *Sœur Jeanne des
Anges*.

16 This fine set of buildings is in Tours opposite the departmental
archives. It illustrates what a fine and successful convent of the time
looked like.

17 Marie de l'Incarnation, *Correspondance*, ed. Oury, letter 140,
444–5. This nun was later sent to Canada (Quebec, New France)
to found the first Ursuline convent in that colony. She has an important place in the religious history of the country. A sensible personality shines through her letters. The quotation throws useful light
upon the mind-set of an intelligent religious woman of the seventeenth century.

18 She gained a reputation as a mystic in her day as the result of the
apparitions and her autobiography and letters. Some modern
authors have made judgments and comments on her as a mystic. See
references to Jeanne des Anges in Timmermans, *L'accès des femmes
à la culture (1598–1715)*, and Le Hir, "L'expression mystique dans
l'autobiographie de Sœur Jeanne des Anges."

19 Rohaut, "Réflections sur Urbain Grandier."

20 AM Loudun, GG21, fol. 31, reverse. This information was kindly
provided to me by Edwin Bezzina from his own research.

21 This story was told to the author by Mme Sylviane Rohaut, the
municipal archivist in Loudun.

Bibliography

ARCHIVES

Archives municipales (AM) de Loudun, GG series
Archives nationales (AN), U832
Bibliothèque de l'arsenal (B arsenal), MSS 4824, 5371, 5423, 5554
Bibliothèque mazarine (B mazarine), MS 1209, collection of spiritual letters of Mère Jeanne des Anges
Bibliothèque municipale, Poitiers (BM Poitiers), A2, MS 303
Bibliothèque municipale, Provins (BM Provins), MS 251
Bibliothèque municipale, Tours (BM Tours), MS 1197, Jeanne des Anges, autobiography. MS 1134, collected manuscripts
Bibliothèque nationale (BN), fonds français:
   n.a. 6764, records of proceedings from 1635
   7618–19, original records, 1630–38
   12017, 12047, 14596, 18695, 19869, 24163, 24380–3, original records, 1632–37
   13055, documents on the possessions of Auxonne (fol. 345) and Loudun (fol. 358)
   19191, on the devils of Loudun (fol. 228)
   20157, memoirs and letters by Trincant (fols. 192, 262, 263)
   17368, 17370–3, writings of Laubardemont on the trial at Loudun and the interrogation of the nuns
   Morel de Thoissy, 92
   Collection Dupuy, 473, 571, 641, 776

MANUSCRIPTS

Champion, Pierre. "Discours sur l'histoire de la diablerie de Loudun et sur la mort de Monsieur Urbain Grandier, curé de laditte ville, fait par Pierre Champion, procureur audit Loudun, pour sa satisfaction," 1634. BN, fonds français, 24380; BM Poitiers, A2, MS 303

"Déclaration de Moussault, proc. du roi à Loudun, sur ce qui se passa le jour de la Fête Dieu." BM Poitiers, A2, MS 303

Exorcism records of the exorcisms performed by Barré and Mignon. BN, fonds français, 7619

"Extrait des preuves." BN, fonds français, 24163, 6764. (Also available in Aubin's *Histoire*, with comments, and at BM Poitiers, A2, MS 303)

"Extrait des registres de la commission ordonnée par le roy, pour le jugement du procès criminel fait à l'encontre de Maistre Urbain Grandier et ses complices." BN, Lb 36.3018. (A printed copy was published in Poitiers by J Thoreau et la veuve Antoine Mesnier)

"Interrogatoire de maistre Urbain Grandier, prestre, curé de Saint-Pierre-du-Marché de Loudun, et l'un des chanoines de Sainte-Croix dudit lieu." BN, receuil Morel de Thoissy. (This can be found as an appendix in Villeneuve's *La mystérieuse affaire Grandier*, 244–7)

"Jugement rendu par les commissaires députés contre Urbain Grandier." (This can be found in Danjou, *Archives curieuses de l'histoire de la France*, ser. 2, 5:273–9)

"Lettre de la cordonnière de la Reine-Mère à Monsieur de Baradat." BN, fonds français, 24382

"Manuscrit d'un habitant de Loudun." BN, Collection Barbier

"Mémoire au vray de ce qui s'est passé en la mort du curé de Saint-Pierre-du-Marché de Loudun." Ex Poitiers, BM Poitiers, A2, MS 303; BN, fonds français, 24382

"Mémoire de ce qui s'est passé à l'exécution de l'arrest contre Me Urbain Grandier, prestre." Ex Poitiers, BM Poitiers, A2 MS 303; BN, fonds français, 24380

"Minutes of the bailli of Loudun." BN, fonds français, 24380

"Procès verbal de la question et mort de Grandier (écrit par Langevin, notaire royal, 18 aoûst 1634)." BN, fonds français, 7619

"Receuil de Thoissy." BN, fonds français. Receuil, Morel de Thoissy, 92

"Relation véritable de ce qui s'est passé en la mort du curé de Loudun, bruslé le vendredy 18 aoûst 1634." BN, fonds français, n.a. 6764 (can also be found in full in Danjou's *Archives curieuses*, ser. 2, 5:273–9)

"Requête au Roy des habitants de Loudun." BN, fonds français, 24380 and 7619 (also quoted in full in Legué, *Urbain Grandier*, 237–9)

BOOKS AND ARTICLES

Abse, David Wilfred. *Hysteria and Related Mental Disorders*. Bristol: Wright 1966

Ankarloo, Bengt, and Henningsen, Gustav, eds. *Early Modern European Witchcraft*. Oxford: Clarendon Press 1989

Aubin, Nicolas. *Histoire des diables de Loudun*. Amsterdam: Abraham Wolfgang 1693

Baird, Henry Martyn. *The Huguenots and the Revocation of the Edict of Nantes*. New York: AMS Press 1972

Ballu, C. "Du rôle des médecins dans le procès d'Urbain Grandier." *Revue poitevine et saumuroise* 4 (1901): 1–17

Balteau, J. *Dictionnaire de biographie française*. Vol. 3. Paris: Letouzey et Ané 1939 (entry on Jean d'Armagnac II)

Barbier, Alfred. *Jean d'Armagnac ii, gouverneur de Loudun, et Urbain Grandier*. Poitiers: Imprimerie générale de l'ouest, Blais, Roy et Cie 1886

Barbier, Charles. "Inventaire des pièces manuscrites relatives au procès d'Urbain Grandier, conservées à la bibliothèque de Poitiers." *Bulletin de la Société des antiquaires de l'ouest et des musées de Poitiers* (1877): 153–4

Bardet, Jean-Pierre. *Rouen aux dix-septième et dix-huitième siècles*. Paris: Société d'Edition d'enseignement superieur 1983

Baroja, J.C. "Witchcraft and Catholic Theology." In *Early Modern European Witchcraft*, ed. Bengt Ankerloo and Gustav Henningsen. Oxford: Clarendon Press 1989

Barstow, Anne Llewllyn. *Witchcraze: A New History of the European Witch Hunts*. San Francisco: Harper 1994

Bayle, Pierre. *Dictionnaire historique et critique*. Basle: Brandmuller 1741 (entry on Urbain Grandier)

Beauchet-Filleau, Henri, ed. *Dictionnaire historique, biographique, et généalogique des familles de l'ancien Poitou*. 2 vols. Poitiers 1840–54

Benoit, A. "Catholiques et protestants en Moyen Poitou jusqu'à la révocation de l'Edit de Nantes 1534–1685." *Bulletin de la société historique et scientifique des deux Sèvres*, 16, no. 2 (1983): 235–42

Bertrand, I. *Les possédées de Loudun et Urbain Grandier*. Paris 1890

Bizouard, Joseph. *Des rapports de l'homme avec le démon*. Vol. 3. Paris: Gaume frères et J. Duprey 1863–64

Bleau, Alphonse. *Précis d'histoire sur la ville et les possédées de Loudun*. Poitiers: H. Oudin frères 1877

Boccaccio, Giovanni. *The Decameron*, translated by Guido Waldman, with introduction and notes by Jonathan Usher. Oxford: Oxford University Press 1993

Bonnelier, Hippolyte. *Urbain Grandier.* Paris: Vernarel et Ternon 1825

Bossy, J. *Christianity in the West.* Oxford: Oxford University Press 1985

Boulliau, Ismael. "Lettre d'Ismael Boulliau à Gassendi," 1634. In Roland Villeneuve. *La mystérieuse affaire Grandier.* Paris: Payot 1980, 229–31. Also in *Le cabinet historique* 25 (1879): 6–12.

Bourneville, D.M. *Leçons sur les maladies du système nerveux faites à la Salpêtrière.* Paris 1877

Brauner, Sigrid. *Fearless Wives and Frightened Shrews: The Construction of the Witch in Early Modern Germany,* ed. Robert H. Brown. Amherst: University of Massachusetts Press 1995

Brémond, Henri. "Surin et Jeanne des Anges." In *Histoire littéraire du sentiment religieux en France, depuis la fin des guerres de religion jusqu'à nos jours,* 5:178–251. Paris: A. Colin 1967

A Brief History of Loudun. Anonymous pamphlet distributed to visitors in Loudun.

Briggs, R. *Communities of Belief: Cultural and Social Tension in Early Modern France.* Oxford: Oxford University Press 1989

– *Early Modern France, 1560–1715.* Oxford: Oxford University Press 1990

– *Witches and Neighbours.* London: HarperCollins 1996

– "Women as Victims? Witches, Judges, and the Community." *French History* 5, no 4 (1991): 438–50

Brossolet, Jacqueline, and Henri Mollaret. *Pourquoi la peste?* Paris: Gallimard 1994

Burckhardt, Carl J. *Richelieu and His Age: Power Politics and the Cardinal's Death,* trans. Bernard Hoy. London: Allen 1971

Carmona, Michel. *La France de Richelieu.* Paris: Fayard 1984

– *Les diables de Loudun: Sorcellerie et politique sous Richelieu.* Paris: Fayard 1988

– *Richelieu: L'ambition et le pouvoir.* Paris: Fayard 1983

Cartwright, Frederick F., and Michael D. Biddis. *Disease and History.* London: Hart-Davis 1973

Cassan, Michel. *Le temps des guerres de religion: Le cas de Limousin.* Paris: Publisud 1996

Cavallera, F. "L'autobiographie de Jeanne des Anges d'après des documents inédits." *Recherches de science religieuse* 18 (1928)

– "L'autobiographie du Père Surin," *Revue d'ascétique et de mystique* 6 (Apr. and Oct. 1925): 143–59, 389–411

Charbonneau-Lassay, Louis. *La tour carrée de l'ancienne forteresse de Loudun.* Loudun: Veuve Blanchard 1934

Charcot, Jean-Martin. *Leçons sur les maladies du système nerveux, faites à la Salpêtrière*. Np 1877

– *L'hystérie: Textes choisis et présentés par E. Trillat*. Toulouse 1971

Charcot, Jean-Martin, and Paul Richer. *Les démoniaques dans l'art*. Paris: Macula 1984

– *Nouvelle iconographie de la Salpêtrière*. 3 vols. Paris: Lecronier et Babbe 1888

Cipolla, C.M. *Faith, Reason, and the Plague in Seventeenth-Century Tuscany*, trans. Muriel Kittel. Ithaca: Cornell University Press 1979

Clark, Jack Alden. *Huguenot Warrior: Rohan*. The Hague: Martinus Nijhoff 1967

Clark, Stuart. "Protestant Demonology: Sin, Superstition, and Society." In *Early Modern European Witchcraft*, ed. Bengt Ankarloo and Gustav Henningsen. Oxford: Clarendon Press 1989

Cohn, Norman. *Europe's Inner Demons*. New York: New American Library 1977

Collin de Plancy, Jacques Albin Simon. *Dictionary of Demonology*. London 1965

Crozet, René, and Hilaire Bouzon. "Le donjon cylindre de Loudun," *Bulletin de la Société des antiquaires de l'ouest et des musées de Poitiers* 12, no. 3 (1973): 165–74

Dagen, Jean. *Bérulle et les origines de la restauration catholique (1575–1611)*. Bruges: Descleé de Brouwer 1952

Danjou, F. *Archives curieuses de l'histoire de France depuis Louis XI jusqu'à Louis XIII*.Ser. 2, vol. 5. Paris: Beauvais 1838

Dante Alighieri. *The Divine Comedy: Hell, Purgatory, Heaven*, trans. and annotated by Dorothy Sayers, completed by Barbara Reynolds. London and New York: Penguin Classics 1949–62

David, Anne. *Les possédées de Loudun*. Paris: Gallimard 1959

David-Ménard, Monique. *Hysteria from Freud to Lacan: Body and Language in Psychoanalysis*. Ithaca: Cornell University Press 1989.

de Certeau, Michel. *La possession de Loudun*. Paris: Archives Gallimard/ Julliard 1970

Dedouvres, Louis. *Politique et apôtre: Le Père Joseph de Paris*. Paris, Angers: G. Beauchesne 1932

Defoe, Daniel. *A Journal of the Plague Year*. London: Bestseller Library 1959

Delaroche, Pierre. *Une épidémie de peste à Loudun en 1632*. Bordeaux: Delmas 1936

– *Loudun*. Loudun: SI et la Société historique du Loudunais 1948

Delaroche, Pierre, and Maryvonne Poupard. *Urbain Grandier: 1590–1634* (Maryvonne Poupard interviews of Pierre Delaroche on Radio Chinon, Val-de-Vienne). Loudun: SI et la Société historique du Loudun 1984

Delfour, Joseph. *Les jésuites à Poitiers (1604–1762).* Paris: Hachette 1901

Delumeau, Jean. *Catholicism between Luther and Voltaire: A New View of the Counter-Reformation.* London: Burns 1971

- *La peur en Occident.* Paris: Fayard 1978

d'Espinay, G. *Le bailliage de Loudun.* Angers 1891

Didi-Huberman, Georges. *Invention de l'hystérie: Charcot et l'iconographie photographique de la Salpêtrière.* Paris: Macula 1982

Duby, G., and R. Mandrou. *A History of French Civilization.* New York: Random House 1964

Dulong, Claude. *La vie quotidienne des femmes au grand siècle.* Paris: Hachette 1984

Dumoulin, Maurice. "La construction de la ville de Richelieu." *Bulletin de la Société des antiquaires de l'ouest et des musées de Poitiers* 10, no. 2 (1935): 520–51

Dumoustier de La Fond. *Essais sur l'histoire de la ville de Loudun.* Poitiers: M.V. Chevrier 1778

Esmonin, E. *Etudes sur la France des dix-septième et dix-huitième siècles.* Paris: PUF 1964

Evans, Martha Noel. *Fits and Starts: A Genealogy of Hysteria in Modern France.* Ithaca: Cornell University Press 1991

Favreau, Robert. *Histoire du diocèse de Poitiers.* Paris: Beauchesne 1988

- "La sorcellerie en Poitou à la fin du moyen âge." *Bulletin de la Société des antiquaires de l'ouest et des musées de Poitiers* 18, no. 4 (1985): 133–54

Febvre, Lucien. "Witchcraft: Nonsense or a Mental Revolution?" In *A New Kind of History and Other Essays: From the Writings of Febvre*, trans. K. Folca, ed. P. Burke, 185–92. London: Routledge and Kegan Paul 1973

Figuier, Louis. *Histoire du merveilleux dans les temps modernes: Les diables de Loudun.* 2nd edn, vol. 1. Paris: L. Hachette 1881

Formon, M. "Henri Louis Chasteignier de La Rocheposay, évêque de Poitiers, 1612–1651." *Bulletin de la Société des antiquaires de l'ouest et des musées de Poitiers* 3, no. 4 (1955)

Foucault, Michel. *The History of Sexuality.* New York: Pantheon Books 1978

- *Madness and Civilization: A History of Insanity in the Age of Reason*, trans. Richard Howard. London: Tavistock Publications 1967

Freud, Sigmund. "A Neurosis of Demoniacal Possession in the Seventeenth Century." In *Collected Papers.* Vol 4. New York: Basic Books 1959

Gagey, Roland. *Les possédées*. Paris 1971

Garnier, Samuel. *Barbe Buvée, en religion Sœur Sainte Colombe, et la prétendue possession des Ursulines d'Auxonne*. Preface by M. le Dr Bourneville. Paris: Progrès médical 1895

Garnot, Benoit. *Le diable au couvent: Les possédées d'Auxonne (1658–1663)*. Paris: Imago 1995

Gayot de Petaval, François. *Causes célèbres et intéressantes avec les jugements qui les ont décidées*. La Haye: J. Neaulme 1747–51

– *Histoire d'Urbain Grandier, condamné comme magicien et comme auteur de la possession des religieuses Ursulines de Loudun*. Amsterdam, 1735 (Although this work is anonymous, the copy in the Archives municipales de Loudun has a hand-written note attributing it to Gayot)

Ginzburg, Carlo. *The Cheese and the Worms: The Cosmos of a Sixteenth-Century Miller*. Baltimore: Johns Hopkins University Press 1980.

– *Ecstasies: Deciphering the Witches' Sabbath*. New York: Pantheon 1991

– *Le sabbat des sorcières*. Paris: Gallimard 1992

– *The Night Battles: Witchcraft and Agrarian Cults in the Sixteenth and Seventeenth Centuries*, trans. John and Anne Tedeschi. London, Melbourne, and Henley: Routledge and Kegan Paul 1983

Goubert, Pierre. *Louis XIV and Twenty Million Frenchmen*, trans. Anne Carter. Vintage Books 1972

Grandier, Urbain. "Factum pour Maistre Urbain Grandier." BN, fonds français, 24163; Dupuy 241; and B arsenal 4824. Copy in F. Danjou, *Archives curieuses de l'histoire de la France*, ser. 2, 5:225–57

– "Remarques et considérations servans à la justification du curé de Loudun, autres que celles contenues en son factum." Appendix in Roland Villeneuve, *La mystérieuse affaire Grandier*. Paris: Payot 1980

– "Requête d'Urbain Grandier, curé de Sainte-Croix de Loudun, au roi. Undated. AN, U832, 80–6, and BN, fonds français, 7169. Copy entitled "Lettre du Sieur Grandier, accusé de magie au Roi," in F. Danjou, *Archives curieuses de l'histoire de la France*, ser. 2, 5:261–74

– *Traité du célibat des prêtres*, with introduction and notes by Robert Luzarche. Paris: Librairie Richelieu 1866. Also in BN, fonds français; Dupuy 571; and B arsenal, 5371 and 5423

Greenblatt, Stephen. "Loudun and London." *Critical Inquiry* (Chicago), 12, no. 2 (1986): 326–46

Griguer, Thérèse. "Historiographie et médecine: A propos de Jeanne des Anges et de la possession de Loudun [Vienne, 1632]." *Annales de Bretagne et des pays de l'ouest* 99, no. 2 (1992): 155–63

Grimaud, H. "Un juge d'Urbain Grandier." *Revue poitevine et saumuroise* (Saumur), 1 (August 1900): 1–4

Grosburin, Louis. *Sur les traces d'Urbain Grandier.* Montreux 1930

Guiley, Rosemary. *The Encyclopedia of Witches and Witchcraft.* New York: Facts on File 1989

Guinoyseau. *La mort d'Urbain Grandier.* Paris 1839

Hanlon, Gregory. *Confession and Community in Seventeenth-Century France.* Philadelphia: University of Pennsylvania Press 1993

Hanotaux, Gabriel. *Histoire du Cardinal de Richelieu.* Paris: Société de l'histoire, Librairie Plon 1932–47

Harline, Craig. *The Burdens of Sister Margaret: Private Lives in a Seventeenth-Century Convent.* New York and London: Doubleday 1994

Hasquin, Hervé. *Magie, sorcellerie, parapsychologie.* Brussels: Editions de l'Université de Bruxelles 1984

Hédelin, Abbé d'Aubignac. "Relation de M. Hédelin, abbé d'Aubignac, touchant les possédées de Loudun au mois de Septembre 1637." BN, fonds français, 12801, and B arsenal 5554. Copy in Robert Mandrou, *Possession et sorcellerie,* 134–94. Paris: Plon 1968

Hemphill, R.E. "Historical Witchcraft and Psychiatric Illness in Western Europe." *Proceedings of the Royal Society of Medecine* 59 (1966)

Hester, Marianne. *Lewd Women and Wicked Witches.* London and New York: Routledge 1992

Hildesheimer, Françoise. *La terreur et la pitié.* Paris: Publisud 1990

– *Richelieu: Une certaine idée de l'état.* Paris: Publisud, 1985

Houdard, Sophie. *Les sciences du diable: Quatre discours sur la sorcellerie (15e–17e siècle).* Paris: Editions du Cerf 1992

Huguet, M. "Expérience mystique, pathologie mentale et condition féminine." *Pénélopé* 8 (1983): 25–8

Huxley, Aldous. *The Devils of Loudun.* London: Chatto and Windus 1952.

Israel, Lucien. *L'hystérique, le sexe, et le médecin.* Paris and New York: Masson 1985

Jacob, Frère. *Les possédées de Chaillot.* Paris: J. Clathes 1983

Jacques-Chaquin, Nicole, and Maxime Préaud. *Le sabbat des sorciers, quinzième au dix-huitième siècles.* Grenoble: Jerome Millon 1993

Jones, E.H. *The Road to En-Dor.* London and New York: White Lion Publishers 1973

Jovy, E. *Trois documents inédits sur Urbain Grandier et un document peu inconnu sur le Cardinal Richelieu.* Paris: Librairie Henri Leclerc 1906

Kors, Alan Charles. *Witchcraft in Europe, 1100–1700: A Documentary History.* Philadelphia: University of Pennsylvania Press 1972

Kraemer, Heinrich, and Jacobus Sprenger. *Malleus maleficarum* [1487]. Dover 1971. Reprint, Salem: Ayer 1978

Kreiser, Robert. "The Devils of Toulon: Demonic Possession and Religious Politics in Eighteenth-Century Provence." In *Articles on Witchcraft, Magic and Demonology*, ed. Brian P. Levack, 9:63–111. New York: Garland 1992

Krohn, Alan. *Hysteria, the Elusive Neurosis*. New York: International UP 1978

Lacombe, Robert. "Analyse comparative des événements de Loudun: La possession et la transe." *L'ethnographie* (Paris), 83 (1984): 93–114

Laingui, A. "Nouveauté et permanence dans le droit criminel au dix-septième siècle." *Destins et enjeux du dix-septième siècle*, ed. M. Bercé et al. Paris: Presses Universitaires de France 1985

La Menardaye, Abbé Jean-Baptiste de. *Examen et discussion critique de l'histoire des diables de Loudun, de la possession des religieuses ursulines, et de la condemnation d'Urbain Grandier*. Paris: Debure l'aîné 1747

La Ménardière, C. de *Quelques épisodes d'histoire Loudunaise*. Poitiers: Blais et Roy 1905

Langlet, Louis. *Une possession au seizième siècle: Etude médicale de la vie et de l'hystérie de Nicole Obry*. Reims: Matot-Braine 1910

Larner, Christina. *Witchcraft and Religion: The Politics of Popular Belief*. New York: Blackwell 1984

Larroque, Tamizey de. *Document relatif à Urbain Grandier*. Paris: Alphonse Picard 1879

Lebrun, François. *Se soigner autrefois: Médecins, saints, et sorciers*. Paris: Temps Actuels 1983

Ledru, Abbé Ambroise. *Urbain Grandier*. Château-Gontier 1884

Legué, Gabriel. *Documents pour servir à l'histoire médicale des possédées de Loudun*. Paris: Delahaye 1874

– *Urbain Grandier et les possédées de Loudun*. Paris: Baschet 1880

Legué, Gabriel, and Gilles de La Tourette, *Sœur Jeanne des Anges, supérieure des Ursulines de Loudon (dix-septième siècle): Autobiographie d'une hystérique possédée*. 1886. Reprint, Editions Millon 1985

Le Hir, Yves. "L'expression mystique dans l'autobiographie de Sœur Jeanne des Anges. *Revue d'histoire et de philosophie religieuse* (Paris), 60, no. 4 (1980): 453–9

Leriche, Pierre Ambroise. *Etudes sur les possessions en général et sur celle de Loudun en particulier*. Paris 1859

Lerosey, Auguste-Louis. *Loudun, histoire civile et religieuse*. Loudun: Librairie Blanchard 1908

Lesourd, Louis. *Notice historique sur J. Martin de Laubardemont*. Paris 1842

Levack, Brian. *The Witch-Hunt in Early Modern Europe*. London and New York: Longman 1995

– ed. *Articles on Witchcraft, Magic, and Demonology*. 12 vols. New York: Garland Publishing 1992

Lévy-Valensi, J. "Urbain Grandier et les possédées de Loudun." *Semaine des hôpitaux de Paris* 15 (1933): 505–27

Lhermitte, Jean. *Vrais et faux possédés*. Paris: Fayard 1956

Livonnière, Claude Pocquet de. *Coustumes du pays et duché d'Anjou*. Paris: Jean Baptiste Coignard 1725

Lorédan, Jean. *Un grand procès de sorcellerie au dix-septième siècle: L'abbé Gaufridy et Madeleine de Demandolx (1608–1670)*. Paris: Perrin 1912

Lucenet, Monique. *Les grandes pestes en France*. Paris: Aubier 1985

Macrin, Salmon. *Un juge d'Urbain Grandier, Louis Trincant*. Loudun: A. Roiffe 1892 (This can be found in AM Loudun)

McKenzie, John L. *Dictionary of the Bible*. New York: Macmillan 1965

Magen, A. "La ville d'Agen pendant l'épidémie de 1628–1631 d'après les registres consulaires." *Bulletin de la Societé de médecine d'Agen*, 1862

Mair, Lucy. *Witchcraft*. London: Weidenfeld and Nicolson 1969

Mandrou, Robert. *Magistrats et sorciers en France au dix-septième siècle: Une analyse de psychologie historique*. Paris: Plon 1968

– *Possession et sorcellerie au dix-septième siècle*. Paris: Fayard 1979

Marcadé, Jacques. "Saint Cyran et l'apologie pour La Roche Posay." *Bulletin de la Société des antiquaires de l'ouest et des musées de Poitiers* 3, no. 5 (1989): 221–30

– "Les protestants dans le centre-ouest de 1534–1660." *Bulletin de la Société des antiquaires de l'ouest et des musées de Poitiers* 1, no. 5 (1987): 99–116

Marie de l'Incarnation. *Correspondance de Marie de l'Incarnation*, ed. Guy Marie Oury. Abbaye Saint-Pierre de Solesmes 1971

Martin, Jean. *Véritable relation des justes procédures observées au fait de la possession des Ursulines de Loudun*. Paris 1634

Marwick, Max. *Witchcraft and Sorcery: Selected Readings*. Harmondsworth: Penguin 1982

Max, Stéfan. *Crescendo satanique: (Théatre)*. Paris: La Pensée universelle 1974

Mémin, Edmond. *L'origin des familles Mesmin: Essais sur leur histoire du quatrième et huitième siècle*. Le Mans, nd

– *René Mesmin de Silly, adversaire d'Urbain Grandier*. Saumur: P. Godet 1916

Micale, M.S. "Hysteria and Its Historiography: A Review of Past and Present Writings." *History of Science* 27 (1989): 3, 223–61; pt 4, 318–51

Michaud, Joseph François, and Louis Gabriel. *Biographie universelle.* Paris: Michaud 1811–62

Michelet, Jules. *La sorcière.* 1862. Rev. ed. with chronology and preface by Paul Viallaneix, Paris: Garnier/Flammarion 1966. English translation, *Satanism and Witchcraft.* New York: Citadel 1936

Midelfort, H.C. Erik. "The Devil and the German People." In *Religion and Culture in the Renaissance and Reformation*, ed. Steven Ozment, 99–119. Kirksville: Sixteenth Century Journal 1989

– "Were There Really Witches?" In *Transition and Revolution: Problems and Issues of European and Reformation History*, ed. Robert M. Kingdon, 189–205. Minneapolis: Burgess 1974

Monter, E. William. *Witchcraft in France and Switzerland.* Ithaca: Cornell University Press 1976

Mora, George, et al., eds. *Witches, Devils, and Doctors in the Renaissance.* Binghampton, NY: Medieval and Renaissance Texts and Studies 1991 (translation of Johann Weyer's *De praestigiis daemonum*, 1563)

Moreau de la Ronde, Joseph. *Les châteaux de Loudun d'après les fouilles archéologiques.* Loudun 1915

Mousnier, Roland. *L'homme rouge: La vie du Cardinal de Richelieu (1585–1642).* Paris: Robert Laffont 1992

– *The Institutions of France under the Absolute Monarchy, 1598–1789*, trans. Brian Pearce. 2 vols. Chicago and London: University of Chicago Press 1979

Muchembled, R. *La sorcière au village, quinzième au dix-huitième siècles.* Paris: Julliard/Gallimard 1991

– *Le roi et la sorcière: l'Europe des bûchers (seizième au dix-huitième siècles).* Paris: Desclée 1993

– *Société et mentalités dans la France moderne, seizième au dix-huitième siècles.* Paris: Armand Colin 1990

– *Sorcières: Justice et société aux seizième et dix-septième siècles.* Paris: Editions Imago 1987

Niau, Des. *The History of the Devils of Loudun.* 1634. English translation, Edinburgh 1887–8

Nohl, Johannes. *The Black Death: A Chronicle of the Plague.* London: Unwin 1961

Olson, Alan M, ed. *Disguises of the Demonic: Contemporary Perspectives on the Power of Evil.* New York: Association Press 1975

Owen, Alan Robert G. *Hysteria, Hypnosis, and Healing. The Work of J.M. Charcot*. New York: Garrett 1971

Palou, J. *La sorcellerie*. Paris: Presses Universitaires de France 1966

Pearl, Jonathan L. "'A School for the Rebel Soul': Politics and Demonic Possession in France." *Historical Reflections/Réflections Historiques* 16, nos. 2 and 3 (1989): 286–306

– "Demons and Politics in France, 1560–1630." *Historical Reflections/ Réflections Historiques* 12 (1985): 241–51

– "French Catholic Demonologists and Their Enemies in the Late Sixteeth and Early Seventeenth Centuries." *Church History* 52 (1983): 457–67

Penderecki, Krysztof. *Die Teufel von Loudun (Devils of Loudun)* (opera score). Mainz, Schott 1969

Potter, Aloys S.J. *Le Père Lallemant et les grands spirituels de son temps*. Paris 1830

Poupard, Maryvonne, and Pierre Delaroche. *Urbain Grandier 1590–1634* A series of radio interviews published by the Office de tourisme de Loudun, 1984

Ranum, Orest. *Les créatures de Richelieu*. Paris: Pedone 1966

Rapley, Elizabeth. *The Dévotes: Women and Church in Seventeenth-Century France*. Montreal and Kingston: McGill-Queens University Press 1990

– "Women and the Religious Vocation in Seventeenth-Century France." *French Historical Studies* 18, no. 3 (1994): 613–31

Richelieu, Armand Jean du Plessis, Cardinal, duc de. *Mémoires*, éd. Michaud et Poujoulat. 3 vols. Paris: Firman-Didot 1837

Robbins, Rossell H. *The Encyclopaedia of Witchcraft and Demonology*. London: Nevill 1959

Rohaut, S. "Réflections sur Urbain Grandier." *Gazette du Loudunais*, July/ August 1995

Roper, Lyndal. *Oedipus and the Devil: Witchcraft, Sexuality, and Religion in Early Modern Europe*. London and New York: Routledge 1994

Rose, Elliot. *A Razor for a Goat: A Discussion of Certain Problems in the History of Witchcraft and Diabolism*. Toronto: University of Toronto Press 1962

Rosen, George. *Madness in Society: Chapters in the Historical Sociology of Mental Illness*. New York: Harper and Row 1968

– "Psychopathology in the Social Process: A Study of the Persecution of Witches in Europe as a Contribution towards the Understanding of Mass Delusions and Pyschic Epidemics." *Journal of Health and Human Behaviour* 1, no. 3 (1990): 206–16

Roy, Alec, ed. *Hysteria*. Chichester: John Wiley 1982

Russell, J.B. *A History of Witchcraft: Sorcerers, Heretics, and Pagans.*
London: Thames and Hudson 1980
– *The Prince of Darkness: Radical Evil and the Power of Good in History.*
Ithaca: Cornell University Press 1988
Sade, Marquis de. *Urbain Grandier.* Paris 1968
Saint-Jure, Jean-Baptiste. "Lettres inéditées à la mère Jeanne des Anges,
ursuline à Loudun," ed. F. Cavallera. *Revue d'ascétique et de mystique*
7 (1926), 9 (1928), and 11 (1930)
Sauzé, J.C. *Essai médico-historique sur les possédées de Loudun.* Paris
1839
Scarre, Geoffrey. *Witchcraft and Magic in Sixteenth and Seventeenth Cen-
tury France.* London: Macmillan Education 1987
Schneidman, Edwin S. *Deaths of Man.* New York: Quadrangle 1973
Schott-Billmann, F. "La possession – protestation: Le diable de Loudun. In
his *Corps et possession,* 200–10. Paris: Gauthier-Villars 1977
Scott, Randy, and Jonathan Pearl. *On the Demon-mania of Witches.*
Toronto: CRRS 1995. (This is a translation of Bodin's book published in
1580)
Senter, Donovan. "Witches and Psychiatrists." *Psychiatry: The American
Psychiatric Association Annual Review* 10 (1947): 49–56
Sirois, François. "Epidemic Hysteria." In *Hysteria,* ed. A. Roy. Chichester:
John Wiley 1982
Shorter, Edward. *From Paralysis to Fatigue: A History of Psychosomatic
Illness in the Modern Era.* New York and Toronto: Maxwell Macmillan
International 1992
– *From the Mind into the Body: The Cultural Origins of Psychosomatic
Symptoms.* Toronto: Free Press, Maxwell Macmillan International 1994
Skelton, R. *Practice of Witchcraft.* Victoria: Porcepic Books 1990
Slavney, Phillip R. *Perspectives on Hysteria.* Baltimore: Johns Hopkins
University Press 1990
Soman, A. "Les procès de sorcellerie au Parlement de Paris." *Annales:
Economies, sociétés, civilisations* 32 (1997): 790–814
– "Sur la fin des sorciers au dix-septième siècle." In *La vie, la mort, et la
foi.* Mélanges offerts à Pierre Chaunu. Paris: PUF 1993
Spanos, Nicholas P., and J. Gottlieb. "Demonic Possession, Mesmerism,
and Hysteria." *Journal of Abnormal Psychology* (Washington: American
Psychological Association), 88, no.5 (1979): 527–46 (has an excellent
bibliography)
Sturdy, D.J. "Social Tensions and Social Control in Seventeenth-Century
France." *Seventeenth-Century French Studies* (Norwich: Society for Seventeenth-Century French Studies) 12 (1990): 206–16

Summers, Montague. *The History of Witchcraft and Demonology*. New York: University Books 1956

Surin, J.J. *Correspondance*, edited, with a biographical note, by Michel de Certeau. Paris: Desclée de Brouwer 1966

– *Histoire abrégée de la possession des Ursulines de Loudun et des peines de Père Surin*. Paris 1828

– *Triomphe de l'amour divin sur les puissances de l'enfer*. Avignon 1829

Tapié, Victor Lucien. *The France of Louis XIII and Richelieu*. London: Macmillan 1974 (trans. of *La France de Louis XIII et de Richelieu*)

Thomas, Keith. *Religion and the Decline of Magic*. London: Weidenfeld 1971

Timmermans, Linda. *L'accès des femmes à la culture (1598–1715)*. Paris: Honoré Champion 1993

Tonquedec, Joseph de. *Maladies Nerveuses ou Mentales*. Paris: Beauschene 1938

Tranquille, Fr. *Véritable relation des justes procédures observées au fait de la possession des Ursulines de Loudun, et au procès de Grandier*. 1634. Poitiers: I. Thoreau et Veuve A. Mesnier. Reprinted in F. Danjou, *Archives curieuses de l'histoire de France*, ser. 2, vol. 5. Paris: Beauvais 1838

Treasure, G.R.R. *Cardinal Richelieu and the Development of Absolutism*. London: A. and C. Black 1972

Trevor-Roper, H.R. *The European Witch Craze of the Sixteenth and Seventeenth Centuries*. 1967. Reprint, London: Penguin 1990

Trillat, Etienne. *Histoire de l'hystérie*. Paris: Seghers 1986

Trincant, Louis. *Abrégé des antiquités de Loudun et pays de loudunois*. 1626. Reprint, Loudun: Roger Drouault 1894

Urbain Grandier and the Devils of Loudun. Anonymous pamphlet distributed to visitors in Loudun

Veith, Ilza. *Hysteria: The History of a Disease*. Chicago and London: University of Chicago Press 1965

Vigny, Alfred de. *Cinq-Mars ou une conjuration sous Louis XIII*. Paris: Gallimard 1980

Villeneuve, Roland. *La mystérieuse affaire Grandier: Le diable à Loudun*. Paris: Payot 1980

Villette, P. *La sorcellerie et sa répression dans le nord de la France*. Paris: Pensée universelle 1976

Walker, Anita M., and Edmund H. Dickerman. "'A Woman under the Influence': A Case of Alleged Possession in Sixteenth-Century France." *Sixteenth-Century Journal* 22, no. 3 (1991): 535–4

Walker, D.P. *Unclean Spirits*. Philadelphia: University of Pennsylvania Press 1981

Wesley, George Randolph. *A History of Hysteria*. Washington, DC: University Press of America 1979

Whiting, John Robert. *The Devils: A Play*. New York: Hill and Wang 1962

Wright, Thomas. *Narratives of Sorcery and Magic*. London: Bentley 1851. Reprint, Detroit: Grand River Books 1971

Zilboorg, Gregory. *The Medical Man and the Witch during the Renaissance*. Baltimore: Johns Hopkins University Press 1935

See also the films *Mère Jeanne des Anges* (1960), directed by Jerzy Kawalerowicz, and *The Devils* (1971), directed by Ken Russell.